FORT
LARAMIE
AND THE
GREAT SIOUX WAR

FORT
LARAMIE
AND THE
GREAT SIOUX WAR

Paul L. Hedren

University of Oklahoma Press

Norman

Library of Congress Cataloging-in-Publication Data

Hedren, Paul L.
    [Fort Laramie in 1876]
    Fort Laramie and the Great Sioux War / Paul L. Hedren.
      p.   cm.
    Originally published : Fort Laramie in 1876. Lincoln : University
of Nebraska Press, c1988.
    Includes bibliographical references and index.
    ISBN 0-8061-3049-0 (pbk. : alk. paper)
      1. Fort Laramie (Wyo. : Fort)—History.   2. Dakota Indians—
Wars, 1876.   I. Title.
    [F769.F6H43   1998]
    973.8'2—dc21   98-19794
                                                                    CIP

This book originally was titled *Fort Laramie in 1876: Chronicle of a Frontier Post at War.*

Oklahoma Paperbacks edition published 1998 by the University of Oklahoma Press, Norman, Publishing Division of the University, by arrangement with the University of Nebraska Press, 312 North 14th Street, P.O. Box 880484, Lincoln, Nebraska 68588-0484. Manufactured in the U.S.A. First printing of the University of Oklahoma Press edition, 1998.

1   2   3   4   5   6   7   8   9   10

To Janeen, Ethne, and Whitney Hedren with warmest affection

Contents

Maps and Illustrations

When I was challenged in 1983 to write what became *Fort Laramie in 1876: Chronicle of a Frontier Post at War,* I at once envisioned an opportunity to combine my passionate interest in the Great Sioux War with an equally trenchant enthusiasm for Fort Laramie history (my National Park Service career began there in 1971). The product, I reasoned, might well be unique to both subject areas. I knew well how Fort Laramie scholars before me had paid so little heed to the outpost's strategic role in the Great Sioux War, preferring instead to tell of a warfare saga focused on the Grattan fight occurring nearby in 1854, and of the 1860s Bozeman Trail War and its especially dramatic finale, the signing of the now infamous Fort Laramie Treaty with the Sioux in 1868. Similarly, historians of the Great Sioux War evidently found estimable challenge in accounting for monumental battles and personalities such as Rosebud, Little Big Horn, Custer, and Crazy Horse than they did the seemingly ignoble story of a distant support base.

To my expected pleasure, of course, I discovered a multifaceted story of Fort Laramie in 1876 that proved to be uncommonly dramatic. To illustrate, the post lay at a strategic transportation crossroads in the mid-1870s that brought to it conspicuous attention during the so-called Black Hills crisis and its related Indian war. From the Union Pacific Railroad's freighting houses in Cheyenne, Wyoming, countless supply wagons rolled northward to the fort and then continued on one of three paths: eastward to the eruptive Red Cloud and Spotted Tail Sioux agencies in Nebraska; straight north to the luring Black Hills on a road that ultimately also bore thousands of gold-seeking "Hillers" and soon the storied Cheyenne and Black Hills Stage; or northwestward along the North Platte River on the Fort Laramie–Fort Fetterman trail, an avenue used chiefly by troops and their contractors bound for that northernmost Wyoming outpost and the principal war front in the Powder River country.

As well, I encountered a delightful cast of characters at Fort Laramie, including a veritable military "Who's Who." Joseph Reynolds, George Crook, Eugene Carr, Wesley Merritt, Phil Sheridan, and Ranald Mackenzie were then and are yet recognized in an instant. So, too, are frontiersmen such as Jack Crawford, Bill Hickok, Bill Cody, and Martha Cannary. A greater pleasure, however, came in discovering Fort Laramie's supporting cast from 1876, soldiers and civilians including "Teddy" Egan, Alfred Morton, Charles Petteys, Samuel Hinman, John Collins, Elizabeth Burt, and Cynthia Capron. Some found their way to combat because Crook routinely rotated fresh troops to the war front. Doctor Petteys and Reverend Hinman, meanwhile, did their best in their own unique ways to avert bloodshed, both on the home front and in Indian country. And Burt and Capron grieved when their husbands marched to war, mothered their children and the remainder of the shrunken Fort Laramie garrison, and anguished aplenty on the margins of America's final Indian frontier.

In all I made a compelling case that for Fort Laramie these months of the Great Sioux War were perhaps *the* most important in its long and storied history. The mix of people and the prolonged, dramatic events of national impact that transpired within its buildings and on its margins were unlike those occurring at any other time in the fort's distinguished chronology, notwithstanding its role in decades of fur trading and overland migrations, treaty negotiations, and ceaseless turmoil with the Sioux. My conclusion has not been challenged.

I vowed at the onset of this project to construct a story as exclusively as possible from primary source materials, particularly the incredible array of military post records preserved in the National Archives. In doing so I blazed a fairly fresh trail in finding records related specifically to Fort Laramie and to associated aspects of the Great Sioux War. In my experience, I've watched few fort scholars successfully mine the veritable mountain of military records preserved at the National Archives. So goes the norm in most treatments, it seems, that to have explored and cited *Post Returns* and maybe *General Orders* constitutes a sense of having exhausted that phenomenal iceberg-like treasure when, in fact, the Archives invariably possesses an original of every document ever produced at an American military post. The sum amounts to thousands of papers in dozens of record types covering the entire span of a post's existence. As well, the army generated mountains of paper in its array of depots, departments, and divisions, and therein, too, awaits treasure to be discovered relating to individual forts and campaigns. In my particular Fort Laramie quest, I think I saw it all. More recently, others such as Tom Buecker, in *Fort Robinson and the American West, 1874–1899* (1998), and Jack McDermott, in *Frontier Crossroads: The History of Fort Caspar and the Upper Platte Crossing* (1997) and *Dangerous Duty: A History of Frontier Forts in Fremont County, Wyoming* (1993), have fully tapped this extraordinary Archives cache. But where are competent, fulsome histories of wartime Forts Fetterman, Abraham Lincoln, Buford, or Keogh?

Similarly, scholars focusing singularly on the combat fronts of the Great Sioux War have yet to craft many stories from National Archives sources, though works from Jerome Greene have narrowed the field measurably. In particular, Greene's history of Nelson Miles's campaigning on the Yellowstone River (*Yellowstone Command*, 1991), which focuses attention on the hitherto neglected conclusion of the Great Sioux War, makes comprehensive use of Archives treasure. My own small story in 1995, *Sitting Bull's Surrender at Fort Buford*, also is largely drawn from well-buried Archives sources. But where yet are histories of Gibbon's Montana Column, Terry's Dakota Column, or Crook's Powder River campaign drawn from relevant post and department records?

Most reviewers hailed my Fort Laramie history as an important and unique contribution to site and Great Sioux War scholarship. I was hopeful of that. Other significant contributions to our understanding of the Great Sioux War have been made since 1988 as well. Our comprehension of the Little Big Horn battle, long in the myopic focus of Sioux War scholarship, has been rounded out importantly in recent years by archaeologists interpreting battle debris and other material remains, and by historians who at long last have begun using critically the phenomenal array of Indian battle accounts.

A well-worn lament for decades was that no historian had undertaken a genuine, comprehensive history of the Great Sioux War, from start to finish, but that complaint was answered with the publication of two highly significant works in the mid-1990s. First was Robert Utley's biography of Sitting Bull, *The Lance and the Shield* (1993). More than an obvious life and times of this extraordinary Hunkpapa Sioux leader, Utley devoted fully the middle third of his book to events of the 1870s, crafting in effect a first-ever Indian account of the Great Sioux War. It's a rivetingly good read. Then, in 1995, came Charles Robinson's *A Good Year to Die: The Story of the Great Sioux War.* Robinson aimed to tell the 1870s Sioux War story in toto, from treaty rumblings in the late 1860s and gold strikes in the early 1870s through the fitful Sioux and Cheyenne surrenders at war's end. He succeeded wonderfully, and for the first time another historian accorded wartime Fort Laramie its due.

In the decade since my history of Fort Laramie first appeared, I've continued to explore aspects of its history, its people, and the engulfing 1876–77 Indian war. I remain particularly fascinated by the lives of the officers who garrisoned Laramie in the 1870s, and I maintain active files on most of them. Occasionally new information appears, such as when Jack McDermott discovered and shared an account he had found by James Regan from the August 1880 issue of *The United Service.* First Lieutenant Regan of the Ninth Infantry toiled as Fort Laramie's commissary officer in 1876, almost singularly tending receipt of and issuing food stuffs to the garrison and outfitting the campaign-bound soldiers at the post.

Regan's seventeen-page essay, titled "Military Landmarks," was partly an epitaph for aging posts such as Forts Kearney and Laramie, which were rapidly disappearing from the mournful gaze of soldiers such as Regan, and partly an insider's history of Fort Laramie as it was known in 1876. Of particular interest is Regan's walking-tour description of the fort and his innumerable asides on its buildings and people. For instance, on the ironic and dangerous location of the magazine literally within a few feet of officers' row, he comments that "the people here treat it with the greatest indifference." On the new grout cavalry barracks and hospital completed in 1874 and 1875 respectively, he notes that they are "superior edifices, and reflect credit upon the government." (The barracks building stands yet today, meticulously preserved and refurnished by the National Park Service.) And on veteran Post-master and Ordnance Sergeant Leodegar Schnyder, the venerable enlisted man who had served continuously at Fort Laramie since 1849, Regan admonished the government—as Schnyder neared retirement—to "be generous to the Old Sergeant." These and other observations were, in all, colorful, revealing thoughts from a soldier who served at Fort Laramie during its illustrious heyday.

Captain James "Teddy" Egan, the indefatigable commander of Lara-mie's resident cavalry company in the summer of 1876, never penned anything of a history like Regan's, yet his story of reliable, steady service is the veritable hallmark of a certain class of officers in the Old Army. Like Regan, Egan was commissioned from the enlisted ranks, but unlike Regan, he was thrice wounded during the Civil War. A gunshot wound to the right humerus, received in the Battle of Cold Harbor in 1864, destroyed nearly two inches of bone. The muscles of that arm atrophied, rendering the limb virtually useless thereafter. An injury to the left palm in another battle impaired the use of that hand thereafter, and a wartime saber wound to the head occasioned complete deafness in Egan's left ear.

Despite such debilities, by all accounts Egan possessed sterling leadership skills and an amiable personality. He was married to a charming wife, Mary Anna, and was one of Crook's favorite officers, the two serving together often on the Plains. Following service at Fort Laramie in 1876, Egan's Company K was assigned to Fort Custer, Montana. While surveying a military road from Fort Custer to the Mussleshell River, his horse plunged over a deep embankment with Egan tight in the saddle. The mount and rider tumbled together a formidable distance. Remarkably, Egan survived but sustained an injury reported as "within his breast and near his heart, a serious hurt from which he never recovered." Captain Egan retired from the army in May 1879 and died in 1883 of a ruptured aorta. The attending surgeon ascribed the cause of death as a lingering effect of his Montana horse-back injury. The grizzled veteran was but forty-five years old.

I tracked Doctor Charles Petteys through his career, too. In 1876 Petteys was one of Fort Laramie's contract medicos. Laramie and other larger posts usually had several physicians in residence, typically a commissioned officer and one or more term doctors such as Petteys.

Petteys was in the thick of Fort Laramie's business during the Great Sioux War, responding to repeated bloodshed on the Black Hills trail and to injury and death at the post, including the tragic passing of the young child Henry Capron. Like most contract doctors, Petteys aspired to the permanence of an officers' commission, but gaining that security eluded him throughout his military career. Though well trained in medicine at the Georgetown Medical School in Washington, D.C., Petteys possessed an inadequate classical education. The army medical examinations of the day probed as deeply into geography, history, mathematics, and classical and modern languages as it did the varied aspects of medicine. Petteys never mastered the exam, and after on-again, off-again employment with the army through 1883, he shelved his military aspirations and established a private practice in the District of Columbia, where he lived for fifty more years.

Another of the curious characters figuring in Fort Laramie's war-time story—an exact opposite of humanitarian Petteys—was "Persimmon Bill" Chambers, the Black Hills outlaw. Like others of his ilk, Chambers was a barely known individual who only emerged from history's shadows when perpetrating outlandish episodes, such as the so-called Metz family massacre, and the murder of stage operator "Stuttering" Brown, both travesties occurring north of the fort on the Black Hills road. Never indicted for these homicides, Chambers simply melted away, the Cheyenne newspapers last reporting on him in mid-1876. But what happened to "Persimmon Bill"? My continuing search for Chambers has mostly run cold. Where his loathsome counterpart in Black Hills mayhem, Jack McCall, was hanged in March 1877 with considerable publicity in Yankton, South Dakota, for killing Bill Hickok, I have yet to discover Chambers's fate. One lead suggests he next ran with the Jesse James gang, while another reports his being hanged in Tennessee for an old murder.

Easily the most melancholy human tale surfacing since this book first appeared is that of First Lieutenant Alfred Morton, Fort Laramie's quartermaster in 1876. At a youthful age Morton emigrated from his birth state of Maine to California, and at the onset of the Civil War he enlisted in a California infantry regiment. During the war California troops, with Morton in tow, served continuously in their home state or in the nearby Great Basin territories. Between 1861 and 1866 Morton rose from the enlisted ranks to that of major. Evidently finding personal satisfaction in military life, at war's end Morton petitioned the War Department for a commission in the Regular Army. In 1866 he was appointed a second lieutenant in the Ninth U.S. Infantry, a unit then, too, stationed in California.

In short order Morton was appointed in 1866 as regimental quartermaster of the Ninth, a role he held until 1879. His regiment, meanwhile, transferred from California to the Department of the Platte in 1869, eventually landing Morton at Fort Laramie with regimental headquarters. But as Morton and colleagues James Regan and "Teddy" Egan came to understand well but deplore greatly, faithful service in Uncle Sam's army was no guarantee of promotion within a well-entrenched seniority system. All officers yearned for promotion, and most deserved it. Morton yearned resolutely and furthermore desired a transfer into a secure department- or Washington-based staff position. He already was performing similar duties, but for a field regiment. Evidently for Morton and his family, civilization beckoned fiercely.

Morton's official Appointments, Commissions, and Personal file in the National Archives brims with letters to the War Department seeking transfer and promotion to the Inspector-General's Department or the Pay Department, with similar inquiries sent in 1888, 1893, and again in 1897. One and all were curtly denied by army headquarters. Morton gained his captaincy in the Ninth Infantry in 1879 but was never promoted beyond that. Frustrated, he finally petitioned Washington in 1897 to be retired and in 1898 he was so ordered. His cumulative military service exceeded thirty-six years, thirty-one being with the Ninth Infantry and nineteen as a captain.

A story so grand as Fort Laramie's in this dramatic centennial year dangles other research threads that I delight in following from time to time. The pleasures of discovery and storytelling continue to have a strong hold on me. And that the University of Oklahoma Press makes this volume available again to a new audience under the more apt title of *Fort Laramie and the Great Sioux War* is an original pleasure renewed.

PAUL L. HEDREN

O'Neill, Nebraska
January 1998

Preface

When I was asked to write about Fort Laramie and the Great Sioux War of 1876 I could hardly refuse. My long-standing interest in the events of 1876 on the American frontier is a matter of record. Moreover, my National Park Service career began at Fort Laramie National Historic Site, an area labeled by one of our esteemed senior colleagues as among the seven most important and representative historic sites in the whole of the American West. From my Fort Laramie days I remembered well the rousing staff debates about park history. Of two or three climactic episodes, we regularly concluded, the Indian war of 1876 had to be represented. We merely echoed, of course, earlier Fort Laramie historians like LeRoy Hafen, Merrill Mattes, David Hieb, and Remi Nadeau, who also paid tribute to that significant event. But despite its widely recognized importance, my colleagues and I had only peripherally related documentary material to base our conclusions on. There are excellent studies of Fort Laramie's neighbors, the Sioux and Cheyennes. The Black Hills gold rush was well chronicled, and Crook and Custer battle studies were rife. These histories faithfully mention Fort Laramie, but always in passing. The real action, if we believe Sioux War historians, occurred in the barren reaches beyond the safety of military posts; forts played minimal roles.

Such a widely repeated idea was patently incorrect—we knew it even by gut reaction. But Sioux War bibliographies remained void of any specific analysis of Fort Laramie in 1876. For that matter, no military post on the northern plains had been so examined. Just as important, students of the 1876 Sioux War have never yet used official army records widely in their chronicles. At each command level—field, post, department, division—a vast body of correspondence, orders, and directives was generated. It all survives and is carefully preserved in the National Archives. At the outset, I intended that this special study be a careful synthesis of primary evidence and secondary literature but that special emphasis be placed on these official documents.

That a field historian—what the National Park Service knows internally as an interpreter—should take on such a time-consuming project was an unusual proposition. Michael G. Schene, regional historian for the Park Service's Rocky Mountain Regional Office, first suggested I do the job. He had already received concurrence from Fort Laramie National Historic Site superintendent Gary K. Howe and my Golden Spike NHS superintendent Edward A. "Ted" Nichols. The diversion of my time from park operations to research and writing posed logistic concerns, and I tried to maintain a balance. Fortunately, my Golden Spike colleagues Jon G. James and Michael K. Johnson admirably filled the void while I was away doing research or otherwise had my attention diverted to events of 1876. In the midst of writing I transferred to Fort Union Trading Post NHS as park superintendent. Tending operations at a developing unit of the national park system and at the same time finishing *Fort Laramie* became a challenge bordering on obsession. I do not think operations at Fort Union suffered, but Theodore Roosevelt National Park superintendent Harvey D. Wickware, who patiently allowed the study to continue, sits in final judgment.

Obviously an undertaking of this size involved the cooperation and assistance of many people. I am grateful to Gary Howe's generous Fort Laramie staff, including John Burns, Louise Samson, Kathie Perry, Michael C. Livingston, and Philip A. Young, for their cordial help. Equally rewarding was the extended opportunity to work in the vast Fort Laramie NHS research collection. Their five-thousand-volume library, comprehensive National Archives microfilm collection, and rich manuscript files are a delightful yet unsung treasure for any western historian.

Others who helped immeasurably during field research are Bill Barton, Jean Brainard, and Paula W. Chavoya of the Wyoming State

Archives, Museums, and Historical Department; Gene M. Gressley, Emmett D. Chisum, Paula McDougal, and Robin G. B. Tully of the University of Wyoming's American Heritage Center; and Robert B. Matchette and Elaine Everly of the National Archives and Records Service.

Winifred E. Popp and William P. Frank of the Huntington Library were gracious correspondents, as were Richard J. Sommers and Michael J. Winey, United States Army Military History Institute; Dave Walter, Montana Historical Society; Hilary Cummings, University of Oregon; Alice Lentz, Laura Glum, and Bonnie Gardner of the South Dakota State Historical Society; and Betty Loudon, John E. Carter, and Marilyn Stewart of the Nebraska State Historical Society.

Photographs were provided by many of the institutions and individuals mentioned above, and also by Mercedes Penarowski, Colorado Historical Society; Neil Mangum, Custer Battlefield National Monument; Marie T. Capps and Wendy Whitfield, United States Military Academy; Towana D. Spivey, Fort Sill Museum; Tracey Baker, Minnesota Historical Society; Bobbie Rahder, Omaha History Museum; Shari L. Small, Buffalo Bill Historical Center; and Charles K. Mills, Geo. V. Allen, B. William Henry, Jr., and Jim Crain. Harvey O. Thompson provided photographic copying services with boundless enthusiasm.

Janice K. Hurley was a faithful typist through several drafts. Also answering the call of friendship and service were John P. Langellier, Joe Porter, John M. Carroll, Paul Fees, Tom Buecker, John R. Markeson, M.D., Rodd Wheaton, and Joyce Pontarolo and the Board of Directors of the Fort Laramie Historical Association.

Edwin C. Bearss, Gordon S. Chappell, Jerome A. Greene, and Robert M. Utley read and commented on an early draft of the manuscript; it has been much improved by their suggestions and advice. And in the finest tradition of Old Army camaraderie, Greene, Marvin L. Kaiser, and Paul A. Hutton supported the project and me in the truest sense of fellowship.

To all I give heartfelt thanks.

Chapter One

A Fort Laramie Perspective
on the Great Sioux War

Buffalo grass flourishes on the plains of eastern Wyoming. A luxuriant green speckled with flowers in the springtime, a muted brown the rest of the year, this living carpet rolls endlessly to the horizon. Only in the west does a low spine of mountains, highlighted by the setting sun, break the undulating prairie. And a lone sentry in the midst of these hills, 10,274-foot Laramie Peak, hints at the formidable Rockies beyond.

Coulees and intermittent watercourses break the eastern Wyoming shortgrass prairie. Gravel bars, cut-banked and timberless, dot these sinuous dry streambeds. For two hundred miles, in fact, between Cheyenne and the Black Hills, only three rivers—the Laramie, North Platte, and Cheyenne—bisect these plains. Fast and deep in the spring, these waterways provide a reliable haven throughout the year. There too, tall, strong cottonwoods shelter the valleys, giving sanctuary to man and animal alike.

This vast grassland was the stage for a cultural drama between Sioux Indians and whites that determined supremacy on the northern plains. Its culmination, the Great Sioux War of 1876–77, was a landmark episode rooted in the earliest Anglo-American advances into the trans-Mississippi West.

Indian-white relations were never comfortable. The Sioux and their neighbors knew well of the white man's pestilence. They observed his ruthlessness in trade and his fever for gold and land. Cautiously they accepted the terms of the Fort Laramie or Horse Creek Treaty of 1851, meant to bring harmony to the plains, but they bristled at immediate violations.

Both groups, of course, were capable of a hard fight. The record of bloodletting on the northern plains, from the Grattan debacle of 1854 and the Blue Water Creek retaliations the next year to the Wounded Knee tragedy in 1890, is a horrific and costly litany. Events of the 1850s, in fact, were a tidy preamble to the 1860s Bozeman Trail War. During the American Civil War long-standing lures propelled whites through the very heart of Sioux country, triggering a conflict remembered so well for the annihilation of the Fetterman command and Chief Red Cloud's total domination over army troops guarding this Wyoming and Montana road.

In final tally Red Cloud's War established temporary order in the Powder River country, but it did little to ease the deep-seated animosity between cultural factions. In a broader sense, as events of the 1850s had foreshadowed this war, so it presaged an even bloodier conflict in the 1870s. It was not intended to be this way: when the United States government sued for peace in 1868, both Indians and whites seemed genuinely interested in an end to warfare.

An impressive assembly of government commissioners, including Nathaniel G. Taylor, commissioner of Indian affairs; Senator J. B. Henderson of Missouri, chairman of the Senate Committee on Indian Affairs; and Generals William T. Sherman, William S. Harney, and Alfred H. Terry came into Fort Laramie, Wyoming Territory, on April 19, 1868, bearing a new treaty document. Word had already been sent to the powerful Dakotas to come to the fort and talk. To the dismay of the commissioners, none of the Sioux had come in April to meet them. Undaunted, the commissioners again sent runners to the camps of these heretofore intractable Sioux asking that they visit Fort Laramie and discuss terms for ending the Bozeman Trail War. Specifically, of course, the commissioners wished to see Chief Red Cloud, leader of the Oglala Sioux, who had masterminded the hostilities on the Bozeman Trail. But they wished to see other leaders as well, since the treaty they bore was intended for all the Sioux people.[1]

Among the first to come in and sign near the end of April were Iron

Shell, Red Leaf, and Spotted Tail of the Brule Sioux. Gradually, as the summer wore on, various bands of Oglalas, Miniconjous, Yanktonais, Hunkpapas, and others came to the fort, and the leaders of these groups set their marks on the treaty document. Throughout the summer proceedings, however, Red Cloud steadfastly held out, despite repeated attempts to coax him to Fort Laramie. He is alleged to have once replied to the commissioners, "We are on the mountains looking down on the soldiers and the forts. When we see the soldiers moving away and the forts abandoned, then I will come down and talk."[2]

The commissioners, concerned over their limited success and eager to meet with the Sioux of the upper Missouri River, left Fort Laramie in May. The treaty document remained in the hands of post commander Lieutenant Colonel Adam J. Slemmer, Fourth Infantry, with instructions for him to obtain Red Cloud's signature. But Red Cloud was still in no hurry to cooperate. After watching the troops leave the Big Horn Mountain country, he destroyed the army posts there and then set about gathering winter meat. Finally, on October 4 he and his followers appeared. After negotiating with government representatives for more than a month, during which time he debated each term of the new treaty, harangued about past injustices, and argued forcefully about the location of the new agency for his people, Red Cloud and several others marked the document on November 6.[3]

Despite Red Cloud's articulate and vehement speech, from outward appearances the Fort Laramie Treaty of 1868 was an impressive document. In its seventeen articles, the Oglalas had indeed won the concessions they most stridently demanded—notably, of course, the closing of the Bozeman Trail and the abandonment of Forts C. F. Smith in Montana and Phil Kearny and Reno in Wyoming. The federal government asserted itself too. Most important, the treaty ended a costly war and provided a mechanism to make the Sioux into farmers. While it conceded that the Sioux could continue hunting buffalo in the Powder River country and elsewhere, at the same time it provided education, clothing, and rations on a newly established reservation. But like any broadly encompassing document, the Fort Laramie Treaty left much unanswered.

Article 2, for instance, established a permanent reservation for the

Sioux that stretched down the Missouri River to the northern boundary of the state of Nebraska, then along that line west to the 104th meridian, north from there to the 46th parallel, and finally east on that line back to the river. In essence this provided nearly a quarter of the existing Dakota Territory as a permanent reservation, or what today is South Dakota west of the Missouri. Significantly, this new reservation contained nearly all of the Black Hills, those beautifully timbered and mineral-rich ancient mountains long held sacred by the Sioux. Even more important was the fact that a reservation was being created at all, because before this the powerful Sioux had ranged over all of the Dakota Territory, as well as most of Montana, Wyoming, and Nebraska. A final clause in Article 2 declared that no one "shall ever be permitted to pass over, settle upon, or reside in" this territory except those agents of the United States government duly authorized to discharge the duties enjoined by law.[4]

Articles 11 and 16 were important in defining other limits on the Sioux. Article 11 contained agreements that the Sioux would henceforth relinquish the right to occupy lands outside the newly created reservation and, furthermore, would withdraw opposition to the construction of railroads; that they would no longer attack or harass travelers, coaches, or animals belonging to whites; and that they would never capture or carry off white women or children or scalp white men. Article 11 did permit the various Sioux tribes to hunt on any lands north of the North Platte River and on the Republican Fork of the Smoky Hill River[5] as long as buffalo ranged there.

These were conflicting dicta. Technically the Sioux were not entitled to live off the reservation, yet hunting incursions guaranteed flight to the buffalo country of the Powder River basin. These tradition-tied Sioux, known eventually as "northern roamers" or "northern Sioux," justified a continued free-roaming existence by the pretense of the hunt, but their prolonged freedom nettled both other Indians and whites. On the one hand, the roamers harassed the Crows and Shoshonis, traditional enemies of the Sioux who also hunted the buffalo country. And with equal impunity the Sioux vexed the mining communities and then freely boasted of their triumphs in the presence of reservation kin. Forcing white law on these northern roamers ultimately became the overriding goal of the Great Sioux War.

Article 16 provided for the abandonment of the Bozeman Trail forts and established the country north of the North Platte River and east of the summits of the Big Horn Mountains as unceded Indian territory that no white could settle or occupy without the prior consent of the Indians. Ideally it was expected that the Sioux would move permanently onto their reservation, but the government understood well the importance of the annual hunts and consented to excursions into Nebraska and Kansas and as far as the North Platte River and Big Horn Mountains of Wyoming. At least south and west these hunting lands approximated the traditional range of the Sioux. Nothing was said about hunting north or northwest of the reservation, an area that was also important to these people.

Other articles provided for the physical well-being and hoped-for transformation of these nomadic prairie peoples. Several defined the government's intent to introduce farming onto the reservation. Article 6, for instance, allowed heads of families to take legal title to up to 320 acres of reservation land so long as it was cultivated, while article 8 provided for seeds and agricultural implements and instruction in farming. Article 7 provided for education for Indian children between the ages of six and sixteen. Article 10 granted clothing, a daily ration of meat and flour, and one cow and one pair of oxen for each lodge of Indians who removed themselves to the reservation. Article 13 stipulated that the United States would provide a physician, teachers, and various craftsmen as might be needed on the reservation. And article 12, as if the government already anticipated a time when different needs would demand the abrogation of treaty terms yet wanted to ensure that such changes would be difficult to effect, stated that any cessions of reservation land held in common by the Sioux would require the consent of at least three-fourths of all the adult male Indians.

The government proposed to administer to the Sioux from an agency to be established at some point along the Missouri River, declared article 4, "near the center of said reservation, where water and timber may be convenient." In final application, five separate agencies were constructed in 1868, and two more were added in following years. The Grand River Agency (relocated and renamed Standing Rock Agency in 1875) administered to Hunkpapa, Blackfoot, and

Yanktonai Sioux. Miniconjou, Sans Arc, other Blackfoot, and Two Kettles Sioux gathered at the Cheyenne River Agency, while the Whetstone Agency served Brules and Oglalas. The Crow Creek and Lower Brule Agencies served Lower Brules as well as other Yanktonais and Two Kettles.[6]

Although most of the Sioux adapted to this new condition, Spotted Tail's Brules and Red Cloud's Oglalas preferred the more traditional haunts in the far western reaches of the new reservation and unceded hunting lands. Although the government had built agencies along the Missouri where they could more easily and cheaply transport Indian goods, these two chieftains forced the creation of separate and distant agencies for their people. In 1870 Red Cloud secured a site in Wyoming, thirty miles southeast of Fort Laramie, on the north bank of the North Platte River. Spotted Tail succeeded in obtaining an agency in Nebraska on the White River about 13 miles south of the reservation and 125 miles from Fort Laramie.[7] Red Cloud's agency was moved once again in 1873 to a site on the White River, about forty miles west of the Spotted Tail Agency. The presence of these two agencies off the reservation in Nebraska, and so distant from the convenience of the Missouri River supply lines, was a point of irritation to the government as well as the citizens of Nebraska, and it figured prominently in eventual military operations against the Sioux. Significantly, Fort Laramie lay on the overland supply route to these two agencies, served as their nearest telegraph station, and otherwise materially supported the camps and their adjacent military structures.

Debate over the interpretation of certain treaty articles began almost immediately. Sioux and whites alike chose to ignore some or, at best, to comply only as long as conditions met their favor. And it appeared repeatedly that the treaty was prejudicially worded to suit white interests at the expense of the Sioux. The much-desired end to bloodshed on the northern plains never really materialized, even though in 1871 General Christopher C. Augur, commanding the Department of the Platte, boasted that no whites had been killed in his military department in that year.[8]

The situation in the vicinity of Fort Laramie after the signing of the treaty points up antagonisms in both quarters. Between 1869 and the formal onset of a major war in 1876, there occurred no fewer than seven formally recorded skirmishes between soldiers and Indians, most of whom were Sioux. The year 1869 was particularly busy for a presumed time of peace: four fights were reported, with six soldiers killed and another three wounded. Single skirmishes were recorded in 1872 (with one soldier dead) and in 1873. First Lieutenant Levi H. Robinson, Fourteenth Infantry, who was memorialized when the military post adjacent to the Red Cloud Agency was subsequently named for him, was ambushed and killed by Miniconjou Sioux near Laramie Peak, Wyoming, in 1874, along with a corporal from the Second Cavalry. Curiously, each of the fights in the Fort Laramie vicinity took place south of the North Platte River, the line of demarcation separating legal and illegal hunting lands.[9]

The incidents of Indian fighting around Fort Laramie were representative of armed clashes on the northern plains. Official accounts tally no fewer than fifty-one armed encounters from 1869 to March 1876. The same official reports record twenty-two soldiers, twenty-five civilians, and sixty-five Indians killed in those fights, with dozens of others wounded.[10] Most of these clashes were small and relatively insignificant, aside from the fact, of course, that they occurred in direct violation of articles 1 and 11 of the treaty. Perhaps none were bolder than the three attacks on Fort Abraham Lincoln, near Bismarck, Dakota Territory. On May 7, 1873, nearly one hundred Sioux attacked the infantry post at Lincoln but were driven off with the loss of four killed and wounded. Barely one month later the Sioux made two other attacks, on June 15 and 17, one while church services were being conducted for the garrison. As in the May fight, the attackers were driven off after lively skirmishing, and though no white casualties were recorded, the Sioux demonstrated a fearful resolve and grew continuously bolder as other pressures mounted on the northern plains.[11]

Closer to Fort Laramie, during the winter of 1873–74, large numbers of northern Sioux had come to the new Red Cloud and Spotted Tail agencies in Nebraska and had succeeded in creating near anarchy. The Red Cloud Agency was particularly hard pressed, and the agent there, J. J. Saville, was nearly powerless to carry out his duties. Friendly Indians and those with political influence, such as Red Cloud, Old Man Afraid of His Horses, and Sitting Bull of the South, refused to intervene. Finally, after a large war party raided the agency in February 1874 and killed several whites, including Saville's assistant Frank Appleton, troops from Fort Laramie responded. They had, of course, experienced their own losses after the killing of Lieutenant Robinson west of the fort.[12]

Lieutenant General Philip H. Sheridan, commanding the military division of the Missouri in Chicago, had been reluctant to answer earlier requests for armed assistance, but as the agency crisis grew he was compelled to act. In early March 1874 he personally oversaw the dispatch from Fort Laramie of Colonel John E. Smith, Fourteenth Infantry, and sixteen companies of infantry and cavalry that had been hastily gathered from Forts D. A. Russell and Laramie. Although the troops suffered greatly in the subzero cold, they quickly reached the Red Cloud Agency and forced the troublemakers back into the Powder River country. The crisis passed, but to stem future troubles Smith's Sioux expedition established military camps at each agency. Camp Sheridan henceforth protected Spotted Tail Agency, while Camp Robinson guarded the Red Cloud Agency. Each of the new military posts played an increasing role in the coming hostilities.[13]

Westerners were quick to point to this increasing bloodshed as evidence of bad faith on the part of the Sioux. But violations of the 1868 treaty by white men were equally numerous. Prospecting for gold, forever a powerful lure, was carried out throughout the northern plains in the 1860s and 1870s despite treaty prohibitions. Strikes of consequence took miners to the South Pass region of Wyoming after 1867. There a number of small towns prospered, but under such a threat of Indian harassment that the army established Camp Stambaugh to provide protection. Elsewhere mining sorties into the Big Horn Mountains in the early 1870s strained relations with the Crow Indians, whose reservation lay directly north of the Big Horns, as well as with the Sioux. But it was two unrelated, bold provocations in the early 1870s that made war seem inevitable.

The nation's first transcontinental railroad, completed at Promontory Summit, Utah Territory, on May 10, 1869, ushered in a new era in western commerce and travel. Journeys that had taken weeks by stage and months by wagon caravan were reduced to a few days by train. The railroad touched every facet of western life. The military, particularly, quickly realized the advantages of supply and mobility and soon redeployed to make maximum use of this new form of travel. The Indians of the plains, notably the Sioux and Cheyennes, also felt the power of the railroad, but for them the ominous changes were adverse. The transcontinental companies, particularly the Union Pacific, strongly promoted western settlement and were heard in eastern cities and by immigrants filled with a pioneering resolve. New people flooded into the Great Plains after 1869. Soon plows broke virgin sod and beef cattle began to displace the once countless bison, sounding a death knell for the first inhabitants of the prairie. Moreover, the success of the Pacific Railway served as a sterling example for other railroads with transcontinental ambitions. One of these, the Northern Pacific, was poised to advance through the very heartland of the Sioux.[14]

Since 1871 Northern Pacific surveyors had been marking out a route west of the Missouri River for the advance of their line. By 1873 the railroad had extended track from Duluth, Minnesota, to Bismarck. Beyond the temporary river terminus, the proposed route extended directly west to where Glendive Creek joins the Yellowstone River in Montana, and from there the survey continued up the south side of the Yellowstone valley. Whether the presence of railroad surveying crews in Montana violated conditions of the 1868 treaty is debatable. Whites were indeed prohibited from trespassing on the reservation or the unceded hunting lands, but the Northern Pacific route never crossed the reservation. And no one has yet decided whether the unceded hunting lands stretched northward as far as the Yellowstone River; the issue was perhaps purposefully avoided in the treaty. Article 11, on the other hand, did expressly prohibit the Sioux from objecting "to the construction of railroads . . . , which may be ordered or permitted by the laws of the United States," and with enabling legislation signed in 1864 by President Abraham Lincoln, the Northern Pacific was sanctioned by law. But permitted or not, the presence of surveyors and formidable military escorts in the Yellowstone country during the summers of 1871, 1872, and 1873 was fiercely contested by the Sioux, who considered it an unprovoked invasion of their buffalo plains.

The Sioux, it seems, drew lessons from the arrival of the Union Pacific Railroad in Nebraska and Wyoming and would not tolerate again the destruction of the buffalo and the influx of more whites into what they felt was their indisputable domain. But pressure from the Yellowstone valley, serious as it was, was not nearly as bothersome as the growing expressions of interest in the Black Hills of Dakota. And these Hills did indeed lie squarely in the midst of the Sioux reservation.[15]

The seemingly inordinate attention given to the Black Hills in the mid-1870s was not spontaneous but was the culmination of decades of suspicion, rumor, and intrigue coupled with a serious national calamity, the Panic of 1873. Contrary to popular views of this famous episode, gold was not "discovered" by the Custer expedition to the Black Hills in 1874, though doubtless news of their finds had much to do with precipitating a rush. Custer's miners merely confirmed what had been known, at least regionally, since the 1830s when trappers and perhaps one major mining party first detected traces of this alluring metal. These early reports were confirmed in the 1840s and 1850s during the explorations of Father Pierre Jean De Smet, but he prudently hushed up the news and counseled the Indians he visited to do likewise. By the 1860s, however, Sioux reportedly were exchanging gold for trade goods at Fort Laramie, and expressions of white interest, already strong in the 1850s, were brisk.[16]

The Black Hills expeditions of First Lieutenant Gouverneur K. Warren of the Topographical Engineers in 1857 and Captain William F. Raynolds, also of the Topographical Engineers, in 1859 each reported finds of gold. Perhaps fortuitously, Warren never filed an official report of his reconnaissance, and the Raynolds report was not published until 1867, when his statement about gold only supported the announcements made in 1866 by geologist Ferdinand V. Hayden, who reported that particles of gold "can be found in almost any stream in the vicinity."[17]

Before the 1868 Sioux treaty, the United States Army thwarted a number of civilian expeditions formed to explore the Black Hills. After the treaty the army had an undeniable mandate to do so, and in the early 1870s they again stopped a number of attempts. Pressure continued to mount, however, and when the Legislative Assembly of Dakota Territory twice petitioned Congress in January 1873 to authorize a scientific exploration of the Hills and, furthermore, to confine the Sioux to a reduced portion of their reservation and open the area to settlement, the government's will was weakened.[18] The army, struggling to quell confrontations between the Sioux and whites throughout the northern plains, was the first to suggest an alternative policy, though General Sheridan seems not to have had in mind precipitating a gold rush when he wrote of the advantages of constructing a large military post in the Black Hills where "by holding an interior point in the heart of the Indian country we could threaten the villages and stock of the Indians, if they made raids on our settlements."[19]

In the spring of 1874 William T. Sherman, commanding general of the army, consented to an official exploration of the Black Hills, on the pretense of siting this military post. The presence of two practical miners on the expedition attests to other motives as well, but it seems impossible to say whether this was the government's calculated response to economic considerations, the army's own desire to hasten a final war with the Dakotas, or the casual irresponsibility of the officer selected to command the survey. The exploration was not a violation of the 1868 treaty, since article 2 clearly permitted entry onto the reservation in the discharge of duties enjoined by law, and, like the Northern Pacific Railroad surveys, this operation was officially sanctioned.

General Sheridan, in whose military division this excursion took place, had first selected Fort Laramie as the base of origin for the expedition, since it was much closer to the Black Hills than any other post. But after personally visiting the fort on two occasions, he concluded that such a reconnaissance would only provoke hostilities.[20] Among many concerns, for instance, were the recently relocated Red Cloud Agency and several thousand Oglala Sioux poised on what might be a direct route to the Black Hills. Sheridan next chose Fort Abraham Lincoln near Bismarck. Garrisoning that post and several others in upper Dakota Territory was the Seventh U.S. Cavalry, with its colorful but controversial junior commander Lieutenant Colonel George Armstrong Custer.

Custer's two-month-long 1874 Black Hills expedition provided just the elixir the country needed. His command of one thousand men, plus wagons, artillery, and the regimental band, explored as if on a picnic. They climbed the highest peaks, hunted, made scientific observations of geology and mineralogy, remarked upon the timber and rich agricultural potential, and played baseball. Although they encountered a few Sioux, never once was the expedition threatened. Most important, on July 30 Horatio N. Ross recovered traces of gold in French Creek near what is today Custer City. These initial finds were dismissed by the officer corps as the sort of "color" one could wash out of any western stream with a bit of luck.[21] More substantial discoveries were made later, however, inducing Custer to report to Sheridan that there was gold among the roots of the grass.

The first news from the Black Hills expedition was dispatched by Custer from French Creek on August 3, coming south to Fort Laramie in the care of Charles A. Reynolds, a popular scout and guide known as "Lonesome Charlie." Riding mostly at night over a route eventually to become the most important way into the Hills, Reynolds arrived at Fort Laramie on August 8. From there the telegraph wires hummed.[22] Within days the nation's newspapers carried columns about Black Hills gold, and even as Custer's troops were returning to Fort Abraham Lincoln, civilian parties were outfitting for their journey to the new El Dorado. Faithful to his original objective, Custer also found a suitable location for a military post.

One other sanctioned exploration of the Black Hills occurred in August 1874, led by the Reverend Samuel D. Hinman, who was escorted by two companies of the Third U.S. Cavalry commanded by Captain Charles Meinhold and First Lieutenant Emmett Crawford. An attempt was being made to placate Nebraskans by relocating Spotted Tail Agency to the reservation in Dakota Territory. Hinman's party crossed Custer's path several times during their stay in the Hills, and though he and Custer viewed the same sights, climbed the same mountain peaks, and worked the same placer deposits, the two produced completely different reports. Where Custer lauded the agricultural and timber potential of the Black Hills, Hinman found the area bleak and uninviting. And whereas Custer wrote of the strong indications of gold (he declined to speculate on the richness of the deposits), Hinman's party could find no traces of gold or any other precious metal. Hinman, of course, was obviously protecting the interests of the Sioux. Regardless, his report, following Custer's welcome news, was ignored.[23]

Throughout the fall of 1874 numerous civilian expeditions were formed to visit the Black Hills. Although nearly every frontier community from Minnesota to Montana announced that its citizens were soon to head out, the government stepped in to quell most dreams of riches. Indisputably, the Black Hills lay in the midst of the Sioux reservation, and despite editorials like the one appearing in the *New York Tribune* that declared, "If there is gold in the Black Hills, no army on earth can keep the adventurous men of the west out of them," Washington had a clear responsibility to try.[24] During the winter of 1874–75, army garrisons from posts along the Missouri River and in Nebraska and Wyoming stepped up their patrols and surveillance and turned back dozens of Hills-bound mining parties. A few managed to get through, only to be summarily ejected once troops discovered them.[25]

The most prominent of these early trespassers was the group led by John Gordon and promoted by Sioux City, Iowa, newspaperman Charles Collins. The Gordon party, twenty-eight strong including Mrs. Annie D. Tallent, remembered as the first white woman in the Black Hills, entered the Hills from the north in December 1874 and followed Custer's path to French Creek, where they erected cabins and a stockade for winter protection. News of their presence in the heart of the Sioux reservation prompted a military response on March 22, 1875, when Lieutenant Colonel Luther P. Bradley dispatched Captain John Mix and Company M, Second Cavalry, from Fort Laramie to arrest the miners. Mix wasted little time organizing, and on March 23 they left the fort. His scouts walked into the Gordon stockade on April 3 and startled the occupants. Within a week Mix had rounded up the intruders and marched them to Fort Laramie, and the party continued to Cheyenne and points east.[26]

The army's valiant policing attempts ignored the obvious fact that interest in the new goldfields was at fever pitch and perhaps only other measures would solve the growing dilemma. The most logical option, naturally, was to acquire the Black Hills from the Sioux. In an attempt first to verify Custer's assertions and determine a negotiable value, Washington authorized a comprehensive survey of the gold region. "Should it be found," wrote Secretary of the Interior Columbus Delano to Secretary of War William W. Belknap, "to contain the precious metal in large quantities it will be very desirable to extinguish the Indian title guaranteed to the Sioux by the treaty of 1868."[27] In charge of the scientific corps of this new Black Hills expedition were geologists Walter P. Jenney and Henry Newton, both from New York City's Columbia School of Mines. Escorting the official party was a sizable military command composed of Companies C and I, Second Cavalry; A, H, I, and K, Third Cavalry; and C and H, Ninth Infantry, all under the immediate charge of Lieutenant Colonel Richard I. Dodge, Twenty-third Infantry, from Omaha Barracks. The expedition formed at Fort Laramie, and on May 25, 1875, it marched northward bent on determining whether gold existed in the Black Hills in paying quantities.[28]

The scientists surveyed late into September, carefully examining the mineral resources and topography of the Hills. Their first dispatches, sent by courier to Fort Laramie, were exceedingly cautious. In Jenney's June 22 report, for instance, he wrote that despite considerable excitement among the soldiers and teamsters about gold on French Creek, "no one obtained even by several hours hard labor more than a few cents worth of gold dust."[29] But subsequent reports continued to speak of gold that, to echo Hayden's 1866 findings, could be found in almost every watercourse in the Black Hills. Dodge was more optimistic about these mineral prospects. In his daily journal he wrote that "a good deal of work has been done, not with very great success, but with sufficient to demonstrate the fact that there is a considerable amount of gold in the bars and placers of French Creek, which though not remunerative to 'pan miners,' will yet pay, when worked properly and scientifically by sluces [sic]."[30] He threw aside caution, however, in his widely circulated promotional book *The Black Hills,* first published in 1876. Although still insisting that pan miners would struggle to make expenses, he reported that sluice and hydraulic mining would pay on French Creek, pay well on Spring Creek, and pay best on Rapid Creek.[31] The nation needed little more of an invitation.

Despite these encouraging reports, the army was still duty bound to protect the Black Hills for the Sioux Indians. The futility of that chore was evident in the dispatches sent by the 1875 expedition. In his July 31 report, for instance, Jenney wrote: "On the 20th of June there were about twenty miners in the Hills and at the present time the number is estimated at between one thousand and fifteen hundred men."[32] Dodge too noted that Spring Creek was filled with miners: "They seem to have suddenly sprung from the earth."[33]

In mid-July Brigadier General George Crook, commanding the Department of the Platte, personally visited the Black Hills to meet with the miners. Coming by way of Fort Laramie, he joined Dodge's command at Spring Creek on July 28. The next day he issued a proclamation ordering all the miners in the Hills to remove themselves by August 15 but first to hold a grand meeting and take the necessary steps to secure their claims against the day when they could legally return. The proclamation brought an unexpectedly cordial response from the miners, who for the most part readily complied.[34]

The miners' good faith was predicated on successful negotiation with the Sioux for the relinquishment or lease of the Black Hills. That effort was inaugurated in June 1875 when the secretary of the interior appointed a commission to meet with the Sioux and discuss the leasing of mining rights for $400,000 per year or the outright purchase of the region for $6,000,000. The commission was also to request the cession of the Powder River country, over which the nonreservation bands continued to roam. Heading the commission that would soon bear his name was Senator William B. Allison of Iowa. Among others serving with him were two who had already figured prominently in Sioux matters. Brigadier General Alfred H. Terry, for instance, had served on the 1868 treaty commission and was intimately familiar with the pitfalls of such negotiations. Another member, the Reverend Samuel Hinman of the Santee Sioux Agency, had just a year earlier unsuccessfully attempted to effect a relocation of the Spotted Tail Agency.[35]

After some confusion over where the meetings would be held, in early September the commission passed through Fort Laramie traveling to the banks of the White River, eight miles east of the Red Cloud Agency. In a series of councils held there beginning September 20, Allison presented the government's desires. Speaking of the country east of the Big Horn Mountains and particularly the Black Hills, he said: "It does not seem to be of very great value or use to you and our people think they would like to have the portion of it I have described."[36] This request for an enormous tract of land, some of which was considered sacred, bitterly divided the Sioux. A majority of the chiefs, including Red Cloud and Spotted Tail, seemed willing to sell the Black Hills, but the prices they asked were incomprehensible to the commissioners—some suggested a price of $30 million to $50 million, others more. Red Cloud wanted money as well as food, clothing, guns, and ammunution for seven generations. Spotted Tail and others demanded that their people be taken care of for all time as long as Indians lived. A minor but still forceful element, composed mostly of representatives from the northern hunting bands, opposed the sale of the Black Hills and other lands at any price. Although Sitting Bull, Crazy Horse, and other prominent leaders of these nonreservation Sioux refused even to attend the councils, their spokesmen managed to keep the meetings in turmoil. In addition to verbal harangue, they threatened the lives of those Sioux who favored the sale and even of the commissioners, and at one point the cavalry escort had to be deployed. After eight days the meetings broke down. Allison later offered five reasons for the failure of his commission. Principal among them was the high value the Sioux placed on the Black Hills, and also the general fear that to open the Hills to whites would only hasten the final expulsion of the Sioux from the whole of their reservation.[37]

The validity of these excuses comes into question when we study other reports of the proceedings. Red Cloud, for instance, once more a principal spokesmen for his people, may not have fully comprehended the worth of $70 million, his asking price. According to a newspaper reporter covering the proceedings for the *New York Herald,* the Sioux did not know the method of counting 1,000,000 and might mistakenly have supposed it to be 100,000. A price of $70 million could therefore have been $7 million, or only $1 million more than the government offered. At the least, historian James C. Olson in *Red Cloud and the Sioux Problem* suggests that "had the Commissioners approached their problem with a little more wisdom and with a little more ability, their chances of success would have been greatly enhanced."[38]

The rush to the Black Hills resumed virtually unchecked after September, though troops from Fort Laramie and elsewhere vigorously policed the region all season and continued to eject miners. But the futility of that exercise was telling. Crook had already received a candid assessment from his trusted aide-de-camp Second Lieutenant

General George Crook, commander of the army's Department of the Platte, and his aides-de-camp, Second Lieutenant John G. Bourke, Third Cavalry (*left*), and Captain Azor H. Nickerson, Twenty-third Infantry (*center*), about 1875. (Arizona Historical Society)

John G. Bourke, Third Cavalry, declaring that all the cavalry in the Department of the Platte could not keep the miners out of the Black Hills.[39] Meanwhile, the Sioux continued to harass the invaders by attacking wagon trains and vulnerable parties. And as if preparing for a general war, the Indians were also alleged to be stockpiling arms, ammunition, and other war matériel from the traders and anyone else who would sell them.[40] Another ominous sign came in October from the Red Cloud Agency when Agent Saville reported to his superiors that many Indians in his charge were leaving the agency and going north. He thought, however, that their purpose was to hunt and said there appeared to be no hostile feeling.[41]

The prospect of a military solution to the Black Hills dilemma materialized in early November. At a small and unpublicized conference held at the White House on November 3, attended by President U. S. Grant, Secretary of the Interior Zachariah Chandler, his assistant secretary Benjamin R. Cowen, Commissioner of Indian Affairs Edward P. Smith, Secretary of War William W. Belknap, and Generals Sheridan and Crook, the entire Black Hills crisis was thoroughly discussed. The men fully appreciated the government's moral and legal obligation to protect the integrity of the Sioux reservation, a task made frustrating by the failure of the Allison commission. At the same time, it was impossible to dismiss the electorate's enthusiasm for the Black Hills, and despite the army's best attempts, thousands of miners were there already. Shouldering this burden, President Grant chose a policy clearly favoring the opening of the Black Hills. Standing orders forbidding the occupation of the area by miners must not be rescinded, he noted, but the military would henceforth no longer resist such incursions. Simultaneously the army would initiate measures to force the hunting bands out of the Powder River country and onto the reservation, a move calculated to end Sioux opposition to settlement in the Black Hills and elsewhere. If the Sioux resisted, Sheridan was to launch a winter campaign against them.[42]

From this point on, larger aspects of the Sioux War of 1876–77 are fairly well known and are cited by those who write about these captivating events. For instance, on November 9, just six days after the consequential White House meeting, Erwin C. Watkins, a representative of the Indian Bureau, filed a report that was sharply critical of the hunting bands. In almost inflammatory language he wrote that they were "untamable and hostile," that they possessed the "best hunting-ground in the United States . . . [and] for this reason, they have never accepted aid or been brought under control," that they raided white settlements and friendly Indian villages with impunity, and that they seduced young warriors away from otherwise friendly bands. Watkins concluded that the government owed it to civilization to "send troops against them in winter—the sooner the better—and whip them into subjection."[43]

The Interior Department endorsed the Watkins report and commended it to the War Department. Following through on December 6, Commissioner Smith instructed his Sioux agents to send runners to all the Indians in the unceded hunting lands and instruct them to move onto the reservation by January 31, 1876, or otherwise be certified as hostile, to be dealt with by the army.[44] When none of the Sioux came in, active military operations commenced, aimed at bringing to an end, once and for all, this persistent Sioux problem.

Chapter Two

Sioux War Geography

President Grant's directive to cease military interference with the Black Hills gold rush circulated quickly. On November 8, 1875, Sheridan wrote a confidential letter to General Terry, commander of the army's Department of Dakota, headquartered in St. Paul, telling him of this new policy. General Crook, Terry's counterpart in the Department of the Platte at Omaha, was present at the White House meeting and telegraphed the affected troops in his command on that same day. The telegram received at Fort Laramie ordered that Captain Edwin Pollock's four companies be withdrawn from detached service in the Black Hills and distributed to their proper stations. Pollock acted quickly, and by the end of the month his command had marched south, with Companies E, Ninth Infantry, and I, Second Cavalry, taking winter quarters at Fort Laramie, while the remainder of the battalion continued to Forts D. A. Russell and Sanders.[1] Although Fort Laramie was still the closest post of consequence to the new goldfields and had already figured prominently in the army's policing actions, as winter spread across the northern plains attention and concern at the post shifted homeward. The holiday season was at hand, and the coming new year was awaited with great anticipation, since it marked the centennial anniversary of the founding of the Republic.

Lieutenant Colonel Luther Prentice Bradley, Ninth U.S. Infantry. (U.S. Army Military History Institute)

The weather thus far had been unusually mild. In the Black Hills miners were still working their placer claims in December and, in fact, were panning gold in their shirtsleeves during midday hours. Lieutenant Colonel Luther Prentice Bradley, Ninth Infantry, who commanded Fort Laramie, was a faithful diarist, and his entries at the close of the year spoke not of looming troubles or other apprehensions but of the "very beautiful winter weather" and the "bright and warm" Christmas Day. The weather on New Year's Eve was just as pleasant, and Bradley's entry was blissful: "Clear and warm, *as fine a wintery day as I ever saw. A good ending to this old year. I never saw a finer De-cember than this one just closed. Altogether 1875 has [been] a pleasant year for army work." But neither Bradley nor anyone else could forecast the tragedies of the coming Indian war. Nor could they know or properly anticipate the significant role their venerable post would play in these matters.[2]

Fort Laramie was one post of many in a giant ring loosely surrounding the Sioux reservation and the unceded hunting lands. A series of forts, some sizable, stretched up the Missouri River from Yankton through all of the Dakota Territory. An enormous and unfortunate gap existed from Fort Buford, in Dakota Territory at the confluence of the Missouri and Yellowstone rivers, to Fort Benton, in western Montana Territory, but three other forts joined Benton to safeguard the numerous white settlements in the vast western mountain country of Montana. In Wyoming and Nebraska other military garrisons closed the ring and performed a variety of services. A string of forts, for instance, had been built in the mid-1860s to protect the transcontinental railroad. By 1876 the importance of these posts had diminished as raiding and other threats from Indians shifted elsewhere. Still, these posts provided a garrison home for two or three companies of soldiers. In the Wind River country of central Wyoming, Camps Brown and Stambaugh watched over the mining communities at South Pass and also the neighboring Shoshone reservation. Military service here could still be lively, especially when the Sioux raided the villages of these traditional enemies. Sidney Barracks, Nebraska, and Fort D. A. Russell at Cheyenne owed their early development to the railroad. But in the mid-1870s each took on heightened importance as the Black Hills gold rush mushroomed and as other attention was focused on the Oglala and Brule agencies in northwestern Nebraska. Fort D. A. Russell had other value too, since on its reservation stood a subpost, the Cheyenne Depot. This depot provided quartermaster and subsistence stores for all the military posts in Wyoming, Utah, western Nebraska, and part of Idaho. Naturally it also figured prominently in the military operations soon to come.

Of nineteen posts in Crook's Department of the Platte, three stood at the cutting edge during the campaigns of 1876. Camp Robinson, the station adjacent to the Red Cloud Agency, was obviously well suited to participate in actions against the Sioux, particularly since the Oglalas reporting there were openly sympathetic with the northern bands. Camp Sheridan, adjacent to the Spotted Tail Agency, was in an equally keen position, but Spotted Tail's Brules were far more am-

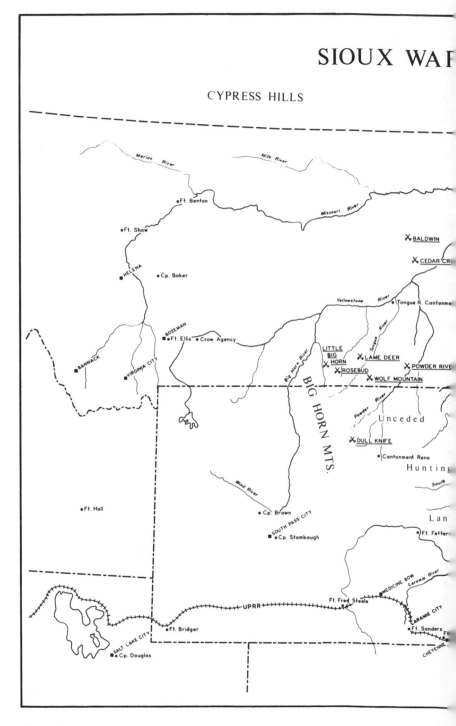

SIOUX WA[R]

CYPRESS HILLS

Marias River

Milk River

●Ft. Benton

Missouri River

●Ft. Shaw

✗ BALDWIN

✗ CEDAR CR[EEK]

■Helena   ●Cp. Baker

Yellowstone   River   ●Tongue R. Cantonme[nt]

●BOZEMAN
■●Ft. Ellis ●Crow Agency

LITTLE
BIG   ✗ LAME DEER
HORN
✗ ROSEBUD
✗ WOLF MOUNTAIN

Tongue River

■BANNACK   ●VIRGINIA CITY

Big Horn River

BIG HORN MTS.

✗ POWDER RIVE[R]

Powder River

Unceded

✗ DULL KNIFE

●Cantonment Reno

Huntin[g]

●Ft. Hall

Wind River

●Cp. Brown

South

Lan[d]

●SOUTH PASS CITY
■●Cp. Stambaugh

●Ft. Fetter[man]

MEDICINE BOW

Laramie River

UPRR   ●Ft. Fred Steele

LARAMIE CITY

●SALT LAKE CITY   ●Ft. Bridger   ●Ft. Sanders

■●Cp. Douglas

CHEYENNE

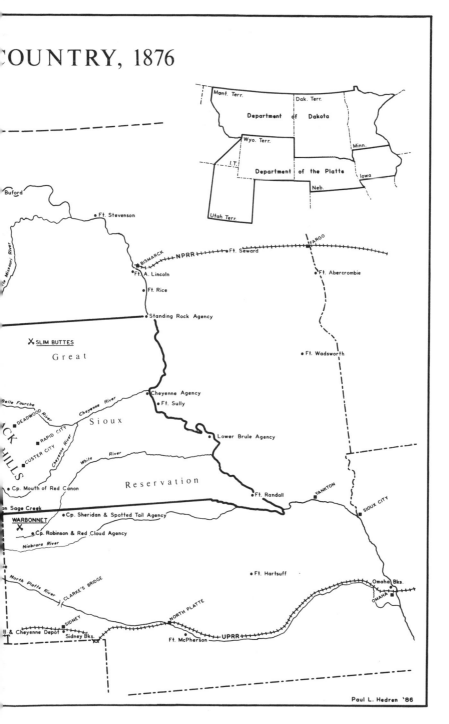

COUNTRY, 1876

Mant. Terr.   Dak. Terr.

Department   of   Dakota

Wyo. Terr.

Minn.

I.T.

Department   of   the   Platte

Iowa

Neb.

Utah Terr.

• Buford

• Ft. Stevenson

BISMARCK →NPRR← • Ft. Seward   FARGO

• Ft. A. Lincoln   • Ft. Abercrombie

• Ft. Rice

• Standing Rock Agency

X SLIM BUTTES

Great

• Ft. Wadsworth

Belle Fourche

DEADWOOD

RAPID CITY

CUSTER CITY

Cheyenne River

Cheyenne River

White   River

Sioux

• Cheyenne Agency

• Ft. Sully

• Lower Brule Agency

CK
HILLS

Reservation

• Cp. Mouth of Red Canon

• Ft. Randall

YANKTON

SIOUX CITY

on Sage Creek   • Cp. Sheridan & Spotted Tail Agency

WARBONNET
X

• Cp. Robinson & Red Cloud Agency

Niobrara River

North Platte River   CLARKE'S BRIDGE

• Ft. Hartsuff

Omaha Bks.

OMAHA

SIDNEY   NORTH PLATTE

ll & Cheyenne Depot   Sidney Bks.

Ft. McPherson →UPRR←

Paul L. Hedren '86

icable toward the whites, and most seemed against the current hostilities. Fort Fetterman, on the North Platte River 145 miles north of Cheyenne, was closest to the Powder River country and had survived the Bozeman Trail War of the late 1860s. It would serve as the springboard for each of Crook's Sioux campaigns. Eighty-one miles down the North Platte lay Fort Laramie. Laramie too would be snarled with military traffic related to the continuous campaigning, but it also lay astride the busiest road to the Black Hills. The steady military traffic, important as it became, paled compared with the stream of emigrants trekking to and from the goldfields. Laramie also sat squarely on the principal road to the Red Cloud and Spotted Tail agencies, and they too provided secondary traffic of consequence.

This loose network of military posts surrounding the Sioux reservation and protecting white settlement on the northern plains was about equally divided for administration into the two departments already mentioned, with the Department of Dakota encompassing the state of Minnesota and Dakota and Montana territories while the Department of the Platte comprised the states or territories of Iowa, Nebraska, Wyoming, Utah, and southeastern Idaho. These departments, along with three others only marginally related to the coming Indian war, were in turn administered by the Military Division of the Missouri, headquartered in Chicago and commanded by General Sheridan. The army's chain of command ultimately continued to the War Department, but rarely did the War Department or the division interfere in the operation of a solitary military post. In a fairly well-defined and even division of functions, Crook and the individual post commanders controlled operations at Fort Laramie and elsewhere.

Fortunately for the Department of the Platte, there were well-maintained connections between the military posts and the railroad. Most east-west passage in the department came first on the Union Pacific Railroad, which provided a selection of daily trains as well as connections for points east at Omaha or west and south at Ogden, Utah. The railroad destination for the posts in southeastern Wyoming and western Nebraska was invariably Cheyenne. One could also reach Cheyenne by rail from Denver via the Kansas Pacific Railroad, with Denver providing eastbound connections on the Kansas Pacific to Kansas City and elsewhere.

Headquarters, Department of the Platte, Omaha, Nebraska, as seen in the late 1860s. From here General Crook ruled an administrative region stretching from Iowa to Utah. (Western Heritage Museum)

The road overland north from Cheyenne followed the telegraph line across high rolling prairie broken conveniently by streams of varying size. In addition to fairly abundant and reliable sources of water, the road also provided wood and grass as well as campsites. For less hearty travelers, a series of road ranches existed along the way. These roadhouses varied greatly in quality, some laying out the barest of accommodations while others resembled full-service hotels. After passing the Schwartz and Fagan ranches and a host of smaller ones in between, northbound travelers came to the John Phillips ranch, fifty-three miles north of Cheyenne near present-day Chugwater. Fourteen miles beyond was the Hunton ranch, also on Chugwater Creek. Here the road forked, with a cutoff branch or left fork continuing north to Fort Fetterman, eighty-four miles beyond. Travelers taking the right fork went twenty-seven miles directly northeast, over highlands and past the Eagle's Nest roadhouse, to Fort Laramie.[3]

John Phillips, a much-respected rancher in the Chugwater valley, operated a roadhouse in the 1870s serving travelers bound for the Black Hills. (Wyoming Division of Cultural Resources)

At the start of 1876 only an informal road existed beyond Fort Laramie to the Black Hills, but established routes radiated from the fort to various other destinations. Two roads, for instance, followed the North Platte River to Fort Fetterman. These were essentially only improvements to decades-old emigrant trails, and military traffic traveled either the north or the south side of the river. The route on the north side was slightly longer—eighty-seven miles all told—and was much less used, since it tended to be hilly and in places sandy. The road on the south side, eighty-one miles long, received most of the traffic and was also the route of the telegraph line. It ran almost due west from Fort Laramie as far as Warm Springs, turned northwest past the Bull's Bend in the North Platte, thirty-four miles out, met the Cheyenne–Fort Fetterman cutoff at about sixty-one miles, and then continued to Fetterman.

Traces of roads, though seldom used in the mid-1870s, headed

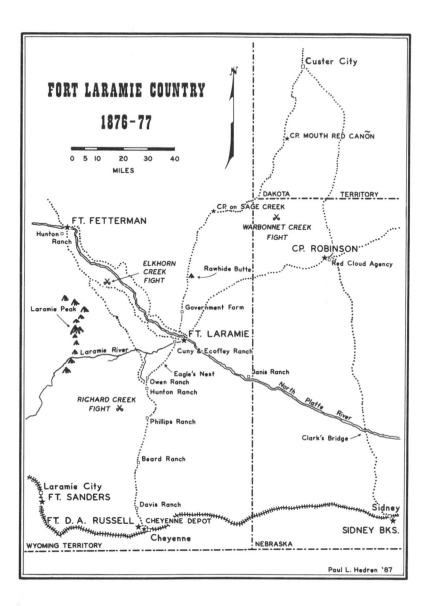

FORT LARAMIE COUNTRY
1876-77

0 5 10 20 30 40
MILES

Custer City

CP. MOUTH RED CANÕN

DAKOTA   TERRITORY

CP. on SAGE CREEK
WARBONNET CREEK
FIGHT

CP. ROBINSON
Red Cloud Agency

FT. FETTERMAN

Hunton
Ranch

ELKHORN
CREEK
FIGHT

Rawhide Butte

Laramie Peak

Government Farm

FT. LARAMIE

Cuny & Ecoffey Ranch

Laramie River

Eagle's Nest
Owen Ranch
Hunton Ranch

Janis Ranch

North Platte River

RICHARD CREEK
FIGHT

Phillips Ranch

Clark's Bridge

Beard Ranch

Laramie City
FT. SANDERS

Davis Ranch

FT. D. A. RUSSELL   CHEYENNE DEPOT
Cheyenne

Sidney

SIDNEY BKS.

WYOMING TERRITORY   NEBRASKA

Paul L. Hedren '87

down the North Platte from Fort Laramie, at least as far as the Janis ranch, near the site of the old Red Cloud Agency thirty miles away. The road to the new Red Cloud Agency in Nebraska was well established. After crossing the newly completed, but not yet fully accepted, iron bridge over the North Platte, this route angled northeastward directly to Rawhide Creek, twenty-one miles away. Across Rawhide the road continued overland to the Niobrara River, then entered the canyon at the head of the White River and finally followed the White to Camp Robinson and the adjacent agency. The distance between these posts was seventy-three miles. Travelers continuing to the Spotted Tail Agency or Camp Sheridan followed an excellent road eastward over level country for another forty-two miles.

Garrisoning Fort Laramie at the New Year were five companies of the Ninth U.S. Infantry, C, E, F, G, and H, along with the regiment's field staff and band, and Companies I and K, Second U.S. Cavalry. These companies represented two field-hardened regiments. The Ninth Infantry, for instance, was employed extensively throughout the Washington Territory in the late 1850s scouting, campaigning, and building posts and roads. By a quirk of fate, it escaped the travails of the Civil War, serving instead as provost guard in and around San Francisco until late 1865, preserving, according to its regimental history, "California to the Union." Between 1866 and mid-1869 the Ninth was again deployed along the Pacific coast, participating in the Indian campaigns in northern California and Oregon. In July 1869 the regiment was ordered to the Department of the Platte, where it was combined with the Twenty-seventh U.S. Infantry. Aside from an interlude during the summer of 1873 when six companies were detailed to the Yellowstone expedition guarding the Northern Pacific Railroad survey in Dakota and Montana, the regiment performed routine garrison and field duties in the department until 1876.[4]

The Second Cavalry Regiment had a longer and even more diverse history dating to the time of the Second Seminole War in the 1830s, and also including service in the Mexican War, on the Great Plains in the mid-1850s, and in the campaign to quell Mormon dissent in Utah in 1857 and 1858. During the Civil War the Second was engaged in the eastern theater, participating in the span of actions from First Manassas to Appomattox. After the war the regiment returned to the plains, with several companies coming to Fort Laramie in 1866. Throughout the later 1860s the Second was continuously engaged against the Sioux and their allies and suffered casualties in the Fetterman fight of 1866 and elsewhere along the Bozeman Trail. In the spring of 1869 a battalion composed of Companies F, G, H, and

Major Edwin Franklin Townsend, Ninth U.S. Infantry, distinguished himself as post commander of Fort Laramie during the active summer of 1876. Townsend is seen here as colonel of the Twelfth U.S. Infantry in the late 1880s. (U.S. Army Military History Institute)

L, commanded by Lieutenant Colonel Albert G. Brackett, was ordered to Montana, where it remained for fifteen years, coming eventually to be known as the "Montana Battalion." The remaining eight companies remained in the Department of the Platte until 1876,[5] garrisoning posts in Wyoming and Nebraska.

Fifteen commissioned officers were present for duty at Fort Laramie at the start of the new year. Commanding the post until January 2 was Lieutenant Colonel Bradley. When he embarked upon a one-month leave of absence, forty-two-year-old Major Edwin Franklin Townsend, Ninth Infantry, assumed command. Townsend, whose role at Fort Laramie would swell dramatically as the Sioux War expanded, was a twenty-one-year veteran officer. An 1854 graduate of the United States Military Academy, he had been commissioned in the artillery but resigned in 1856 to follow civil pursuits. At the onset of the Civil War Townsend again received a regular army commission, this time with the Fourteenth Infantry. He was briefly regimental adjutant but was rather abruptly promoted to captain and transferred to the Sixteenth U.S. Infantry in 1861, where he served for the rest of the war. During the postwar army reorganizations Townsend transferred to the Twenty-fifth Infantry in 1866, was promoted as a major into the Twenty-seventh Infantry in 1868, and joined the Ninth Infantry after the 1869 consolidations. With his stocky build, white beard and hair, and gentle demeanor, Townsend was a reassuring presence all year.[6]

Assisting the post commander was First Lieutenant Leonard Hay, Ninth Infantry, who was both regimental and post adjutant. As adjutant, Hay held a critical role in the day-to-day functioning of the post. All official communications were channeled through him; he kept the headquarters books and files; he paraded and inspected escorts, guards, and other armed parties before they went on duty; and he otherwise saw to it that the orders of the commanding officer were carried out. Two others in positions of authority were First Lieutenant Alfred Morton and First Lieutenant James Regan, both of the Ninth Infantry. As regimental and post quartermaster, Morton's responsibilities included the assignment of quarters and the procurement and distribution of clothing, forage, fuel, and all other quartermaster supplies, a duty that would grow to enormous proportions as the 1876 Indian campaigns progressed. Regan, the post's commissary and subsistence officer, principally tended to procuring and issuing food and related supplies.[7]

Among other officers present at Fort Laramie before the rolls began to read like a veritable Who's Who in American Military Affairs were Captains Andrew Sheridan Burt, Thomas Bredin Burrowes, Edwin Pollock, and Samuel Munson, all of the Ninth Infantry, and Captains Henry Erastus Noyes and James R. Egan of the Second Cavalry. Noyes, an 1861 USMA graduate, was the sole West Pointer among these captains. All except Pollock had seen Civil War service, and

First Lieutenant Alfred Morton, Ninth Infantry and Fort Laramie quartermaster, as photographed in Omaha by E. L. Eaton, 1882. (Lee Banicki)

Noyes, Burt, and Burrowes had each been breveted major for gallant and meritorious service. These same three officers were also veterans of the Bozeman Trail War, which was finally concluded by the Fort Laramie Treaty of 1868; Burrowes, in fact, had established Fort C. F. Smith, the northernmost Bozeman Trail military post. Burt, Pollock, Munson, and Egan had each served in the enlisted ranks before receiving their commissions.

Among Fort Laramie's captains, certainly thirty-eight-year-old James "Teddy" Egan was a dynamic though unheralded force in 1876. A well-educated Irish immigrant, Egan enlisted into the Second U.S. Cavalry in 1856 and reenlisted in the First Cavalry in 1861. In 1862 he participated in the Peninsular Campaign in Virginia and in various actions, including Antietam, in Maryland. In early 1863 Egan's company was assigned to the Army of the Cumberland, and in Tennessee he fought in numerous engagements and was wounded three times. For his sterling gallantry First Sergeant Egan received an appointment as a second lieutenant, Second Cavalry, in August 1863. Egan returned to the Army of the Potomac, and at Cold Harbor he was seriously wounded. This time a bullet shattered his right arm and thereafter he was partly disabled and relied on his left hand to hold a pistol or saber. After the war Egan came to the plains. Twice earlier he had been stationed at Fort Laramie, and he had most recently rejoined the post in October 1875. Egan's wiry build and competent, action-filled background suggest unbounded nervous energy. Like Townsend's, his presence at Fort Laramie in 1876 assuredly comforted the post's inhabitants.[8]

The post medical staff in January included captain and assistant surgeon Albert Hartsuff of the U.S. Army Medical Department, and acting assistant surgeon Adoniram Judson Gray, a citizen under contract to the army and routinely assigned to Fort Laramie. Both Hartsuff and Gray had seen Civil War service, but whereas Hartsuff formally entered the military in 1861, Gray preferred a citizen's role even though from 1863 onward it was in affiliation with the army and included frontier duty at such southwestern posts as Fort Concho, Texas, and Forts Craig, Bayard, and Cummings in New Mexico.[9]

Among the fifteen officers and the contract surgeon present for duty at Fort Laramie on January 1 were a number of junior officers plus twelve others who were assigned to the fort but were absent either on detached service or with leave. Some of these officers, like First Lieutenant Thaddeus Hurlbut Capron, Ninth Infantry, and Second Lieutenant James Nicholas Allison, Second Cavalry, would return from their absences and figure prominently in Laramie's affairs. Others, however, like Colonel John Haskell King, Ninth Infantry, who was detached as superintendent of the General Recruiting Service in New York City, would not return, despite a major Indian war on the northern plains.

Rounding out the official complement at Fort Laramie were the post's three staff noncommissioned officers, led by the venerable ordnance sergeant Leodegar Schnyder, along with commissary ser-

Ordnance Sergeant Leodegar Schnyder in 1876. This Fort Laramie veteran
served at the post from 1849 to 1886. D. S. Mitchell photograph. (Fort Laramie
National Historic Site)

geant A. A. Goodson and hospital steward Theodore V. Brown.
Schnyder, the old man of the post, had entered the army in 1837 and
was among the first soldiers to garrison Fort Laramie in 1849 when
the existing fur-trading post called Fort John was purchased by the
army. Schnyder's appointment as ordnance sergeant became effective in December 1852, and in 1876 he still maintained Laramie's
ordnance, arms, ammunition, and related stores. Similarly, Goodson
received, stored, issued, and sold subsistence stores at the fort, while
Brown, under the guidance of the post's doctors, made up prescrip-
tions, administered medicines, and generally supervised the sick at
Fort Laramie's new hospital.[10]

The seven companies of Second Cavalry and Ninth Infantry constituting Fort Laramie's garrison early in 1876 were among six regiments at Crook's disposal in the Department of the Platte. At nearby Camp Robinson were other companies of the Ninth Infantry and one company from the Third Cavalry Regiment. Up the Platte at Fort Fetterman were three companies of Fourth U.S. Infantry and one company from the Second Cavalry. Elsewhere in the department were the remaining companies of these regiments, along with all of the Fourteenth and Twenty-third Infantry regiments. Virtually every company of these six regiments, either singly or in battalion formation, would pass through Fort Laramie at one time or another in 1876. So too would a panoply of other regiments—infantry, cavalry, and artillery alike.[11]

Bearing heavily on the actions of Fort Laramie's garrison and its post commander at the dawn of the new year was the comprehension that thousands of Sioux and their allies, including the Northern Cheyennes, were very close at hand. By the most direct route, the Great Sioux Reservation was less than sixty-five miles away. The Red Cloud Agency, seventy-three miles distant, was home to an estimated 9,000 Oglala Sioux, 1,200 Northern Cheyennes, and another 1,500 Northern Arapahoes, while as many as 8,000 Brule Sioux drew rations at the Spotted Tail Agency.[12] Although these figures later proved to be inflated, this was a fearful presence given the generally antagonistic attitudes exhibited by the Sioux just months earlier at the Allison Commission meetings and the knowledge that Indians were still hunting throughout the unceded lands, which came as close as the North Platte River, only three miles from the fort.

Even though the Bureau of Indian Affairs had issued an ultimatum ordering the northern bands to return to their agencies by January 31 or be declared "hostile," the roamers were not coming in. Such movement as existed in the dead of winter was still outbound on what was known as the Powder River Trail. This broad trace led from the agencies northwestward into Wyoming, passed Sage Creek just north of the Pine Ridge, crossed the South Fork of the Cheyenne River, and continued northwest past Pumpkin Buttes and into the valleys of the Powder and Tongue rivers.[13] Traffic on this trail was almost constant in the fall and became so steady again by spring as to figure in army deployments throughout all of 1876. In addition to the trafficking of war materials between the agencies and the northern Indian camps, the fact that the Powder River Trail bisected the Black Hills road between Fort Laramie and Custer City was of enormous consequence.

In many ways Fort Laramie in 1876 was an imposing sight. It was not necessarily prettier, at least architecturally, than other conventional, wide-open, plains military forts, but it was sprawling, with more than seventy buildings spread out over half a square mile along the Laramie River. With at least two of those buildings dating from 1849, it was not among the newest forts on the Indian frontier—in fact, it was one of the oldest active military installations west of the Mississippi River. Fort Laramie's significance lay in the fact that seven companies of soldiers resided there through the winter of 1875–76. Sheridan rated the fort as an eight-company installation in his 1876 "Outline of Posts," but even with the seven present Fort Laramie held the largest garrison in all of General Crook's Department of the Platte.[14]

Fort Laramie's center was a small parade ground, only about 350 by 450 feet, situated on a bench above a bend in the Laramie River. The earliest army developments were laid out there, and "Bedlam," the already famous officers' quarters dating from 1849, still loomed imposingly from the midst of officer's row on the west side. Elsewhere were buildings of greater importance: the guardhouse, up against the river on the east side of the parade; Adjutant Hay's office in the southeast corner, to the east and rear of the board-and-batten 1870 officers' quarters; and post headquarters in the southwest corner of the parade ground attached to the commanding officer's quarters. The five infantry companies were also housed around the parade ground, two in double barracks on the east side and three in a triple set on the immediate north side.[15]

Most of Fort Laramie's buildings stretched north beyond the parade ground. To the northwest at the end of officers' row was the all-important post trader's store run by John S. Collins and many subordinates. Next door was Collins's handsome gingerbread-trimmed residence, called by Cynthia Capron "the finest in the post." On a hill overlooking Collins's home and virtually all of Fort Laramie was the imposing twelve-bed hospital completed for occupancy in January 1875. Just below and to the east was the two-story, two-company cav-

Fort Laramie in 1876. This D. S. Mitchell photograph shows the sprawling character of this venerable military post. The buildings at left, painted a deep red, surround the original parade ground. The stark, untrimmed two-story cavalry

alry barracks completed except for porches in 1874. These large buildings were made of poured lime grout, a mixture of local lime, coarse gravel, and a small measure of concrete. Grout was an economical construction material used at Fort Laramie and a few other locations and was popular because it provided a more lasting and warmer building than wood or stone. Adjacent to the barracks were four sets of stables for the cavalry and quartermaster animals.[16]

East of these buildings and closer to the river stood the bakery, telegraph office, offices for the quartermaster and commissary, all of the storehouses, assorted shops, a large fortified corral, quartermaster employees' homes known as "Dobie Row," hay and wood yards, and other outbuildings and sheds important to the operation of the post. Across the Laramie River over a log bridge stood several additional buildings, one of which was laundresses' quarters converted from the former cavalry barracks.

The post cemetery stood on the plain one-half mile north of the

barracks, home of Company K, Second Cavalry, sits at center. On the hill behind it is the new post hospital, while at the right are laundress quarters, stables, and warehouses. (National Archives and Records Service)

fort. And about two miles northeast stood what may have been Fort Laramie's most important asset, the new iron bridge over the North Platte River. Authorized by Congress in 1874 principally to facilitate the transportation of men and supplies from the railroad to the new Sioux agencies, the significance of the structure was widely recognized. Built in 1875 by the King Bridge and Manufacturing Company of Cleveland, Ohio, under the supervision of Captain William Sanford Stanton, Corps of Engineers, this three-span bridge was substantially complete by December 1875 and had even been rigorously tested by leaving thirteen army wagons loaded with stone on each arch for several days. Even though the army delayed formal acceptance of the bridge until February 1876 while certain minor conditions were corrected, Cheyenne's promoters were already ballyhooing their route to the Black Hills as the unqualified best. It had, they reported, substantial army protection midway north and an iron bridge across the treacherous North Platte.[17]

John Collins's post trader's store at Fort Laramie, 1877. Photograph attributed to D. S. Mitchell. (Fort Laramie National Historic Site)

Fort Laramie's iron bridge in 1876. This vital crossing of the North Platte River gave supremacy to the Cheyenne–Black Hills road as the leading route to the new goldfields. D. S. Mitchell photograph. (U.S. Military Academy Library)

Cheyenne's boosterism notwithstanding, none of the other routes to the goldfields could compare with that running north by way of Fort Laramie. Along the Missouri River, Bismarck, Fort Pierre, Fort Randall, Yankton, and Sioux City each vied for recognition as "the" jumping-off point for the Black Hills. Each community, moreover, organized and sent out parties of miners. But to their ultimate dismay, none of these cities attracted strong national attention. Most were isolated from principal avenues of inbound transportation, and all required extensive overland travel across the Sioux reservation, which, as one Black Hills guidebook put it, was "a country infested by hostile Indians."[18] Along the Union Pacific Railroad in Nebraska towns like Fremont, Kearney, Plum Creek, North Platte, and Sidney tried hard to lure travelers to their stations. The Union Pacific served as a cordial partner providing the steady inbound traffic that the Missouri River points simply could not muster. But logically, if a prospector could afford the price of a train ticket to begin with, it only made sense to pay to the transfer closest to one's ultimate destination, and so the numerous stations east of Sidney failed to garner serious attention. Sidney, however, came close. A widely known trail northward had already been marked out and was used with some regularity, at least as far as the Red Cloud Agency. Like the Cheyenne road, this one offered military protection, both from the garrison at Sidney Barracks and also from the troops at Camp Robinson. But the citizens of Sidney were too slow to aggressively promote their route, and they did not have a secure crossing over the North Platte River until a toll bridge was completed near present-day Bridgeport on May 10, 1876. In the meantime, Cheyenne had already capitalized on its strong assets and was offering regular stage service, endorsements from nearly all the travel-guide writers, and other important inducements, enabling it early on to eclipse its rivals.[19]

To one seeing Fort Laramie for the first time, the lackluster colors of its buildings and landscape may have created a pallid vision. Only for a few months in spring and early summer did green cover the surrounding prairies; during the rest of the year shades of tan and brown predominated. A few scrubby bushes grew along the rivers, but there were no trees except one—the big box elder down the Laramie from "Dobie Row." This was the papoose tree, the final rest for the bodies of forty or more Indian children.[20] Elsewhere other dusky tones prevailed. Although much of the fort had recently been painted, the predominant color in 1876 was a local variation of Venetian red. Aside from trim, the grout buildings were left unpainted. With weathered wooden roofs throughout, the whole must have been unprepossessing. One visitor in 1876 remembered it this way:

> The rear windows of the commanding officer's house looked out upon a rushing torrent, and where the surgeon lived, at the southwest angle, the waters lashed against the shabby old board fence. . . . South and west the bare, gray-brown slopes shut out the horizon and limited the view. Northward the same brown ridges were tumbling up like a mammoth wave a mile or so beyond the river.

Elsewhere, this visitor saw "the unpicturesqueness of the yards, the coal- and wood-sheds, the rough, unpainted board fences; the dismantled gate, propped in a most inebriate style against its bark-covered post."[21]

The vitality of Fort Laramie fortunately was not measured by the appearance of its buildings. The fort was home to nearly four hundred soldiers plus hundreds of other civilians who were either army dependents, quartermaster employees, or other citizens under contract or engaged in commercial activities such as the post trader's store and the mail and stage services. To nearly all, Fort Laramie seemed a comfortable station. Cynthia Capron, for instance, remembered the gracious hospitality shown her family upon their arrival at the fort. "We drove to Captain Munson's," she wrote, "and they both gave us a warm welcome. We remained there until Tuesday [three and a half days], Mrs. Munson in particular doing everything she could to make it pleasant for us."[22] The Caprons soon settled in Bedlam, the old officers' quarters. Her letter offers details about that famous structure:

> We live in a large building containing four setts of quarters, two below and two above. The rooms are quite large and there are plenty of them. We are fixed very comfortably. We have a good man to cook but I have all of the rooms except the kitchen and dining room to take care of. Parlor, bedroom, with three beds, dressing room, a store room and hall. I don't sweep it all everyday, I can't.

"Bedlam" in 1876. This 1849 officers' quarters, which is now the oldest surviving building in the State of Wyoming, was immortalized by Captain Charles King in his 1889 romantic novel of the Sioux War era, *Laramie; or, The Queen of Bedlam*. Photograph by D. S. Mitchell. (Archives, American Heritage Center, University of Wyoming)

We stay in the bedroom a good deal so that I don't have to sweep the parlor thoroughly more than once or twice a week and the children play out of doors some, so that helps keep clean. They have a nice play house in the back yard under the stairs to the upper sett of quarters. Hazen and the man made it. It is enclosed, has a floor carpeted with a gunny sack, and has a door.[23]

Elizabeth Reynolds Burt had other recollections of the fort during this time. The isolation so common to the frontier experience could be dealt with, but winter posted its own problems:

A daily mail and telegraphic communications with Cheyenne and the world beyond were blessings. So my husband's rank gave him better quarters than many of the other officers had, even if they consisted of only six rooms poorly constructed. With wood stoves and plenty of wood we could keep comfortable in our living room at least. At night it was impossible to make the dining room and kitchen warm. Milk was found frozen solid in the pan in the morning. Jack Frost played havoc with everything. The precious sack of potatoes was covered with a buffalo robe and placed near the stove in the living room each night.[24]

As Mrs. Burt points out, mail and telegraph services were extremely important to the garrison, both for the orderly carrying out of military responsibilities and for the general well-being of the inhabitants. In these respects, fortunately, Fort Laramie was well tended. Telegraph connections to the fort had been made in 1861 upon the completion of the first transwestern line, Omaha to San Francisco. Although the line was rerouted southward in the late 1860s, a generally reliable Western Union connection to Cheyenne still existed. And the daily mail brought letters from home, along with magazines and newspapers. Cynthia Capron remembered that the post had an excellent library, subscribing to *Harper's* and *Scribner's* magazines and to various papers.[25] Beyond some hometown favorites, undoubtedly the most influential newspapers received at the fort were the *Cheyenne Daily Leader* and the *Army and Navy Journal*. Published daily except Monday, the four-page *Leader* offered an array of national and international news and always had a full page or more covering local events. Heading all coverage through the winter of 1875–76, naturally, was news about the Black Hills gold rush. There were continual, sometimes multiple, reports from returning Hillers, stories about new parties forming up for a springtime departure, hot strikes, and ceaseless endorsements of the Cheyenne route to the new El Dorado. Of greater appeal certainly in military circles was news of transfers, the coming and going of military personages in Cheyenne, and soon, lengthy and quite reliable reports from the battlefields. The *Army and Navy Journal*, published weekly in New York City, carried news from the army and navy headquarters in Washington as well as the various division offices, extracts from military memoirs, and bulletins from points of action nationally and internationally, plus reports and enticing gossip of interest to officers, enlisted men, and families alike.

As at any military post, a system of bugle calls regulated Fort Laramie's day, not only for the troops but for all residents. The current schedule was first published in 1872 and remained virtually unchanged through nearly all of 1876. The calls, detailed below, allowed for an orderly carrying out of military routine and responsibility:

First Call for Reveille	5:30 A.M.
Reveille	5:45
Police Call	Immediately after
Stable Call	Immediately after
Breakfast Call	6:30
Surgeon's Call	7:30
Fatigue Call	7:30
First Call for Guard Mounting	8:50
Guard Mounting	9:00
Band and Field Music Practice	Immediately after
Water Call	11:00
First Sergeant's Call	11:30
Recall from Fatigue	11:45
Dinner Call	12:00
Fatigue Call	1:00 P.M.
Stable Call	4:00
Recall from Fatigue	Thirty minutes before Retreat
Retreat	Sunset
Tattoo	8:30
Taps	9:00
Sunday Morning Inspection	9:00 A.M.
Guard Mounting	Immediately after
Church Call Sundays	10:45
Dress Parade	When ordered[26]

A highlight of this official schedule was the daily mounting of the guard. The twenty-four-hour rotating guard detail provided continuous internal security at the post. Each morning this soldier complement was changed in an elaborate parade ground ceremony involving several inspections, a demonstration of the manual of arms, and musical accompaniment by the Ninth Infantry Regimental Band. Invariably the guard mounting attracted attention, and it was a rare day when the children of the post and the officers' wives failed to turn out. Citizens too, especially miners passing through who might otherwise be unaccustomed to such a formal military ceremony, paused to watch the proceedings.[27]

Beyond the dependents in the military garrison, two other sizable groups of civilians figured in the day-to-day operation of the post. One, briefly alluded to already, comprised the quartermaster employees in the charge of Lieutenant Morton. Through the winter, Morton's roll of citizen employees dwindled from fifty-two in October 1875 to thirty-four in January 1876. Most of these men—twenty-four in January, for instance—were teamsters. But the rolls also carried specialists, such as quartermaster clerk I. G. Thomson; John W. Ford, the telegraph operator; D. C. Chatterton, post engineer in charge of the steam sawmill; Indian interpreter John Farnham; and two blacksmiths, a saddler, a wheelwright, and two wagonmasters. The monthly wages paid to these civilians varied widely according to the skills required and the responsibilities exercised. Thomson, the clerk, received $125 a month—exactly the monthly pay received by Lieutenant Morton. The scale dropped from there, with the telegraph operator, engineer, and interpreter each receiving $100 a month; the blacksmith and wheelwright $90; the saddler $80; the two wagonmasters $75 and $50; and the teamsters $35 each. This pay rankled many of the soldiers. An enlisted cavalry saddler received $15 a month, and noncommissioned officers, who formed the backbone of the enlisted force, received base pay topping out at $23 for a first sergeant. It was no surprise then that as Morton's quartermaster employee rolls grew, which they did considerably in 1876, discharged soldiers were often among the newly hired.[28]

Another group of citizens who considered Fort Laramie home were the numerous ranchers living in the vicinity, particularly to the west and south. Although they may not have resided on the post, their appearance there was routine as they came for mail, to purchase goods at the well-stocked post trader's store, or perhaps to use the Western Union telegraph. These ranchers, of course, did not live on the Fort Laramie Military Reservation, which, as declared in 1869, encompassed the land within a six- by nine-mile rectangle around the post. Nor was trespassing allowed on the reservation extension added in

Jules Ecoffey (*left*) and a friend in the mid-1870s, at his Three Mile Ranch along the Laramie River west of Fort Laramie. (Fort Laramie National Historic Site)

1872, embracing another 125 square miles east along the south bank of the North Platte River. Elsewhere, however, ranchers thrived in surprising numbers.[29]

Fort Laramie's closest ranch neighbors were probably Adolph Cuny and Jules Ecoffey, who owned the Three Mile Ranch west of the fort on the Laramie River. Both Cuny and Ecoffey were old-timers in the area. Ecoffey, for instance, had a long history of friendship and association with the Sioux, serving in the 1860s and 1870s variously as trader, interpreter, and confidant to Red Cloud and his Oglalas.[30] In 1876 these partners operated a ranch in the traditional sense, at least according to J. H. Triggs, who in the extensive discussion of grazing and stock growing in southeastern Wyoming that appeared in one of his guidebooks, listed 2,000 head of cattle and 150 horses and mules on their place.[31] Cuny and Ecoffey offered other services too. Morton, the post quartermaster, would contract with them for wagons and teams later during the summer. And in the true spirit of frontier entrepreneurs, they operated a roadhouse for Black Hills travelers, offering meals, an outfitting store, a billiard hall, a blacksmith shop, and a corral with hay and grain. Appealing to baser instincts, they also ran a saloon and brothel, principally for Fort Laramie's soldiers. The unvarnished nature of that concern was described with some detail by General Crook's aide-de-camp Lieutenant Bourke:

Several times, on mild afternoons, Lieut. Schuyler and myself went riding, taking the best road out from the post. Three miles and there was a nest of ranches, Cooneys and Ecoffey's and Wrights, tenanted by as hardened and depraved a set of wretches as could be found on the face of the globe. Each of these establishments was equipped with a rum-mill of the worst kind and each contained from three to half a dozen Cyprians, virgins whose lamps were always burning brightly in expectancy of the coming bridegroom, and who lured to destruction the soldiers of the garrison. In all my experience, I have never seen a lower, more beastly set of people of both sexes.[32]

The combination of brothel, roadhouse, and legitimate ranch may have been unique to the partnership of Cuny and Ecoffey. But these three enterprises each appeared independently elsewhere around Fort Laramie, such as Wright's brothel, mentioned above, which was also three miles west but on the south side of the Laramie River. The Six Mile Ranch southwest of the fort doubled as a genuine roadhouse in 1876 as well as a house of prostitution, a tradition that dated from years earlier. Other ranches, such as those owned and operated by John Phillips and John Hunton, were true cattle spreads, with incidental, often elaborate, services for travelers. William G. Bullock, another Fort Laramie old-timer, operated a ranch up the Laramie beyond Cuny and Ecoffey's, and he also partnered with Hunton on the Chugwater. All together there were at least three cattle ranches on the Laramie River, ten on Chugwater Creek, and dozens more on the road to Cheyenne. Small and large, these establishments interacted in countless ways with Fort Laramie, especially during the event-filled year of 1876.[33]

Fort Laramie's winter routine, calm as it may have appeared, concealed the undercurrents of a looming war. Soldiers comprehended better than anyone else that it would be their sweat and blood that would ultimately effect the changes demanded in the existing order on the northern plains. Gold in the Black Hills was precipitating this Indian war, but it had antecedents much older than that. Some soldiers, probably mainly the officers, understood these emotionally laden issues, but while they might sympathize, it was not their duty to

Freighters' camp at the Eagle's Nest Stage Station, fifteen miles south of Fort Laramie. This 1876 photograph by D. S. Mitchell provides a glimpse at freighting operations during the Black Hills gold rush. (Geo. V. Allen)

question, only to carry out the decisions of the president. This Great Sioux War did not envelop Fort Laramie and its officers and men overnight. Rather, as in a great symphonic crescendo, it built up deliberately, unfolding with ever larger movements to engulf, but never destroy, the post. Laramie was, after all, well tempered, and though eventually taxed to the limit, it never skipped a beat. For examining a post at war, barely behind the scenes as it was, there could be no better example.

Chapter Three

Campaigning Begins:
January–March 1876

Attention turned to war almost immediately after the November 1875 White House conference. General Sheridan, returning to Chicago, outlined an overall campaign strategy that recalled the successes against the Southern Cheyennes in 1868–69 and in the more recent Red River War of 1874–75. He would deploy semi-independent forces against the Sioux, with General Terry mustering those troops at his disposal in Minnesota, the Dakota Territory, and Montana and General Crook leading troops from the Department of the Platte. Timing was critical. The generals understood that if these nomadic Sioux were to be driven back to their agencies, the action must occur in winter while the Indians were most vulnerable. Should a winter campaign fail and the Sioux be reinforced by the usual springtime defections from the agencies, Sheridan feared they might never be caught. At the onset there was every expectation of success. The newly deemed hostile Sioux, led principally by Sitting Bull and Crazy Horse and numbering, according to Sheridan's early intelligence, no more than 160 lodges and about 270 warriors, were wintering somewhere in southeastern Montana and would be no match for any of the commands sent against them.[1]

General Crook received his official directives on February 8, 1876. Sheridan could not tell him specifically where the Sioux might be

Lieutenant General Philip H. Sheridan, commander of the Military Division of the Missouri, was the army's chief strategist in the protracted war against the Sioux. (U.S. Army Military History Institute)

found—a moot point anyway since, as he noted, they might be one place today and somewhere else tomorrow. Crook learned that he was not expected to work in concert with Terry, though he would receive information and intelligence from him as rapidly as it could be relayed through the channels and was to reciprocate in sharing information as expeditiously as possible.[2]

During this period Fort Laramie divided its attention between the continuous and ever growing promotion of the Black Hills goldfields and the brewing campaign, which one could read about in the newspapers and trace through the telegrams from department headquarters in Omaha. The otherwise normal winter quiet had already been jarred on December 2 when the post conducted memorial services for Vice President Henry Wilson, who died in Washington on November 22. All of the garrison, which with Captain Pollock's recent addition from the Black Hills totaled seven companies and nearly four hundred men, paraded in battle order at 10:00 A.M. The flag flew at half-staff, and the somber day was broken by cannon salutes of thirteen guns at dawn, seventeen guns at meridian, and a national salute of thirty-seven guns at retreat.[3]

In a logistical sense Fort Laramie's normal seasonal responsibilities continued even though attention was increasingly being diverted elsewhere. On January 11, for instance, Corporal John McFarlane of Company H, Ninth Infantry, was detailed for one month to the iron bridge as the soldier "in charge," relieving a fellow noncommissioned officer who was returned to his company. Bridge duty was a continuing chore in addition to the daily guard, drills, and fatigues. Also, a special order issued January 23 detailed a sergeant and sixteen men of Company C, Ninth Infantry, as escort for the timber train to and from Laramie Peak. Escort duty in one form or another was one of those tasks that grew to enormous proportions as the campaigns got under way. Some of it, in fact, had already irked the post commander until in early December he wrote to Omaha complaining that the depot quartermaster in Cheyenne was sending Fort Fetterman's freight trains via Fort Laramie, obliging him to furnish separate escorts for each. Although he called the arrangement "unfair" and almost pleadingly asked whether it was to stand, Omaha turned a deaf ear.[4]

Travel to and from the Black Hills abated considerably in January, winter weather having replaced the earlier unseasonable conditions that Luther Bradley recorded in his diary. This slowdown, however, had little effect on the ongoing planning and anticipation for the coming rush, nor was it any reason for newspapers like the *Daily Leader* to let up in their incessant promotion of Cheyenne and the Black Hills. Naturally all of this had a strong impact on Fort Laramie. The January 12 *Daily Leader*, for instance, reprinted an extensive interview by the *Omaha Republican* with Captain Pollock, who, as the paper noted at the onset, had spent from July to November 1875 in the Black Hills expelling miners. Pollock, whether or not he knew about other routes, strongly endorsed the Cheyenne road. Even though it was slightly longer than that out of Sidney, he said, the "Fort Laramie route gives miners the advantage of a substantial bridge across the Platte." Pollock was necessarily frank about the dangers from Indians and warned that miners would most likely meet "red men" between the head of the Running Water and the Cheyenne River—not coincidentally, that same area where the Indians' Powder River Trail bisected this gold route. Pollock then offered an appraisal of the goldfields. There was indeed precious metal in all the creeks and bars, and "a man willing to work can make good wages." These comments, reprinted in other newspapers and even in one of J. H. Triggs's widely circulated Black Hills guidebooks, helped fuel enthusiasm for the new El Dorado.[5]

Businessmen, anticipating gain not from their own arduous labors in the Black Hills but from miners headed there, were preparing for this expected mass movement. J. W. Dear, the Indian trader at Red Cloud Agency, spent January establishing five ranches for travelers between Fort Laramie and the Hills. Conveniently situated about a day's walk apart, facilities were soon established at the Government Farm, at the head of Running Water, on the Old Woman's Fork of the Cheyenne River, on Horseshoe Creek, and on the Cheyenne River itself. Even though this was still only a roughly blazed trail, Dear anticipated the day when regular stage service would travel an improved road using most, if not all, of his stops. Such stage travel too was well along in planning. Station stops between Cheyenne and Custer City were being marked out, and some were already stocked with hay and grain for commencement of service in early February. Fort Laramie's trader, John Collins, likewise spent January laying in what the *Daily Leader* called an "immense quantity" of flour, bacon, and other provisions for miners.[6]

Stage service, intermittent at first and destined to change ownership repeatedly in the early going, was finally realized north of Fort Laramie beginning February 3 when the first coach run by the "Cheyenne and Black Hills Stage, Mail, and Express Line" stopped at Cheyenne's Inter-Ocean Hotel to take on passengers for the Black Hills.

This service, announced as semiweekly, augmented existing coach travel between Cheyenne, Fort Laramie, and the Red Cloud Agency but, of course, had as its destination Custer City.[7] John Collins, sizing up the opportunity to operate his own accommodations for these stage travelers and others at Fort Laramie, announced in the February 24 *Daily Leader* that he was building a new hotel at the fort, to be ready for guests in ten days. The "Rustic House," as it was first known, was built on the flats southwest of the post hospital and opened March 15, replete with furnishings delivered directly from Omaha.[8]

In Omaha General Crook had wasted little time in December and January preparing for the campaign, which was officially announced on February 8. He had already queried the commanding officers of the Second and Third Cavalry regiments, at Fort Sanders and Fort D. A. Russell, respectively, on the number of new horses required to fill out their companies.[9] Then, in characteristic fashion, he had Major Marshall Independence Ludington, chief quartermaster for the Department of the Platte, locate and transfer to the Cheyenne Depot all the available mules from posts in Nebraska and Wyoming. Crook's predilection for mules as pack animals was gained in the early 1870s campaigns against the Apache Indians in Arizona, and in fact mules had been an object of lifelong interest and study for him. Crook not only had mules gathered but specifically imported packers and specially fitted pack saddles, known as *aparejos,* to make this facet of his operation the envy of other field commanders.[10] Similarly, Crook redistributed many of the wagons at his disposal in the department, and a number, including extras at Camps Robinson and Sheridan, were transferred to Fort Laramie for immediate use.[11]

Crook's general plan for this late-winter march into the Powder River country was a simple one, based on the essential information from Sheridan suggesting that a relatively small number of Sioux would oppose him, assuming he found these Indians before Terry did. To meet this enemy, Crook ordered elements of the Second and Third Cavalry and a modest infantry escort to consolidate at Fort Fetterman, the post nearest to the roamers' wintering ground. From there he would "move, during the inclement season, by forced marches, carrying by pack-animals the most meager supplies [and] secretly and expeditiously surprise the hostile bands, and, if possible, chastise them before spring fairly opened."[12] Gathered for this campaign, soon to be labeled the Big Horn Expedition, were twelve companies: A, D, E, F, and M, Third Cavalry, representing the total mounted complement at Fort D. A. Russell; B and E, Second Cavalry, from Fort Sanders, near Laramie, Wyoming; three of the four companies stationed at Fort Fetterman—A, Second Cavalry, and C and I, Fourth Infantry; and from Fort Laramie its two mounted units, I and K, Second Cavalry.[13]

Specifics about this winter campaign had a mixed reception at Fort Laramie. Its inevitability, of course, had been foreseen for months as military effort steadily changed from peacetime to wartime conditions. While some of the soldiers, perhaps the enlisted men more than others, may have actually welcomed the prospect of field service, Elizabeth Burt, wife of Captain Andrew Burt, Ninth Infantry, recalled that the garrison, which in her frame of reference surely meant the officers and their families, received the news of the campaign as a "dreadful shock" that totally disrupted the pleasant harmony of garrison life. "Fortunately for us 'Infantry' wives," she noted, however, "the expedition was to be composed of cavalry with only two companies of Infantry."[14]

Fort Laramie, designated as a rendezvous for the companies ordered to participate, had its first field sortie in mid-February. In response to what John Hunton calmly labeled in his diary "Indian rumors," post headquarters issued special order 29, dated February 14, 1876, directing Captain Henry Noyes and twenty men of Company I, Second Cavalry, to leave February 15 on a scout in the neighborhood of the Old Red Cloud Agency, endeavoring to intercept a small party of Sans Arc Sioux "intent on a marauding expedition." These same orders directed Captain James Egan with twenty men of Company K, Second Cavalry, to proceed at once as far as Bridgers Ferry, an old Bozeman Trail river crossing about sixty miles from the fort. Egan was specifically directed to go up the north side of the North Platte River to the ferry site and return down the south side, scouting all the while for a small band of Sans Arcs reportedly stealing stock from the Laramie River valley. Both detachments were to be rationed for five days and furnished with one hundred rounds of ammunition per man. Noyes and Egan each returned on February 17 reporting "no results," but their marches after marauding Indians established a routine that would soon become common. Surprising was the alleged presence of Sans Arc Sioux. The Sans Arcs reported to the Cheyenne River Agency, near the confluence of the Cheyenne and Missouri rivers. Their presence in southeastern Wyoming, if indeed they were correctly identified, demonstrated the astonishing mobility of the Sioux.[15]

By mid-February quartermaster and commissary activities at Fort Laramie, Fort Fetterman, and the Cheyenne Depot had been stepped up to meet the needs of Crook's pending expedition. Troops from Fort Laramie were regularly escorting Fetterman-bound public stores, which were still coming by way of Laramie rather than directly northward from Cheyenne to Fetterman on the cutoff road. Typically the escort was small, such as that described in special order 35 consisting of a sergeant, one corporal, and eight privates, all in this case from Company F, Ninth Infantry. These soldiers were rationed for five days and furnished with one hundred rounds per man for their Springfield rifles. Fortunately, they were also provided with a wagon for conveyance to Fort Fetterman and back.[16] These public stores consisted of a broad range of goods necessary to the campaign, including ammunition, rations, grain and forage for the animals, and what the army conveniently labeled "clothing, camp, and garrison equipage," or "CC&GE." Individual posts were also receiving these essential items, in addition to stocks of related goods required for general operations.

Central to the proper functioning of quartermaster and commissary operations during Crook's campaigns was the wholesale receipt and issuance of military supplies at the Cheyenne Depot. Divided by function, this immense operation was under the control of Captain James Gilliss, an assistant quartermaster for the Department of the Platte with duty station at the depot, and Captain William H. Nash of the army's Commissary and Subsistance Department, who was the depot commissary. These officers received contract goods, arsenal shipments, animals, wagons, and thousands of related issues by the train carload, stored them temporarily in immense corrals and warehouses adjacent to the Union Pacific sidetracks, and issued them on requisition to the posts or the field. Although the Cheyenne Depot was

Cheyenne Depot, Wyoming. The numerous warehouses, yards, and corrals were a prime source of supply for General Crook's campaigns in 1876. (Wyoming Division of Cultural Resources)

on the Fort D. A. Russell Military Reservation, it functioned in every respect, as an independent military post. Garrisoning the depot throughout 1876 was Company E, Twenty-third Infantry, commanded by Captain George K. Brady. While the rest of the Twenty-third participated in the larger events of 1876, the monthly Record of Events for Company E read routinely and simply: "Performed garrison duty and guarded quartermaster and commissary supplies at the Depot."[17]

Lieutenant Alfred Morton's quartermaster employee rolls at Fort

Cheyenne in 1876. This view looks west, with Union Pacific Railroad yards at the left, and the business district westbound at the right. Photograph attributed to D. S. Mitchell. (National Archives and Records Service)

Laramie grew appreciably as military operations expanded during February. The thirty-four employees reported in January nearly doubled in the following month to sixty-three. Most of these new civilians were teamsters, and many had transferred from Camps Robinson and Sheridan when Crook redistributed wagon transport to better meet the needs of field service. Wagons and teamsters coming and going must have presented a spectacle, especially in conjunction with the eventual surge of civilian traffic on the Black Hills road. Moreover, the regular availability of quartermaster transportation became a critical issue as the Sioux War blossomed beyond the limited scope of the earliest movements. Often, as the record glaringly showed, Fort Laramie did not have the transportation to meet its needs, and the system by which Cheyenne Depot could on February 10 simply ask Fort Laramie to send down all but ten of its wagons, on the promise in a telegram dated February 15 that it would return twenty wagons as soon as they off-loaded at Fetterman, simply collapsed.[18] In February, however, this round-robin utilization of transport still worked, and late in the month Fort Laramie did receive twenty wagons that, perhaps of equal significance, came loaded with 100,000 pounds of grain to augment the post's own stocks, which had dwindled to about 100,000 pounds.[19]

Lieutenant Colonel Luther Bradley returned from his six-and-a-half week leave of absence on February 16 and resumed command of the post. He had traveled as far east as New Haven, Connecticut, visiting family and friends including General Sheridan in Chicago,

Cheyenne in 1876. This view looks northwest. The central business district is to the left, out of the picture. Photograph attributed to D. S. Mitchell. (National Archives and Records Service)

Colonel John H. King, his regimental commander who was temporarily assigned in New York City, and Major General Winfield Scott Hancock, also in New York City commanding the Military Division of the Atlantic.[20] Also arriving during this period was acting assistant surgeon William E. Brandt, who reported for duty January 18. Brandt, however, did not stay long, for when the department denied his request for a leave of absence on February 16, stating that he had been selected to accompany Crook into the field, he had his contract annulled and left the post on February 19.[21]

Crook and his entourage left Omaha for the field on February 17, traveling on the Union Pacific Railroad to Cheyenne, where they arrived amid considerable fanfare on the eighteenth. Over the next several days Crook attended to details related to the expedition, received courtesy calls from most of the officers stationed at Fort D. A. Russell and Cheyenne Depot, and visited with reporters from the *Cheyenne Daily Leader*. The February 19 issue of the paper was effusive over the general and the coming campaign, noting that he had proved in Arizona to be "the best Indian fighter America has yet produced" and, if allowed to have his own way, would "make short work of this Indian business."

Lieutenant John Bourke, Crook's plucky aide-de-camp, was particularly impressed by the character of Cheyenne. The city was wild over the prospects of an Indian war, but more so over the settlement of the Black Hills. Along the streets, he wrote, were long trains of wagons loaded for the Hills; every store advertised supplies suited for the Hillers; hotels were crowded with men on their way north; "even the stagedrivers, boot-blacks, and bellboys could talk of nothing but Black Hills—Black Hills."[22] Cheyenne too, according to Bourke, was maturing. Great numbers of new brick buildings had been erected in recent months, "giving the town a bustle and activity as well as an appearance of advancement in favorable contrast with Omaha, Denver and Salt Lake."[23]

Those cavalry companies from Fort D. A. Russell that had been assigned to the expedition departed on February 21, marching north to the Hunton ranch. There, rather than turning northeast to Fort Laramie, they continued on the cutoff road directly to Fort Fetterman. The two Second Cavalry companies from Fort Sanders marched north from Laramie City, crossed through the Laramie Mountains following the route known as the Collins Cutoff, passed the Hunton ranch on February 22, and likewise continued directly to Fetterman. Crook and Bourke, however, left Cheyenne on the twenty-second, spent the night at John Phillips's ranch where, as Bourke recorded in his diary, they were entertained by "interesting reminiscences of the Fort Phil Kearney massacre," which had occurred near Fort Phil Kearney while Phillips was at that post, and then went on to Fort Laramie, arriving on the afternoon of the twenty-third.[24]

The post was alive with the excitement and bustle attendant on the departure of two of its companies, I and K, Second Cavalry, plus three officers, Captains Noyes and Egan, and First Lieutenant Christopher Tomkins Hall of Company I. Assistant Surgeon Curtis E. Munn, normally assigned to Camp Robinson but detailed as the expedition's chief medical officer, had arrived several days earlier and was busy requisitioning supplies needed for the field. That evening these guests were treated to theatrical entertainment presented by the ladies and officers of the post. The plays *Faint Heart Ne'er Won Fair Lady* and *A Regular Fix* were "capitally interpreted," according to Bourke, with the best performances in his opinion given by Andrew Burt, Miss L. Dewey, Miss Lucy Townsend, Luther Bradley, and John Ford, the telegraph operator.[25]

Crook spent all of the twenty-fourth on matters related to the expedition. One important item not yet completely resolved was which scouts would accompany his command. Crook had already arranged

First Lieutenant Christopher Tomkins Hall, Company I, Second U.S. Cavalry, seen in 1868 when he graduated from West Point. (U.S. Military Academy Library)

to have Ben Clark, a close acquaintance from their southwestern campaigns, join him from the Indian Territory, and he directed that local scouts be hired, who knew the country and "had good judgment." This brought to him at Fort Laramie and later at Fort Fetterman a motley assortment of frontiersmen, including such local notables as Frank Grouard, a resident of the Red Cloud Agency who had spent many earlier years in the camps of Sitting Bull and Crazy Horse; Jules Ecoffey, from the nearby Three Mile Ranch; Baptiste "Big Bat" Pourier, a scout and interpreter often on the Fort Laramie rolls who was living along Chugwater Creek; and Louis Richard, another Fort

Laramie regular and an intimate friend of Chief Red Cloud. Before Crook departed from Fort Laramie, the list of scouts reached nearly forty. Most were mixed-bloods hired from the settlements below Fort Laramie and from the Red Cloud Agency. All were put in the charge of Major Thaddeus Harlan Stanton, a paymaster in the department who doubled as troubleshooter and frequent chief of scouts for Crook.[26]

While Crook attended to last-minute details, several other participants arrived at the fort. Colonel Joseph Jones Reynolds, commanding officer of the Third Cavalry, for instance, came in on the twenty-fourth along with First Lieutenant George Augustus Drew, regimental quartermaster, and Second Lieutenant Charles Morton, battalion adjutant. Reynolds, fifty-four years old and an 1843 graduate of the United States Military Academy with Ulysses Grant, was a congenial veteran who had risen to the rank of major general during the Civil War. He would presently command the Big Horn Expedition, with Crook ostensibly along only as an observer.[27]

The Fort Laramie contingent, along with Crook, Reynolds, and their parties, departed on February 25 with a minimum of fanfare. The three officers and 103 men of Companies I and K, Second Cavalry, doubled as escort for these ranking officers. Elizabeth Burt recalled that the morning was bitterly cold, with snow on the ground. Her "heart ached for General Reynolds braving the winter elements on this march to surprise the Indians. His gray hairs proclaimed that such hardships were better suited to a younger man."[28] Reynolds, as events would shortly prove, did not acquit himself well on this expedition, but that did not diminish the goodwill and rapport he enjoyed in this garrison and others.

Crook and Reynolds completed the organization of the Big Horn Expedition at Fort Fetterman, where they arrived on February 27. Theirs would be a formidable command, numbering ten companies of cavalry and two of infantry, plus scouts, packers, and other auxiliaries—nearly nine hundred men. Their departure on March 1 for the Powder River country marked the first movement in the Great Sioux War. At Fort Abraham Lincoln, meanwhile, General Terry was stymied by the weather, which prevented the early departure of his principal command and in fact had virtually halted all supply traffic on the Northern Pacific Railroad between Minnesota and Bismarck.

Colonel Joseph J. Reynolds, Third U.S. Cavalry, seen here as a brigadier general of volunteers during the Civil War. (Paul L. Hedren)

In western Montana Terry had also ordered into action Colonel John Gibbon with his Seventh Infantry and the "Montana Battalion" of the Second Cavalry. But at the time of Crook's movement, they too lay inactive because of the weather.[29]

Before Crook marched from Fort Fetterman he issued a final flurry of orders. Several of these affected Fort Laramie. On February 27, for instance, Bradley received a telegram that expanded the escort role his troops were already performing. Now, instead of merely ushering depot trains northward out of Fort Laramie to their proper destinations, Crook desired that Laramie's troops also provide escorts between that post and the depot itself in Cheyenne. Furthermore, Bradley was to ensure that the telegraph line was kept open.[30] On the twenty-eighth he received a general order from Omaha that had a profound impact on the role his post played in this and later campaigns. In accordance with orders originating at division headquarters in Chicago, Fort Laramie and a number of other posts in the Department of the Platte, including Sidney Barracks, Forts D. A. Russell and Fetterman, and Camp Robinson, were designated "cavalry stations." Sheridan, perhaps anticipating a prolonged campaign season, required that these posts maintain ammunition and various ordnance stores beyond their immediate needs for transfer to officers and commands as necessary.[31] Each of these posts increased its stocks accordingly, and henceforth, in addition to the routine movement of supplies between the depot and individual garrisons, shipments between posts would grow to noteworthy proportions.

Despite Mrs. Burt's lament that the absence of the officers on the expedition "made a great vacancy in our social life," there was still abundant official and social activity to occupy the garrison. For one thing, the post thespians continued their regular productions, with Captain Burt and others playing in *Everybody's Friend* and *Camille* during March.[32] Escort duty by now was entrenched as part of the routine, with small details leaving the post once or twice a week throughout the month, principally to guide supplies to Fort Fetterman.[33] And increasingly, attention was drawn to the Red Cloud Agency.

Conditions had not been good at the Red Cloud and Spotted Tail agencies all winter. The ultimatum issued by the Interior Department the previous December brought back none of the winter roamers, and the looming military campaign against these northern Sioux caused considerable uneasiness and uncertainty at the agencies. Furthermore, the agents were continually restricting the hunting of those living peaceably on the reservation. Until this time it had been possible to obtain authority to go south after buffalo. But various military correspondence shows that tolerance for this activity, even though it was still officially permitted by article 11 of the 1868 treaty, was changing. Sidney Barracks received telegrams from the department in November 1875, for instance, that ordered the commanding officer to investigate a party of Sioux headed south to hunt. If they did not have permission to do so, the telegram read, the commanding officer was to order them back "and see that they go back." Captain Frederick Van Vliet, Third Cavalry, received that order and investigated, but Omaha did not appreciate his response and telegraphed again that the Indians in question should show authorization for their absence or go back, and that Van Vliet should "take no nonsense from them."[34] By March 1876 permission to hunt was officially denied, and with the various Sioux agents no longer issuing licenses or passports to the Indians for excursions south of the North Platte River, Bradley and other post commanders received orders from Omaha to "attack and destroy" any Indians who attempted a crossing.[35]

Aside from the fact that hunting had been a privilege guaranteed by the treaty, the matter of food was unquestionably related to a more serious dilemma at the Red Cloud Agency through the winter. The agent, James S. Hastings, who came to that duty December 3, 1875, replacing J. J. Saville, found the supply of rations nearly exhausted and the routine issue already so small as to not permit any further reductions. In a letter to the commissioner of Indian affairs dated January 10, 1876, Hastings described this dangerous situation. Before the end of the month his information was forwarded to Congress with a request for a deficiency appropriation of $225,000. The House Committee on Appropriations passed a resolution requesting an investigation into the causes of this exhaustion, and a special order from the Military Division of the Missouri on February 29 sent Lieutenant Colonel Wesley Merritt, Ninth Cavalry, to Red Cloud on this mission. Hastings, meanwhile, stretched and borrowed to maintain a semblance of propriety with the ration.[36]

Merritt, a trusted associate of Sheridan's from Civil War days and already in the general's immediate command as a special cavalry inspector for the Division of the Missouri, departed promptly for Red Cloud. Coming by way of Cheyenne and Fort Laramie, he reached the post on March 4. The fort provided a small escort and transportation

Colonel Wesley Merritt, Fifth U.S. Cavalry, 1870s. (Custer Battlefield National Monument, National Park Service)

when he continued the next day. In a report filed on March 17, Merritt found the shortages real and warned that these Indians must be supplied or they would leave to join the northern bands. He also speculated on the causes of the deficiency, which by his reckoning were the result of feeding visiting Indians from other agencies as well as the northern tribes and also reflected a short appropriation for the year. Merritt's report was critical of the Indian Department's system of requisitioning and accountability, but he could find no chicanery on the part of the agent or his employees, and he strongly endorsed a supplemental appropriation, which Congress finally enacted in April. Flight from the agencies became ever more common as summer drew near, however, in part because of this problem.[37]

Merritt returned through Fort Laramie on March 11. Over the next several weeks there was a marked increase in military traffic to and from the post. Some of this was related to the campaign, but much more was routine military business. On March 12, for instance, Captain Andrew Burt, Ninth Infantry Regimental Sergeant Major William H. Donaldson, and a private from Company H escorted an insane soldier, James Dunbar of Company I, Ninth Infantry, to an asylum in Washington, D.C. Burt's enlisted companions returned directly to Fort Laramie, but he continued on other business until May. On March 17, Lieutenant Colonel Michael Vincent Sheridan, aide-de-camp to his brother General Sheridan, passed through the post en route to Fort Fetterman, where he was investigating the progress of Crook's campaign. Fort Laramie, naturally, provided the necessary escort for Sheridan's travels. Also on the seventeenth Captains William S. Stanton, Corps of Engineers, and Martin L. Poland, Crook's chief ordnance officer in Omaha, arrived to confer with Bradley and Townsend on the completion and acceptance of the new iron bridge. From a practical standpoint this bridge had been completed and tested even before January 1, but months later the army was still bound in an impossible snarl of red tape, particularly over whether the bridge, as built, conformed to the contract with the King Bridge and Manufacturing Company. To settle the matter, Omaha issued orders directing that a board of officers consisting of Bradley, Townsend, Stanton, and Poland investigate the case. They met on the seventeenth, found matters in order, and recommended that the structure be accepted.[38]

The government's indecisiveness over the Platte River bridge had no effect at all on civilian use of the structure, which grew considerably as the month of March drew on. The weather, at least according to Bradley's diary, was typical for the season, with extremes of 60° on one day and only 3° above zero the next. All of this, of course, mattered little to the Black Hillers, who recognized that spring was very near at hand and that if they were to have a full season in the goldfields, the time to travel had come. John Hunton, from his ranch at

Black Hills placer gold mining near Deadwood. This D. S. Mitchell photograph taken in the fall of 1876 documents the labor-intensive extraction common during the early Dakota gold rush. (Jim Crain)

Bordeaux, had noticed the surge for almost a month, and there were frequent references in his diary to "many Black Hillers passing" (February 22), or "large party of Black Hillers staid all night" (March 5).[39]

The *Cheyenne Daily Leader* measured the pulse of this traffic all winter and spring and did its best to sustain the enthusiasm, especially when it meant travel via Cheyenne. Letters to the paper extolling the virtues of the Hills were common, written by those who were on the scene. Jack Crawford, "poet-scout" of the Hills, was a regular correspondent to the *Omaha Bee*, and his letters were often reprinted by the *Leader*. A Crawford letter on February 24 ran for nearly two full columns on the attractiveness of the new El Dorado and the industriousness of its inhabitants. New cabins were everywhere, he wrote, and miners in from Deadwood, eighty-five miles north of Custer, reported fine digging "from top clear down to bed rock," while on Calamity Bar, three miles from town, miners were taking from five to fifteen cents per pan.

On March 14 the *Leader* carried two columns, "The Inter Ocean on the Routes to the Black Hills," and "The Black Hills: Information of Interest to Those Who Are Going There," which were reprinted verbatim in many subsequent issues. Both were detailed travelogues covering among many topics the cost of passage on the Union Pacific from Omaha to Sidney and to Cheyenne ($21 vs. $25, special rate to Black Hills, first class; or $13 vs. $15, special Black Hills rate, third class); specifics about the trip north, with many references to Fort Laramie, noting that John Collins has just finished his hotel, "the Rustic," and that "his store house and larder are well supplied with all the necessaries, and not a mean picking of the luxuries, of life"; and much more of practical interest to prospective Hillers.

Among the thousands of northbound travelers during this period were those who did not conform either racially or legally to certain norms. A "Special to the Leader" from Fort Laramie dated February 6, for example, reported on fifty Black Hillers who had passed the fort that morning, and in a contemptuous aside it added that "Hop Lee, Ding Dong, Heap Wash, and Hang Jeff, all as their cognomens indicate, Celestial chuckleheads from the Flowery Kingdom," had departed the day before. The road was also frequented by flotsam and jetsam who thrived by preying on others. "Persimmon Bill" Chambers, for one, was a scourge in southeastern Wyoming. He first gained notoriety when he robbed and murdered a sergeant from Company F, Fourth Infantry, near Fort Fetterman on March 6, then fled to the Hills. His travels made sensational reading in the *Leader* for months to come.[40]

Fort Laramie continued to tend supply trains bound for Fort Fetterman, but more often, especially as the weather moderated, escorts traveled first to the cutoff road near the Phillips ranch to meet their charges. Sometimes the duty was urgent, as on March 18 when Bradley received a telegram reporting that a trainload of grain was snowbound on the cutoff near Bitter Cottonwood Creek. Bradley was ordered to dispatch an officer to investigate and to do everything he could to assist.[41] These huge and constant loads to Fort Fetterman were mostly support material for Crook's operations. Increasingly during this time Fort Laramie too was receiving trainloads of goods, especially after the post was designated a "cavalry station." Each load of supplies coming into the fort required a board of survey, called by special order, to examine the goods and report on their condition and quantity as compared with a bill of lading. Usually three officers made up these boards. They would meet at the proper quartermaster or commissary storehouse, where the attendant assistant quartermaster or assistant commissary officer certified the shipment as it was unloaded.[42]

Since leaving Fort Fetterman on March 1, Crook's Big Horn Expedition had had little contact with the outside world. Enduring bitter cold and an immense four-day "norther," they grimly marched northward into Montana, finally following the Tongue River. On the sixteenth scouts saw two Indians headed east. Following them, that night they located an Indian village numbering about one hundred lodges nestled along the Powder River. The camp was thought to belong to the Oglala chief Crazy Horse. Crook, electing to stay behind with the pack train and escort, gave the attack to Colonel Reynolds. By daybreak on March 17, Reynolds had closed on the village and had loosely deployed his forces, with Fort Laramie's two-company squadron directed to sweep the camp and carry off the horses while other companies engaged from the bluffs above the river. Egan's Company K gallantly charged shortly after 9:00 A.M. to open the fight. Bourke, riding with Egan, recorded the initial action: "The command—'Left Front into Line'—was given, and the little company of forty-seven men formed a beautiful line in less time than it takes to narrate the movement. Egan ordered us to keep at a 'walk' until we had entered the village or been discovered by the enemy, then to charge at a slow 'trot,' (our animals being too tired and cold to do more) and upon approaching closely to fire our pistols and storm the village."[43]

Noyes's Company I started in with Company K but wheeled off to round up the horse herd before any cavalrymen entered the village. After these first successful movements, the attack at Powder River went awry. Several of the support companies from the Third Cavalry failed to engage, and when the warriors later counterattacked, Reynolds and several of his squadron commanders proved no match for them and, as one historian later put it, "withdrew with more haste than dignity."[44]

The battle, all told, lasted five hours. Most of the village was destroyed, but the departure, when it came, was so hasty that four dead soldiers, including Private George Schneider of Company K, Second Cavalry, were left on the field. That night, before Reynolds rejoined Crook, the Indians recaptured nearly all their ponies.[45] When Crook found Reynolds at noon on the eighteenth and learned about the previous day's engagement, he showed his disappointment and chagrin. Reynold's failings were many: he had not followed up on the initial surprise attack; he destroyed provisions in the camp that his own command could have used; he lost the ponies; and he abandoned his dead to the enemy. His men exhausted and demoralized, Crook saw no option but to abandon the expedition. En route south he forwarded a dispatch to Sheridan by courier, and when this reached the telegraph at Fetterman on March 23, the first news of the Powder River fight was made public. By this time Crook had learned that what Reynolds had struck was actually a village of Cheyenne Indians, with only a few visiting Oglala Sioux in their company.[46] The Cheyennes, strongly allied with the Sioux anyway, henceforth openly warred against the army as the 1876 campaign continued.

The Big Horn Expedition tramped back into Fort Fetterman on March 26. It was a bitter homecoming, with humiliation covering the command. Before Crook allowed the expedition to be disbanded so that the troops could return to their proper quarters to recuperate, he filed charges against Colonel Reynolds for his general mismanagement of the engagement. Mortified by this personal affront, Reynolds, after failing to persuade Crook to drop these charges, in turn filed charges against Captain Henry Noyes, Second Cavalry, for ordering his company to unsaddle during the fight, and later against Captain Alexander Moore, Company F, Third Cavalry, for neglect of duty. Noyes was shortly tried by general court-martial at Fort D. A. Russell. The courts-martial of Reynolds and Moore were repeatedly postponed but finally took place in January 1877 at Cheyenne.[47]

Reynolds dissolved the expedition on March 27. Fetterman's three companies moved back into their barracks immediately, while Fort Laramie's two companies began their return on the twenty-eighth and the Fort Sanders and Fort D. A. Russell companies left on the twenty-ninth. What few Indian ponies remained in army hands were distributed among the scouts, and then they too went home.[48]

Companies I and K, Second Cavalry, marched into Fort Laramie to a modest heroes' welcome. Despite Reynold's allegation about Noyes's action in the Indian camp, both companies had acquitted themselves well on the campaign. Noyes all along freely admitted that his company had unsaddled and made coffee during the fight, but in his opinion at no time had he compromised his ability to respond as needed. Noyes and Reynolds, despite the difference, remained on the best of terms, and Reynolds claimed that General Crook had ordered him to file the indictment. Egan, on the other hand, came back with his impeccable reputation showing new luster. As Bourke recorded it in his diary, Egan "during the whole affair was under fire, displaying distinguished gallantry, coolness and fine soldierly qualities." After parading for the post and visiting miners, Companies I and K tended their mounts at the stables, then happily returned to the new cavalry barracks just in time to ride out the hardest snowstorm of the winter, which left, as the post's unofficial meteorologist Colonel Bradley recorded it, "a good ten inches on a level."[49]

Reynolds returned to Cheyenne by way of Fort Laramie, but Crook and Bourke went south on the cutoff. On the way they passed a constant stream of people headed to the Black Hills. "They were," according to Bourke, "well provided with supplies, but ignorant of the dangers and trials in store for them." Crook then went directly to Omaha. His winter campaign had been foiled both on the battlefield and to a large measure by the weather. Significantly, his troops had engaged Northern Cheyennes. But the resulting belligerence from the Cheyennes was perhaps a surprise only by its timing, not by its inevitable occurrence. After Powder River the Indians became more defiant than ever, and more and more of them left the agencies to join those known to be hostile. But Crook was not dwelling on failings. Sheridan had already ordered the campaign to continue, and every available man in the Departments of the Platte and Dakota was placed in readiness to take the field.[50]

Crook's winter operation did establish important patterns and direction, for Fort Laramie certainly as well as for other posts. Even before the campaign, two of Laramie's companies had responded to the reports of Indian raiders south of the Platte. Although their subsequent scouts were fruitless, the movements were timely and helped establish a broader presence in southeastern Wyoming. These same companies then marched north with the Big Horn Expedition and experienced, in a month of field service, the harsh realities of winter duty and combat. They returned mourning one comrade killed and three others wounded.[51] Fort Laramie's infantry companies were busy too, with the less glamorous escort of supply trains. Simultaneously, the whole garrison watched the explosive surge of miners from Cheyenne to the Black Hills. These varied patterns repeated themselves continually in 1876. What changed, beyond the constant addition to these duties, was the way Fort Laramie faithfully shouldered its responsibilities with what would soon prove a shrinking garrison.

Chapter Four

Recovery and the Second Movement: April–May 1876

After General Crook's initial foray into the Powder River country, attention shifted to other concerns. Fort Laramie, while certainly not dismissing the inevitability of renewed movement against the Sioux, did enjoy in April the usual springtime diversions of garrison life. Crook, from his headquarters in Omaha, divided his attention between the needs of the next field operation, which was at most a month away, and the political imbroglio in Washington, D.C. Crook was not personally involved in Washington, but several of his contemporaries, including George Custer, were. It all began with a dramatic exposé in February. The secretary of war, William Belknap, had been accused of selling post traderships on the frontier. An investigation by the House Committee on Expenditures, chaired by Congressman Heister Clymer, obtained proof that Belknap had indeed accepted cash payments in exchange for the appointment of the post trader at Fort Sill, Indian Territory. Upon learning of this irrefutable evidence, Belknap resigned on March 1, 1876. The congressional investigations then turned to other alleged malfeasance in the War Department, and later to every department in President Grant's cabinet. Much of this, it seems, was election-year power playing; all of it made sensational reading in the nation's newspapers.[1]

Despite Washington politics and intrigue, in southeastern Wyo-

Custer City, Dakota Territory, 1876. D. S. Mitchell photograph. (Jim Crain)

ming attention was still riveted on the Black Hills. Traffic north out of Cheyenne was heavier than ever. One traveler who had just come into Cheyenne from the Hills reported passing 978 persons, including 27 women, on the road headed north. The population of Custer City about this time had grown to 500 or 600 citizens, and the town now boasted six general stores, two bakeries, and numerous saloons. Placer mining continued to be profitable along French Creek, but fresh reports were filtering down from the northern Hills telling of impressive strikes in Deadwood Gulch and on Whitewood Creek.[2]

The stage service inaugurated in early February was now leaving Cheyenne for the Black Hills every other day, and its proprietors were promising daily trips as quickly as travel justified it. When not disrupted by the weather, the journey to Custer City could be made in three days. Rates of fare for a through ticket were $20 first class, $15 second class, and $10 third class. Augmenting the stage was a "pony packet line" operating from Fort Laramie to all points in the Hills. This service, begun April 11, carried only mail and light express matter.[3]

The stage, pony line, and independent travelers coming by way of Fort Laramie all followed what had become by April a well-marked,

Freighters' camp at Cold Springs, six miles north of Custer, 1876. Traffic of this nature was common on the Black Hills road through all of the centennial year. D. S. Mitchell photograph. (Jim Crain)

well-beaten trail north from the post. After crossing the Platte River bridge, the road followed the north bank of the river as far as Cottonwood Creek. There it turned directly north, continuing past the Government Farm and Rawhide Buttes, and went down Sage Creek and Old Woman's Fork to a crossing of the South Cheyenne River. Just a few miles beyond the South Cheyenne the road turned to the northeast, where it entered the southern Black Hills by way of Red Canyon and Pleasant Valley, arriving at Custer City after covering just over 147 miles. The stage company utilized a number of the convenient stops opportunely prepared in January by J. W. Dear, but it also established others on its own as needs were better defined by use.[4]

Indian depredations, always a threat on the Black Hills road, increased substantially after the fight on the Powder River. The local newspapers repeatedly published accounts of raids and harassment. Human casualties were few, but the loss of livestock was common.[5] William "Persimmon Bill" Chambers proved equally menacing to the Hillers. The accused murderer was frequently seen on the Black Hills road, and the April 6 *Daily Leader* noted that he made an "appearance at a camp five miles south of Hat Creek, five days ago. He had supper and breakfast, and stayed overnight in the camp. When last heard of he was at Raw Hide Buttes, very drunk, and having considerable money." A follow-up report in the *Leader* dated April 21 told how a Black Hills adventurer made the acquaintance of Chambers, who admitted killing the soldier who had come with orders to arrest him. Bill elaborated on his modus operandi, according to the report, telling how he and his band of outlaws stole stock in Wyoming, trailed it to the San Juan country of southwestern Colorado for sale, and rustled horses there to sell in Wyoming or the Dakotas. The account noted that Persimmon Bill was then in the Hills and, when not thieving, "loafs about the towns there, having plenty of money and spending it freely."

In early spring the troops at Fort Laramie, occupied as they were with logistical support and their own unvarying garrison routines, offered little protection to the Hillers beyond their mere presence in and around the fort. Although not at the moment related to the Sioux War, troop movements did remain constant. On March 31, for instance, fifty General Service recruits for the Ninth Infantry arrived at Fort Laramie in the charge of Captain Samuel Munson of Company C. Twenty-seven of these new men were immediately distributed to the infantry companies at the post. On April 5 Second Lieutenant Thomas Sidney McCaleb escorted the remaining twenty-three recruits to Camp Robinson, where they filled out the ranks of the four Ninth Infantry companies stationed there. Also at the end of March Dr. Charles V. Petteys, a "contract" or, as he was more commonly known by the army, "citizen" physician, reported for duty from Camp Robinson. Petteys promptly took a leave of absence for seven days, but when he returned from Cheyenne on April 6 he became the third permanent member of the post's medical staff, augmenting the services of Dr. Hartsuff and Dr. Gray.[6]

As if to mark an ominous transition, a series of deaths rocked the post in late April. The first involved one of the fort's Ninth Infantrymen, Corporal John A. McKenzie of Company F. The corporal drowned in the Laramie River on the twenty-first while fishing, and his body was not recovered until April 23. A funeral detail was promptly organized, and the next day twelve privates from the post's infantry companies reported to Corporal R. V. Clinton, Company F,

Captain Samuel Munson, Company C, Ninth U.S. Infantry. (B.William Henry, Jr.)

as a firing escort, while the Ninth Infantry Regimental Band re-ported to First Lieutenant William W. Rogers, who commanded the company in the absence of their captain. At 1 P.M. a somber proces-sion carried Corporal McKenzie from the hospital to the cemetery for burial.[7]

About the same time that Fort Laramie was conducting river searches for the body of Corporal McKenzie, a string of ghastly mur-ders occurred on the Black Hills road north of the post. The first in-volved the family of Charles Metz of Laramie City. Metz had been in Custer, working as a baker. He had just sold his business for three thousand dollars and was leaving the Hills when his party was am-bushed on April 16 in Red Canyon. Metz and his wife, their black maid, and several companions were killed and terribly mutilated. Only

Red Canyon in 1876. Very near this location in April 1876 the Charles Metz family were murdered by white outlaws as they traveled from Custer City to Fort Laramie and Cheyenne. D. S. Mitchell photograph. (Jim Crain)

W. G. Felton escaped, though five times wounded, by cutting loose a wagon and dashing southward out of the valley. Felton later testified that his attackers had been Indians, but later evidence suggests that white outlaws, possibly including Persimmon Bill, may have also participated. Bill, of course, was widely known by now, and friends of Metz asserted that he had slipped out of Custer about the same time they left. More substantial testimony came from Jesse Brown, another Hiller. He passed the scene of the slaughter just a few days later, and in looking over the site he found the place where the attackers had concealed themselves behind pine bushes cut and planted in the ground. There he saw boot and shoe tracks, and knee prints in the ground showed the weave of cloth. This led Brown and others to conclude that white men, perhaps helped by Indians, had killed Metz for his money.[8]

Following what was being called the "Metz massacre" came the death of H. E. "Stuttering" Brown on April 21. Brown, a respected

Utah resident and business scout for the stage and freighting firm of Gilmer, Salisbury, and Patrick, had come to the Cheyenne in February and arranged to purchase the infant Cheyenne and Black Hills Stage, Mail, and Express Company. Subsequently appointed agent for the reorganized company, Brown was a regular visitor to Fort Laramie and all the stops on the road. Then came news that he had been fatally wounded by Indians during a night attack eighteen miles north of the Hat (Sage) Creek station. Friends and associates rallied to his aid. News of his shooting even reached Omaha and brought a hurried telegram from Crook ordering Bradley to send an ambulance to Sage Creek and bring in Brown, who, as Crook had heard it, was lying wounded beside the road. Bradley promptly dispatched two ambulances, Dr. Petteys, and a mounted escort to the scene. Although Brown was still alive when the soldiers arrived, there was little Petteys could do, and the stage man died at a nearby station. An attacker's bullet had hit Brown in the abdomen, first striking a cartridge in the belt he wore and driving it into his body. The soldiers brought Brown's body back to the post on April 25, and he was later taken to Omaha for burial.[9]

Like the Metz murders, Brown's death was at first attributed to Indians. But subsequent investigations again linked Persimmon Bill Chambers to the bloodletting. Some questioned whether Indians ever attacked at night. Others pointed out that Brown had confronted Chambers on the very day he was shot and accused him of stealing horses from the company. Moreover, Brown had told Bill that if he did not leave the stage road he would kill him. Against the advice of his companions, who urged him to stay over at the Hat Creek station, Brown pushed on for Custer after dark and was shot.[10]

Other distressing attacks by Indians and outlaws alike followed these killings, prompting Wyoming's governor, John M. Thayer, to telegraph General Crook on April 24 asking for military protection on the road between Fort Laramie and Custer City. To this Crook responded the next day with assurances that troops would be sent to protect citizens. Then, with characteristic savvy, he boarded a train for Wyoming to look into these matters and other pressing issues himself. Crook did not advance beyond Cheyenne, but he did promise, particularly to the press, that troops would shortly be patrolling the Custer City road providing "perfect security." Crook also met with Luther Bradley and received an appraisal of the conditions at the Red Cloud and Spotted Tail agencies. On April 14 Crook had ordered Bradley to look into affairs there and, specifically, to ascertain whether Indians were leaving in any numbers. Defections were noted, but more important, Bradley reported that the Sioux were suffering from hunger and that their tempers were getting short.[11]

The conditions at the agencies in fact had not changed appreciably since Merritt's investigations in mid-March, and despite the recent congressional appropriation to cover the deficient ration, supplies were not getting through. The Department of the Platte, in whose military jurisdiction these two agencies fell, was fully apprised of these deteriorating conditions, and Crook in turn was faithfully communicating with Sheridan in Chicago. On April 27, for instance, he warned Sheridan that the Indians at Red Cloud were starving owing to neglect in forwarding supplies and that unless beef arrived soon they would be compelled to raid or join the roamers. Then came Bradley's information via Fort Laramie, and Crook's follow-up to Sheridan explaining that it was of great importance to his future movements that these Indians be kept friendly. Could he lend the agents there some beef cattle? On April 29 Sheridan telegraphed Crook, who was now in Cheyenne, to say that the secretary of the interior had reported that cattle were to have been delivered at Red Cloud on the twenty-fifth, but if that failed the agent could purchase beef on the open market. Despite Crook's valiant efforts to correct this festering sore, cognizant as he was that the Sioux were defecting and raiding, he could do little more than watch. Agency affairs, after all, remained in the domain of the Interior Department, not in his or the War Department's.[12]

It was no coincidence that Lieutenant Colonel Bradley happened to be in Cheyenne at the time of Crook's visit. In mid-April Fort Laramie's commanding officer received orders from General William T. Sherman to report to Philadelphia for duty with the nation's Centennial Commission. Leaving Captain Burrowes in charge of the post until Major Townsend returned, Bradley left Fort Laramie on April 27. Philadelphia would host the long-awaited Centennial Exhibition, and from its grand opening on May 10, which Bradley attended as official escort to the president of the Centennial Commission, through its six-month run, over eight million citizens would be astonished by the giant Corliss steam engine and eight thousand other machines; an electric lamp; six thousand silkworms from China; "Old Abe," the celebrated eagle mascot of the Eighth Wisconsin Infantry from Civil War days; and countless other attractions and novelties that filled every corner of the 450-acre exhibition grounds.[13]

Crook's final and perhaps most important business in Cheyenne was the court-martial of Captain Henry E. Noyes, which commenced in late April. Noyes, who had been detached to Fort D. A. Russell since April 22, was charged with "conduct to the prejudice of good order and military discipline," specifically that during the recent engagement of March 17 he had ordered the horses of his company unsaddled, thereby rendering him unable to respond promptly to any urgent commands to move. Noyes pleaded not guilty, and in a short trial presided over by Colonel John E. Smith, Fourteenth Infantry, testimony was presented to clarify Noyes's actions. He had indeed ordered his company to unsaddle the horses, but at the time he believed that the fight had become nothing but a small long-range skirmish. Furthermore, his men and horses needed rest and food. Listening to the testimony, in addition to Smith, were Colonel Franklin F. Flint, Major Alexander Chambers, and Captain William S. Collier, all of the Fourth Infantry; Major Andrew W. Evans, Third Cavalry; Major Edwin F. Townsend, Ninth Infantry, from Fort Laramie; and Major Alexander J. Dallas and Captains John J. Coppinger and George K. Brady of the Twenty-third Infantry.[14] Despite his convincing arguments, Noyes was found guilty as charged and sentenced to be reprimanded by the department commander in general orders.

When the proceedings of the court were published on May 2, Crook added his censure as follows:

Referring to the sentence, in the foregoing case, the Department Commander deems it proper to remark that Captain Noyes' reputation during the late war, supported as it is by the evidence adduced, is ample assurance that in unsaddling his horses, at the time and place he did, he simply committed an error of judgment, and that he was not actuated by a desire to evade or shirk any duty that he might be called upon to perform.

Captain Henry E. Noyes, Company I, Second U.S. Cavalry, as he appeared in the 1890s after promotion through the ranks to lieutenant colonel. (Colorado Historical Society)

In the opinion of the Department Commander, no terms that he can use, will add to the punishment of a soldier of Captain Noyes' sensibilities, more than that of the opinion of a Court, composed of his fellow officers, that his error merits their censure; as expressed in the sentence.

Captain Noyes, 2d Cavalry, will be released from arrest and restored to duty.[15]

Noyes's court-martial was a short one, and the sentence, deserved or not, amounted to a slap on the wrist. As J. W. Vaughn, the principal historian of the Big Horn Expedition and himself a lawyer, wrote, "One gets the impression that all were going through a good-natured farce for public consumption."[16]

Even with attention diverted to the killings on the Custer road, the difficulties at the Sioux agencies, or the court-martial of one of Fort Laramie's favorites, the broader activities related to the next phase of the Sioux War continued without letup. Crook was waiting for the spring grass to sprout and the land to dry out before mounting another campaign, and though undoubtedly he had already selected most if not all of the troops who would participate in the coming operation, formal announcements and orders at the end of April were still not forthcoming. These few uncertainties notwithstanding, the garrisons at Forts Fetterman and Laramie and the citizens of Cheyenne could see all around them the bustle of support activities. The *Daily Leader* regularly provided campaign updates, as on April 28, when they reported that "nearly a quarter of a million pounds of army supplies are now on the way to Fort Fetterman for Crook's second campaign in the Big Horn region. Pack trains composing the expedition started out yesterday, heavily laden, and will go to Laramie river, and return for another cargo. Recruits for the thinned-out companies have arrived, and fresh mules, wagons, supplies, etc., for the campaign are coming in almost daily." The *Leader* noted in the same column that the chiefs at the Red Cloud and Spotted Tail agencies planned to send three hundred of their "best braves" out with General Crook, but it added skeptically that "they may do it, but the chances are that they will send them out before Crook starts, and that he will then have three hundred extra to fight."

Fort Laramie's role in the movement of war goods had not changed appreciably from the pattern established in January and February, but the tempo had quickened considerably. The commanding officer was regularly receiving telegraphed orders from Omaha directing him to have escorts meet depot trains, usually at the Phillips Ranch, and accompany them to Fetterman. Infantrymen were also occasionally escorting supplies to the Red Cloud Agency, particularly at the first of May when the long-overdue food went forward. The post's own quartermaster wagons were in constant motion as well, shuttling grain, subsistence stores, and other supplies from disabled Fetterman-bound trains or, more likely, from the post's storehouses.[17] Lieutenants Morton and Regan, Laramie's quartermaster and commissary officers, dutifully monitored the forwarding of these supplies and ensured that sufficient stocks remained on hand to meet the post's own needs. Often supplemental requisitions were needed, as on April 26, when the Cheyenne Depot was notified that Fort Laramie's grain stores were low; only 50,000 pounds were on hand, and daily usage was 4,000 pounds.[18]

In the midst of this campaign preparation, Fort Laramie faced a different demand on its quartermaster and commissary supplies and medicines. The commanding officer explained the predicament in a letter to Omaha dated April 23:

> A good many miners are coming from the Black Hills through this Post in a destitute condition, out of rations and money. They need assistance to reach the railroad, or, to reach any point where they can get work. We have aided these people, many of them sick and wounded, until it has become a serious tax on private means. . . . I respectfully request that the General Commanding will give such orders as will allow the Post Commander to issue rations to these destitute people in limited quantities. And medicines to such as are in immediate danger from sickness or wounds.

Response from headquarters was slow in coming but nevertheless positive; limited issues for "destitutes" could be provided, "but with decided caution."[19]

General Crook had promised during his recent visit to Cheyenne that troops would soon be on the trail north of Fort Laramie patrolling and protecting the road to the Black Hills. The Sioux, embittered by the endless problems at the agencies and by the general press of miners not only from the south but from the east and north as well, and impressed by the Cheyennes' prowess at Powder River in mid-March, kept up a persistent harassment in southeastern Wyoming. Deaths of stockmen and travelers were common news, but the attack and killing of James Hunton on May 5 at the Hunton ranch on Chugwater Creek finally triggered widespread and long-awaited military response.

John Collins, Fort Laramie's trader, was one of the first to come upon the trouble at the Hunton ranch. He was returning from Cheyenne and had spent the previous night at the Kelly ranch, as had Major Townsend, who was returning to Fort Laramie after the Noyes court-martial and other business. Collins left the Kelly ranch alone early on the morning of May 5 and soon came to the Hunton place, ten miles north. He noticed that no one was in sight, but in the usual custom of the country, shouted a greeting. Soon a door opened and a Hunton brother hailed him with the alarming news that Indians had driven off the horse herd only an hour ago and that Jim Hunton had taken off after them in the direction of Goshen Hole. Moments later, the report continued, Jim's horse came back saddled and bridled but riderless. About this time Townsend also came up and heard the news. Turning to Collins, he asked him to hurry on to the post and have the commanding officer order out a sergeant and twenty men after the Indians.[20]

By his own recollection, Collins made the ride of thirty-one miles in "two hours flat." At Fort Laramie he delivered Townsend's message both to the officer of the day and to Captain Thomas Burrowes, who temporarily commanded the post. Burrowes wasted no time in executing the spirit of Townsend's order, although rather than sending a sergeant he ordered Second Lieutenant James N. Allison and fifteen men of Company I, Second Cavalry, mounted, armed, and equipped with one hundred rounds of ammunition per man and rations for three days, to proceed down the North Platte in pursuit of the Indians. Though Allison was the junior officer of Company K, he was commanding Company I in the absence of Noyes and the other regularly assigned lieutenants. Allison was off in half an hour, according to Collins, heading east over the Goshen Hole mesa.[21]

Meanwhile Baptiste "Little Bat" Garnier, Charles F. Coffee, John Sparks, and several others, hearing that a fellow rancher was in peril, rode to the Hunton place and soon continued eastward following the broad trail left by the Indian raiders, the stolen horses, and Hunton. In ten or twelve miles they came upon Jim Hunton dead and scalped. Allison, too, soon came up with his men. The thirteen raiders had managed to cross the North Platte ahead of the troops. The cavalrymen then backtracked on the raiders' trail, came to the huddle around Hunton's body, and finally returned to the fort. Little Bat and the

Second Lieutenant James Nicholas Allison, Company K, Second U.S. Cavalry, seen in 1871 at the time of his graduation from West Point. (U.S. Military Academy Library)

others carried Hunton back to the ranch.[22] John Hunton, meanwhile, was at the Milk Ranch just south of Fort Fetterman. There he learned of the horse raid and of Jim's disappearance, and the next day he received word that his brother had been killed. It took John Hunton another day to get to Bordeaux, and from there he took Jim's body on to Cheyenne, where he was buried on May 9.[23]

The death of Hunton and the boldness of the Sioux attack on that ranch were symptomatic of widespread raiding under way throughout southeastern Wyoming and Nebraska. Along Indian Creek in Red Canyon on May 2 Indians attacked a civilian freight train, and only after a prolonged stand were they driven off, leaving one white badly wounded and fourteen horses dead. Just two days before, in central Nebraska, near the one-company infantry post of Fort Hartsuff, Sioux raiders clashed with a detachment of Twenty-third Infantrymen, leaving one warrior killed and several wounded and one soldier dead. These attacks prompted the *Daily Leader* to editorialize that "the starving Indians from Red Cloud agency, having been supplied recently with a surfeit of flour, sugar and coffee, have recovered sufficient strength to go on their annual horse stealing expedition. . . . Not satisfied with stealing the white man's property, their savage instincts led them to thirst for his blood, and poor James Hunton, being in their path, was murdered by them and his scalped remains left to bleach on the prairie. And what are we going to do about it?"[24]

Crook's essential plan to protect the Black Hills road had already been discussed when he and several post commanders met in Cheyenne at the Noyes court-martial. As the *Daily Leader* reported on May 2, Captain James Egan's "gallant 'Grays'" and a company of infantry would soon march north to the scene of the recent Indian atrocities and patrol the country of the Powder River and Red Cloud trail to "make the heart of the gold-seeker glad." Specific orders for the movement were read on May 7. Company K, Second Cavalry, and Company F, Ninth Infantry, equipped with two hundred rounds of ammunition per man and rations for twenty days, would proceed on detached service along the Black Hills road. Egan would lead his company and the expedition, while First Lieutenant William W. Rogers commanded Company F. Also accompanying the force were post guide and interpreter Louis Richard, who was signed onto the quartermaster rolls April 1, along with contract surgeon Charles V. Petteys, Lieutenant Allison, and a sergeant and seven privates of Company I, Second Cavalry. The expedition of nearly one hundred men departed from Fort Laramie on the morning of May 8 amid a barrage of incoming orders affecting other elements of the garrison. General Crook's second major movement was almost at hand.[25]

The shower of orders that rained on virtually every post in Crook's Department of the Platte beginning May 8 startled no one. Nearly every available company in the department had been in readiness for weeks, and perhaps the only uncertainties remaining were specifically who would join the expedition and when. The basic plan was to assemble troops again at Fort Fetterman and march northward into the Powder River country. This time Crook would not take the field alone, for Colonel John Gibbon and his Montana Column, composed of six companies of the Seventh Infantry and four companies of the Second Cavalry, had already left Fort Ellis, Montana, on March 30, just as the Big Horn Expedition was returning to Fetterman from its first movement. Gibbon, at last report, was scouting as ordered along the Yellowstone River. Also soon to leave Fort Abraham Lincoln was the Dakota Column, composed of all twelve companies of the Seventh Cavalry, two companies of the Seventeenth Infantry, one company from the Sixth Infantry, and a detachment from the Twentieth who would serve three Gatling guns. This column would be commanded directly by General Alfred Terry from St. Paul.[26]

The orders of May 8, along with follow-up directives over the next week, would consolidate twenty companies of infantry and cavalry for Crook's campaign. Fifteen of the twenty cavalry companies in the department would participate, including nine that had already served on the Big Horn Expedition. In drawing cavalry companies for the movement, Crook stripped a number of posts of their whole mounted arm. Fort Fred Steele, Wyoming, for instance, gave Company D, Second Cavalry; Sidney Barracks gave Companies C, G, and I, Third Cavalry; Fort Fetterman provided Company A, Second Cavalry; and Fort D. A. Russell provided Companies A, D, E, F, and M, Third Cavalry, along with Companies B and E, Second Cavalry, which were temporarily assigned there from Fort Sanders. Henceforth only foot soldiers remained at these posts for the duration of the Sioux War. The final cavalry companies to march with Crook included Companies B and L, Third Cavalry, from Fort McPherson, Nebraska, and Company I, Second Cavalry, from Fort Laramie. Rounding out this force, principally as the escort for the supply train, would be three companies of the Ninth Infantry, also from Fort Laramie, along with two of the Fourth from Fetterman.[27]

With half of the companies in the whole of Crook's department soon to join him for field service, a second series of orders appeared on May 8 to redistribute other infantry companies for temporary duty at certain posts. Companies of Twenty-third Infantrymen, for example, would soon go from Omaha Barracks to Forts Hartsuff and

McPherson and to Sidney Barracks, while single companies of Fourth Infantry were dispatched from Forts Bridger and Fred Steele to Forts Sanders and Fetterman. Crook's intent, obviously, was to consolidate a substantial fighting force with him in the field, while still providing a sufficient garrison at each station to maintain order and perform any additional tasks required.[28] Fort Laramie's neighbors were affected in varying ways by these orders. Fort D. A. Russell, so far behind the front lines, was stripped of all but its single Twenty-third Infantry company. Camps Robinson and Sheridan were unaffected, while Fort Fetterman lost its lone mounted company plus two resident infantry companies but shortly gained another of infantry. Sidney Barracks lost its three mounted companies, its whole precampaign garrison, but these were replaced by two companies of infantry. Fort Laramie, with two companies already in the field guarding the Black Hills road and four others scheduled to go with Crook, would soon be left with only a single company in its garrison.

The orders rearranging the troops in the Department of the Platte were predicated on movement from these stations so that the different commands would arrive at Fort Fetterman near the same time, calculated to be about the fourth week in May. As supplies poured in, Fetterman was already bursting at the seams. Before the commencement of the campaign, Crook had amassed there 277,000 pounds of grain, and another 112,000 pounds were en route. In addition there were thousands of pounds of pork, beans, coffee, sugar, and other commissary essentials, plus ammunition, crates of rifles, wagons, and even a herd of over two hundred beef cattle.[29] Increasingly, troops and those supplies destined for Fort Fetterman, which did not have to come via Cheyenne Depot, traveled on the Union Pacific as far as the Medicine Bow station and then overland northward to the post. Medicine Bow, a town of just over one hundred people, was midway between Laramie City and Rawlins and only eighty-five miles southwest of Fetterman. But the road, short as it was, crossed the Laramie Mountains, which were blocked by snow from November until May.[30]

Orders received at Fort Laramie confirming Crook's second movement against the Sioux were but one of many concerns at headquarters. Just two days before Captain Egan departed on his extended service along the Black Hills road, his first sergeant, John

Fort Fetterman, Wyoming Territory, 1876. D. S. Mitchell photograph. (Nebraska State Historical Society)

McGregor, drowned in the Laramie River twelve miles above the post. He had been hunting deserters and was crossing the river when his horse bolted and they both went under in deep water. Through the second week in May his body had still not been found, and waiting at the post were his grieving wife and two children.[31]

Townsend was also soon to be involved with the extension of the telegraph line north of Fort Laramie. This had long been favored by the citizens of the Black Hills and was strongly endorsed by Generals Sheridan and Crook. Cheyenne's promotors too, with their obvious purpose, appreciated the advantages of this extension, as the *Daily Leader* editorialized: "With stage, mail and telegraph lines in operation over the Cheyenne route to the Black Hills, and with the military protection Capt. Egan and his soldiers will extend to travelers over this route, we shall not need to use further arguments to convince people that the Cheyenne route is the best and safest for all who desire to go the new Eldorado."[32] Official communications of May 5 and 6, both to Townsend at Fort Laramie and to W. H. Hibbard, superintendent of the Western Union Telegraph Company in Salt Lake City, outlined the army's role. Fort Laramie would furnish escorts to protect the parties building the line, and the troops so engaged would also aid in the construction as much as possible. And though public transport, taxed as it was in carrying supplies for the posts and campaigns, could not be provided directly, wagons on an empty leg to or from Fort Laramie would haul poles along the line so long as this did not interfere with public service.[33]

Other communications bearing on operations were continually arriving at headquarters. On May 10, for instance, assistant surgeon Albert Hartsuff was notified that he was to be senior medical officer of the expedition and would accompany Fort Laramie's contingent when they departed for the campaign. Hartsuff was further directed to assemble medical supplies for the field from those on hand at Forts Laramie and Fetterman. Townsend was to see that Fort Laramie's troops took no more baggage or equipment than was absolutely necessary, and further, he was to ensure that if Hartsuff depleted the post's medical stores, additional supplies were requisitioned without delay.[34] On May 11 Captain Noyes, who was still under arrest pending receipt of the published orders of May 2, sent a scathing internal letter to Townsend calling attention to recent desertions from his company and to the men's general poor condition. There were occasions, he observed, when no commissioned officer had been assigned to oversee the company. And though he was not in command, he visited the company quarters and saw more men drunk than at any time since they came into this garrison. He noticed broken barracks windows and a general demoralization as well. Noyes was finally released from arrest several days later and immediately commenced reorganizing and outfitting his cavalrymen for the field.[35]

Townsend also learned that remounts from the Cheyenne Depot were coming for the Second Cavalry companies at his post. Noyes would get thirty for Company I, and Egan would receive thirty-five for Company K. When the question of remounts had come up earlier, Captain Egan had specifically requisitioned gray horses to maintain his company's color distinctiveness, which was a long-standing regimental tradition. Egan's desires had somehow gained Crook's attention, and when Captain Gilliss at the depot received instructions about remounts for the various cavalry companies it contained a postscript declaring that the department commander wished to grant Egan's wish.[36]

With the formal campaign startup still several weeks away, General Crook and his aide-de-camp Lieutenant Bourke left Omaha on May 9 bound for the Red Cloud Agency. Stopping first at Cheyenne on the tenth, the general met with Gilliss and then a number of Third Cavalry officers at nearby Fort D. A. Russell. There he learned, if he had not had intimations before, of the strongly divided sympathies and widespread demoralization in that regiment after the discredit of the March 17 fight. There were many, apparently, who believed that the charges against Reynolds and Moore would be dropped and that these officers would never be brought to trial once their colonel's influence in Washington was brought to bear on the case. Intent on quashing that speculation, Crook placed both Reynolds and Moore under arrest and put Lieutenant Colonel William Bedford Royall in command of the regiment. Then without delaying further, on the twelfth Crook and Bourke retraced their steps of the previous February, traveling north as far as the Phillips ranch, where they spent the night, and arrived at Fort Laramie on the thirteenth. After meeting, as Bourke described it, "the same officers almost seen there last February," plus Frank Grouard, who had come in from Fort Fetterman at Crook's request, they enjoyed the evening hospitality of Captain and Mrs. Samuel Munson and then continued to Camp Robinson and Red Cloud Agency, with transportation and an escort provided by Townsend.[37]

Crook's trip to Red Cloud was motivated by a strong desire to enlist Sioux scouts for the coming expedition. In other campaigns Crook had demonstrated the advantages of employing scouts from the same tribe he was warring against. Such auxiliaries knew the haunts and trails and could often predict the responses of their kin. And it was much easier to employ restless young men for white men's objectives than to fight them if they were to abandon the agencies in favor of the warring camps. Crook may also have understood that employing scouts in this manner helped break tribal cohesion and undermined the authority of the leaders, and this ultimately led to a larger goal of assimilation. The warriors often found such overtures an appealing alternative to the baseness of reservation life or resistance to death.

Warring for rather than against the army did, after all, allow one to "retain the dignity of horses, arms, and the manly occupation of violence."[38]

At Red Cloud Crook found Agent Hastings temporarily absent on business, but he sent word to the nearby camps that he wished to meet with the Oglalas on May 15 to discuss the matter of scouts. A number of important Sioux leaders came in for the meeting, but not Red Cloud. After listening to Crook, they expressed a strong willingness to cooperate with him in driving the roamers back to the reservation. Crook then met with Agent Hastings, who had just returned from the Spotted Tail Agency, and told him about the meeting just concluded. Hastings proved cool and uncooperative; he probably still harbored resentment over remarks Crook made after the March 17 fight, which suggested that the abundant ammunition and other war materials found in that village had come directly from the Red Cloud Agency. Hastings brought up this issue and then told Crook that though he would not forbid any Sioux to join the expedition, he would not recommend it. But interfere he did. The willingness so many of the Sioux leaders had expressed at their conference with Crook quickly deteriorated, and when the general departed on the sixteenth not one Sioux warrior rode with him. Afterward Crook learned that Hastings had explicitly forbidden the Indians to join him.[39]

Crook, chagrined at this inability to enlist allies, still had a profitable look at the agency. He saw firsthand that the Sioux were indeed leaving to join the northern roamers, which, he wrote to General Sheridan, might have been prevented had some of these men joined him as allies. And in a talk with Chief Red Cloud he received a stern, almost taunting warning about Sioux resolve. Said Red Cloud, the Sioux "have many warriors, many guns and ponies. They are brave and ready to fight for their country. They are not afraid of the soldiers nor their chief. Many braves are ready to meet them. Every lodge will send its young men, and they all will say of the Great Father's dogs, 'Let them come!'"[40]

Crook, Bourke, and several other departmental officers who had come into Camp Robinson on other business rode through scattered Sioux villages for three or four miles as they began their return to Fort Laramie. Their united escort totaled about sixty-five men; too many

Oglala Chief Red Cloud, about 1876. (U.S. Military Academy Library)

for a small party of Indians to attack, thought Bourke. But the soldiers could not help noticing Indians stationed on prominent points looking as if they expected something. Shortly afterward a big smokesignal appeared from the bluffs overlooking the White River, but the soldiers did not know its exact meaning. About noon, as Crook's entourage was stopped for lunch, Charles Clark, the mail carrier from Fort Fetterman, passed by. Compliments were exchanged, and Clark continued toward Camp Robinson. He never made it. A few miles beyond he was ambushed and killed by a small party of Sioux. Crook learned of this when he reached Fort Laramie on the seventeenth, and only then did it dawn on the officers that the Indians and the smoke signal they had seen might well have been part of a plot against them. This was later confirmed; only the unusual size of the escort had prevented an attack.[41]

When Crook returned to Fort Laramie on May 17 he found the post in a state of anxiety. The body of First Sergeant John McGregor had been recovered from the Laramie River that very day and had been taken to the hospital before burial. The four companies selected to participate in the campaign, I of the Second Cavalry and C, G, and H, Ninth Infantry, had nearly finished packing their garrison possessions and were laying out the last of their campaign gear. A platoon of newspapermen representing many of the nation's largest papers had come in. So too had miners and other civilians, including Isaac Bard, who remembered May 17 with the following entry in his diary: "Seen General Crook today. He looks like some old farmer, is very sociable."[42]

General Crook's first stop at Fort Laramie was at post headquarters. There he received the latest intelligence from Omaha and Chicago, including news from Sheridan that General Terry's command had left Fort Abraham Lincoln on May 16 and that hostile Sioux, according to a variety of sources, numbered about fifteen hundred lodges and were now on the Little Missouri River. Sheridan further warned that the Indians were prepared to fight, and he wanted Crook to come as quickly as possible.[43] Crook also received an update on Egan's movements along the Black Hills road. Skirmishes and casualties between whites and Indians were still common, and one major wagon party had even been turned back, but that train was now being escorted northward by troops, and Egan's command seemed finally to be establishing its presence on the road. Bearing in mind his visit to Red Cloud, Crook issued orders broadening Townsend's jurisdiction to temporarily include Camp Robinson, for the purpose of protecting the country between that station and Fort Laramie as well as the road to the Black Hills. The general had only recently discontinued the administrative District of the Black Hills, which embraced much of southeastern Wyoming, western Nebraska, and southwestern Dakota Territory and which had been administered by the commanding officer at Fort Laramie. But now, with much of the same territory and the same essential purpose, Townsend again exercised authority beyond the limited confines of his post.[44]

Crook's party moved out for Fort Fetterman early on May 18. He had with him Bourke; Major Thaddeus H. Stanton, the paymaster and chief of scouts; Frank Grouard and several locally hired scouts; and the newspaperman Robert E. Strahorn, writing under the pen name "Alter Ego" for the *Rocky Mountain News*. Strahorn, in fact, had already participated in the March campaign, but in the coming expedition he would be among many other journalists reporting on events. That afternoon the officers and soldiers of the post who were not otherwise engaged were invited to attend the funeral of First Sergeant McGregor. The turnout at the cemetery was modest, since nearly all of Company K was on detached service and the rest of the post was occupied with the campaign.[45]

Fort Laramie's three-company infantry contingent marched northwest on Monday, May 22. The previous weeks had been busy. Garrison possessions were packed away. Single officers transferred their belongings into the quartermaster storehouses, and the married officers saw to it that their families were as secure as possible. First Lieutenant Thaddeus Capron, for example, moved his wife and children from their apartment in Bedlam to another on the south side of the parade ground. The whole garrison, naturally, turned out to watch Companies C, G, and H, Ninth Infantry, as they left the post. The soldiers first paraded down officers' row to be reviewed by Major Townsend and Adjutant Hay. The garrison wives and children ringed the parade ground, and the regimental band played a round of stirring melodies. Elizabeth Burt, writing perhaps for all the wives of the post, remembered that they "knew the inevitable danger to all in the field. With aching hearts we watched the soldiers march away while the band played, 'The Girl I left Behind Me.' So many times have I listened to that mournful tune played when a command marches out of garrison to take the field. This time we knew so well there was to be fighting to the death."[46]

Company I, Second Cavalry, departed on May 23. All together, Fort Laramie's four-company contribution to Crook's next campaign totaled 9 officers and 164 men. Among the officers leaving were Cap-

Elizabeth Reynolds Burt, wife of Captain Andrew Burt, Ninth Infantry, who chronicled life at Fort Laramie during the Great Sioux War. She is seen here many years after her western odyssey. (Fort Laramie National Historic Site)

tains Samuel Munson, Thomas Burrowes, and Andrew Burt of the Ninth Infantry and Noyes of the Second Cavalry. Infantry lieutenants included Capron and Edgar Brooks Robertson. Company I's junior lieutenant Frederick William Kingsbury returned from a leave of absence just in time to repack and march for the field. And Company G's first lieutenant, William Lewis Carpenter, returned from detached service May 25 and left for the campaign the very next day. Assistant surgeon Albert Hartsuff marched with the infantry. Remaining behind were Major Townsend, Adjutant Hay, Lieutenant Morton, A.A.Q.M., Lieutenant Regan, A.C.S., Dr. Gray, now the post's only medical officer, the band, and one company, E, Ninth Infantry, commanded by Captain Edwin Pollock.[47]

Other campaign-related troop movements commenced in earnest at this same time. As ordered, a number of companies, including those from posts along the Union Pacific Railway, traveled to Fort Fetterman via Medicine Bow. The Fort D. A. Russell contingent marched north on May 17. This battalion, when it finally merged after a two-day shakedown march, totaled seven companies commanded by Lieutenant Colonel Royall. Among other prominent cavalrymen present in the files were Captains Guy Vernor Henry, Alexander Sutorious, and Anson Mills, along with Second Lieutenant Bainbridge Reynolds, all of the Third Cavalry. Reynolds, son of the regiment's disgraced colonel, commanded Company F. Traveling with these Second and Third Cavalry companies were three newspapermen: Reuben Briggs Davenport, from the *New York Herald,* Thomas C. MacMillan, representing the *Chicago Inter-Ocean,* and John Finerty, writing for the *Chicago Times.* Finerty, whose newspaper accounts of the campaign were later compiled into an important book about the war, seemed not at all impressed by the landscape between Cheyenne and Fort Laramie, calling it at one point "a country greatly devoid of beauty" and elsewhere "monotonously ugly." He spent most of his ride north adjusting to the regimen of the march, enduring before reaching Fort Laramie alkali dust, stiff knee joints from short stirrup leathers, an unquenchable thirst, and standard army rations consisting of raw bacon, hardtack, and coffee that he called "a tin of abominably bad weather."[48] Curiously, Finerty did not mention the wholesale desertions from this Second and Third Cavalry command on May 19.

No fewer than sixty-five men, mostly new recruits, bolted from the battalion but were soon tracked down and captured. One deserter explained that most of them left because they had heard that in the event of a defeat the wounded would be left in the hands of the Sioux, as had happened, so it was said, at Powder River in March. The *Daily Leader,* in reporting the incident, observed that "Gen. Crook is too good and too brave an officer to tolerate anything so barbarous. If the soldiers will stick by him he will stick by them, and the whole command will either conquer or fall together."[49]

Royall's column marched via Fort Laramie, arriving there on the afternoon of May 23. It would have been shorter to travel the cutoff route, but Crook was intent on this show of force on the Black Hills road, at least as far as Laramie. Indians remained a persistent threat south of the North Platte River, and at the end of May the *Daily Leader* continued to flash headlines like "Indian Scare on the Chug" and "Indians Reconnoitering Fort Laramie." Some threats may have been more perceived than real, especially along the Chug, but around Fort Laramie Indian sightings were well verified and fairly constant. Newsman Robert E. Strahorn, for instance, reported that Indians were occasionally to be seen on the ridgetops only a mile or two from the post, and the trails of small war parties were frequently encountered as one traveled away from the fort in almost any direction. On May 20 a rancher gathering stock just two miles south of the post on Deer Creek was fired upon by two warriors. He was not harmed, however, and escaped to the Six Mile Ranch southwest of the fort on the Cheyenne road.[50]

Royall, fearful of missing the rendezvous at Fort Fetterman, continued from Laramie early on May 24, traveling the left or north bank of the river. Although rarely used and slightly longer, this route made unnecessary a costly and time-consuming crossing of the river at Fetterman. Meanwhile, Crook was overseeing from this forward post the ferrying of troops and supplies across the North Platte. The river was swollen and rapid, and the operation proved exceptionally dangerous.

Before the Big Horn and Yellowstone Expedition, as it was soon to be christened, departed from Fort Fetterman on the afternoon of May 29, General Crook issued a final series of orders to his department and, more directly, Fort Laramie, and these would ultimately restructure that post's role in the ever-growing military campaign against the Sioux. Remembering Fort Laramie's plight after the recent departure of four of its companies to join the expedition, and noting that two companies were already guarding the Black Hills road, Crook sent telegrams on May 27 to the commanding officers at Fort Bridger and Omaha Barracks ordering them to designate one company each of the Fourth and Twenty-third Infantry regiments to proceed to Fort Laramie without delay. Crook then advised Townsend of these actions and directed him to deploy these additional companies on the various routes of travel so as to give the best protection possible. Then on May 29 Crook ordered Dr. R. M. Reynolds, A.A.S., to report from Fort Sanders to Fort Laramie for field duty with the incoming troops. Sheridan, too, interceded with telegrams on the twenty-ninth. One went directly to Townsend commanding him to investigate affairs at the Red Cloud and Spotted Tail agencies. Sheridan wanted to know if there were still defections to the enemy camps and if so in what numbers, and whether the Indians were taking their families. And Sheridan asked Crook how he felt about dispatching most of the Fifth Cavalry to Red Cloud and Spotted Tail from their home stations on the central plains.[51]

Townsend probably little appreciated the significance of these varied orders from Crook and Sheridan beyond the obvious relief of knowing that additional troops were en route and, once deployed, would modestly restore his garrison. His small force was still actively forwarding supplies, an unrelenting chore all season long. But the composition of the usual escort, as described in special orders on May 25, had been reduced to a mere sergeant and four privates.[52] Moreover, Major Townsend, in accordance with Crook's directives, quickly drew on the Camp Robinson garrison for Black Hills duty. Thus far that post had been strengthened, not reduced, by Crook's troop movements. Immediately, however, Captain William Henry Jordan, Ninth Infantry, commanding Camp Robinson, was to order out Company K, Third Cavalry, and twenty infantrymen to patrol the road from the Red Cloud Agency to Red Canyon. There a camp would be made by the infantry, while the cavalry patrolled the road as far as Custer City as well as westward to the Powder River. In carrying out this assignment, Captain Gerald Russell, who commanded this Third Cavalry company, was to work in concert with Captain Egan. No sooner had these orders been transmitted on May 26 than Townsend learned he was to receive the two additional companies, so on the twenty-seventh he amended Jordan's directives slightly, explaining that he would deploy the new infantry companies on the Black Hills road at Sage Creek and on or near the Cheyenne River and ordering that Robinson's troops instead establish a camp on the "Running Water" or Niobrara River at some point midway between the two posts. Jordan learned too that instead of sending twenty men to the field, he was now to detail a full company. The various infantry units would take supplies for one month at a time and remain in the field indefinitely. The cavalry companies were to return to their posts only to refit.[53]

Once the troops were fully deployed the Black Hills road would finally be guarded by two full infantry companies operating out of new, semipermanent stations on the trail, and the Laramie-Robinson road would also have full-time infantry protection. Augmenting them would be two companies of cavalry in constant motion between Fort Laramie, Camp Robinson, and the Black Hills. The *Daily Leader* rejoiced. Besides being the shortest and best route, they boasted, theirs was now "the only safe route leading to the Hills from *any* point."[54]

Increasing troop movement, however, still could not guarantee absolute protection. On May 28 Captain Egan led his company back into Fort Laramie and reported to Townsend a brush he had just had with Indians along the Powder River Trail near Sage Creek. As many as seven or eight hundred Indians were harassing a civilian wagon train bound for the Hills. As Egan overhauled them the Sioux withdrew to the north. As it was later telegraphed to both Sheridan and Crook, Egan stated that "he did not think it prudent to attack and they did not molest him." This chance encounter faded almost as quickly as it had happened, and Egan, marching via Red Cloud, was further able to report that the agency was nearly deserted. About eight hundred to a thousand warriors had gone to the mouth of the Powder River, he told Townsend, and most had taken their families. At Spotted Tail about fifty lodges were reportedly gone, some with families.[55]

It is easy and almost natural to second-guess Egan's chance encounter in late May. He did not engage the Sioux even though the fighting odds seemed about even and he could have and maybe should have done so. But in all deference to his on the spot judgment, the Sioux and their allies had not yet become the all-pervading menace of the northern plains. Although they continually harassed miners and stockmen, particularly those who traveled alone or in small parties, the Sioux had not yet destroyed elite army regiments. In these circumstances it was probably difficult for Egan to read ENEMY every time Indians were encountered. Circumstances changed dramatically and rapidly in the coming months, and the next comparable encounter between soldiers and Indians in Fort Laramie's area of operations—an episode remarkably similar to Egan's May confrontation—resulted in a noteworthy victory for the army, the first in what was soon to become a frightfully costly campaign.

Chapter Five

An Uneasy Summer:
June–August 1876

General George Crook's release of additional troops to protect the Black Hills road reaffirmed Fort Laramie's role as the guardian of the most popular route to the goldfields. As spring waned the Hills retained the nation's attention, though increasingly they competed with national politics—this was an election year. And the country was also celebrating its centennial in Philadelphia and widening a military campaign against the Sioux. Despite Sheridan's worries over a summer war, he had already committed more than twenty-five hundred men to field service, and each of the commands was sufficiently strong—so everyone felt—to demonstrate complete prowess over the northern Indians.

Each command—Terry's, Gibbon's, and Crook's—had its own support system. Whereas Missouri River steamboats played an important role in the northern operations, Crook received aid through conventional channels, either through the Cheyenne Depot or through the Medicine Bow station and Fort Fetterman. War matériel and troops flooded those two routes. Communications came more directly by telegraph line to Fort Fetterman and then were taken north by special courier service. Isolated now from the mainstream of the campaign but integrally protecting Crook's lower right flank were the infantry and cavalry detailed by Major Edwin Townsend from Fort

Laramie and Camp Robinson. In a dual role, these soldiers safe-guarded the Cheyenne–Black Hills road and watched over two Sioux agencies. As if on a second front, Townsend's men were in every way as campaign employed as Custer, Gibbon, or their own department commander.

In early summer General Sheridan remained justifiably concerned about conditions at the Red Cloud and Spotted Tail agencies. In the preceding month, reports from Crook, Townsend, Egan, and others had described a precarious state of affairs. Desertions to the northern camps had been rife all spring, yet a considerable number of Sioux and Northern Cheyennes remained behind, and their sympathies worried him. To measure their temper, Sheridan ordered his cavalry inspector, Lieutenant Colonel Wesley Merritt, to the agencies to check on current affairs again. This time Sheridan was determined to receive Merritt's report personally in Cheyenne or even at Fort Laramie. The *Cheyenne Daily Leader* noted Merritt's passing northward on May 31, though the paper announced that it was in connection with the protection of the road between Fort Laramie and the Hills. On June 4 at Fort Laramie, Merritt picked up an eighteen-man escort from Company E, Ninth Infantry, commanded personally by Captain Pollock, and continued on for Camp Robinson and the agencies.[1]

Meanwhile, in response to Crook's orders dispatching two additional companies of infantry to Townsend's command, Colonel Jefferson C. Davis, commanding the Twenty-third Infantry Regiment and Omaha Barracks, ordered Company H to the field, while at Fort Bridger, in southwestern Wyoming, Colonel Franklin F. Flint likewise detailed out Company K, Fourth Infantry. These companies organized quickly and traveled on the Union Pacific Railway to Cheyenne and then overland to Fort Laramie, where Company H arrived on June 5 and K on June 7. Special order 119 of June 6 described the services Townsend wished these companies to provide. Company H, Twenty-third Infantry, led by First Lieutenant George McMannis Taylor, with Second Lieutenant Julius Hayden Pardee, was to march to the head of Sage Creek, some sixty miles north of the post, and establish a temporary field camp. Company K, Fourth Infantry, commanded by Captain William S. Collier, with First Lieutenant Rufus

Porter Brown, would likewise travel north and establish a similar camp five miles north of the South Cheyenne River at the mouth of the Red Canyon. Both companies were to take light field equipment, a plentiful supply of ammunition, and thirty days' rations, which would be renewed from time to time from the post. Dr. R. M. Reynolds, newly arrived from Fort Sanders and outfitted with medical supplies and hospital stores obtained from Dr. Gray at the post hospital, would accompany Collier to his temporary station.[2]

Amid the hustle connected with Merritt's investigations and the outfitting of these new infantry companies for the field, tragedy struck the post when two-year-old Henry Capron died on June 6. Henry, the third and youngest child of Thaddeus and Cynthia Capron, had been sickly since the family arrived at the post in April. Cynthia's and Thad's family letters are filled with references to their baby, and these remarkable documents tell the melancholy tale of his last days. Lieutenant Capron and many of his fellow Ninth Infantrymen marched from the fort on May 22 to join General Crook's new command at Fetterman. In a series of daily letters to Thaddeus beginning May 23 Cynthia reported that "Henry inquired for Papa this morning" but "he is no better today," or "I wish I could tell you that Henry is better but he is not." The letter of May 25 opened with the cheery greeting "Henry is a very little better . . . I think," but concluded with a heart-tugging account of how he asks for "Fad" and says, "Where is Papa, take Henry to Papa." Other letters at the end of May added to the drama, and news on the twenty-eight that "the doctor discovered today for the first time that [Henry's] condition is more serious than he supposed" may even have been telegraphed directly to Fetterman.[3]

All of this, naturally, left Thaddeus emotionally drained. Amid the sunup to sundown campaign preparations at Fort Fetterman, Thaddeus found time late on the twenty-eight to respond, and his letter closed on this note: "I sometimes fear that I may never see little Henry again. May God in his kindness leave him to us. Love him for me and also the little girl and boy older. In case death should remove any of them during my absence send for a casket and have them interred at Laramie. Then we can remove them when we desire. Take good care of them and yourself darling and may we all meet again soon."[4]

Then for a week the letters stopped, but finally on June 7 Cynthia

Henry Capron. This two-year-old child, son of Thaddeus and Cynthia Capron, died at Fort Laramie in June 1876. (Archives, American Heritage Center, University of Wyoming)

wrote to Thaddeus that "our little Henry has passed away," a victim of tubercular meningitis. Only as she wrote to other family members did the larger story unfold. Henry, it seems, had taken a serious fall half a year earlier and thereafter suffered intermittent bouts of what was called "catarrhal fever," which she misunderstood to be a milder form of the disease that ultimately killed him.[5]

Henry's illness and death touched everyone and brought Fort Laramie's small garrison together in a most sympathetic manner. The post wives rallied to help Mrs. Capron however possible. Some, like Mrs. Noyes, cared for the children, while others, including Mrs. Burt, Mrs. Townsend, Mrs. Egan, and Mrs. Burrowes, assisted in the home. When daily concerts by the regimental band seemed to make Henry restless, Mrs. Noyes marched over to Major Townsend and "had it stopped, and it has not played since." Even Lieutenants Allison and William Foster Norris, Ninth Infantry, stayed in the house helping wherever they could, and Mrs. Munson "sat up with Baby three nights out of six, and [takes] the lead in seeing to things now."[6]

The post's favorite newspaper, the *Cheyenne Daily Leader,* ran a full-column advertisement for Converse and Warren retailers in every issue, and among the varied items available from them were "metallic burial cases." Thaddeus may have remembered that bold-print advertisement when he advised Cynthia about burial wishes on May 28, for a metallic casket was indeed ordered from Cheyenne. Post Chaplain Jeremiah Porter came from Fort D. A. Russell to conduct the service. Cynthia, prostrated by the long ordeal, did not attend, nor did she assist much in the preparation, but Henry was laid out in a Swiss muslin dress made by Mrs. Munson and Mrs. Burrowes and was interred on June 8. Pallbearers included Captain Egan and Lieutenants Rogers and Hay. Most of the garrison turned out for the funeral, but only Hazen, Henry's older brother, represented the family, attending in the care of Mrs. Munson.[7]

Lieutenant Colonel Merritt returned from his inspection of the agencies on June 8. He had found conditions there essentially as described in earlier reports. Significantly, however, he had received ominous and seemingly reliable intelligence from a Sioux, Yellow Robe, who had just come in from the roamer camps. Yellow Robe reported that 186 lodges on Rosebud Creek were about to leave for the Powder River below the point of the March 17 fight. Furthermore, these Indians were ready to fight and numbered, in his estimation, about three thousand warriors. Merritt dispatched this information to Fort Laramie by courier, and it was sent east by telegraph. His on-site checks collected little more, but before departing Merritt reaffirmed the responsibilities of the commanders at Camps Robinson and Sheridan to notify higher authority if they noticed unusual activities at their agencies. Merritt barely paused at Fort Laramie on his return, continuing to Cheyenne to await General Sheridan, who was by then en route.[8]

Since returning to Fort Laramie on May 28, Company K, Second Cavalry, had remained at home refitting. Special order 119, which had detailed the new infantry companies to the Black Hills road, also contained a provision that Egan's cavalrymen would join them as a continuous patrol on the road between their stations. The infantry column was nearly ready to march when on June 10 hurried orders came for Egan to investigate reports of Indian raiding on Chugwater Creek in the vicinity of the Kelly ranch. No sooner had he departed down the Cheyenne road than he was overtaken by a courier from Townsend and directed to return through the fort, cross the Platte at the bridge, and "pursue the Indians who are known to have come up, by Goshen's Hole, and crossed the river, endeavoring (as is supposed) to escape toward Red Cloud Agency." Egan's troopers gallantly scouted as directed but returned to the post on the twelfth without finding Indians.[9]

Captain Collier's and Lieutenant Taylor's Fourth and Twenty-third Infantry companies spent a hurried week collecting a full range of commissary stores and camp and garrison equipage. Fort Laramie would serve as a refitting station, but it was expected that each new subpost would be sufficiently stocked to serve not only its own extended needs, but also those of the cavalry companies who would regularly travel the road. Quartermaster Morton also provided each company with a six-mule team and wagon, plus a horse and equipment for conveying dispatches. Captain Collier assumed command of the combined companies on June 8, and on the twelfth they marched north toward the Black Hills. Within several days the column reached its first destination, the head of Sage Creek. There, just beyond the rugged breaks of Pine Ridge, Taylor's Company H, Twenty-third Infantry, was detached to establish the first of the new camps.[10]

At Sage Creek Taylor's soldiers hurriedly erected wall tents and then a substantial log palisade, using timbers cut from nearby Pine Ridge. Dubbed "Camp on Sage Creek," the completed outpost presented a formidable image at the intersection of the Indians' Powder

River Trail and the Black Hills road.[11] Collier, meanwhile, continued to the Mouth of Red Canyon, where he arrived on June 17 and established a semipermanent cantonment three and one-half miles north of the South Cheyenne River. Called "Camp Mouth of Red Canyon," and in finished state looking much like Taylor's fortifications, this station too quickly helped establish military permanence and protection on the road to the goldfields.[12]

The daily routine at these outposts changed little in subsequent months, though as the records showed both companies participated in a broad range of campaign and protection activities. And as at any military post, permanent or not, a schedule of bugle calls regulated the official day. The following list of calls demonstrates the range of fixed duties at these isolated stations:

FOR BOTH COMPANIES
June 8, 1876

Reveille First Call	5:00 A.M.
Reveille	5:10
Assembly	5:15
Breakfast Call	6:00
Surgeon's Call	7:00
Guard Mounting	8:00
Dinner Call	11:30
Retreat	Sunset
Taps	9:30

CAMP MOUTH OF RED CANYON
August 18, 1876

Reveille First Call	4:45 A.M.
Reveille	5:00
Fatigue Call	6:00
Surgeon's Call	6:00
Drill Call	7:00
Recall from Drill	8:00
Dinner Call	11:30
Guard Mounting First Call	Thirty minutes before sunset

Guard Mounting	Twenty minutes
	before sunset
Retreat	Sunset
Tattoo First Call	8:50 P.M.
Tattoo	9:00
Taps [13]	9:30

At Fort Laramie the transitional calm between the departure of the new field companies and the arrival of others was short-lived. Company F, Ninth Infantry, part of the permanent garrison, did return to barracks after Egan's scout in May. But the plucky Second Cavalrymen were home only long enough to repack, and on June 14 they marched north for another extended tour of the Black Hills road. With them again went Dr. Petteys. No sooner had these soldiers departed on the fourteenth than in rode General Philip H. Sheridan from Chicago, along with six companies of Fifth Cavalrymen commanded by Lieutenant Colonel Eugene Asa Carr and a host of staff officers and other notables.

The arrival of these soldiers in Cheyenne during the preceding week had already caused considerable stir. The deployment of the Fifth Cavalry came in response to Sheridan's offering the regiment to Crook late in May. Until now the Fifth had been dispersed across Brigadier General John H. Pope's Department of the Missouri. These troops, coming from outside the previously affected departments, had not been Crook's for the taking, though in private correspondence he may have told Sheridan he needed additional cavalry support. By early June eight of twelve Fifth Cavalry companies were en route from Kansas, Indian Territory, and Colorado. All traveled on the Kansas Pacific Railroad through Denver to Cheyenne, where they began arriving on June 7. One incident marred what otherwise would have been a routine troop movement for the Fifth. Near Cheyenne Wells, Colorado, sparks from a locomotive ignited hay in one of the stock cars, and despite the best attempts to extinguish the flames the fire consumed the car and sixteen cavalry horses belonging to Company A.[14]

Arriving with the Fifth Cavalry, but from Wilmington, Delaware, not Kansas, was the regiment's trusted scout from earlier campaigns, William Frederick "Buffalo Bill" Cody. Cody had long since proved

William F. "Buffalo Bill" Cody in 1876. During the Sioux War Cody often donned this colorful scouting outfit to dramatize his theatrical persona. (Buffalo Bill Historical Center)

himself as a tracker and frontiersman, but more recently he had developed himself as a showman in an act known as the "Buffalo Bill Combination." Spurred on by his theatrical success, yet shrewdly realizing the publicity gain if he were to join the present campaign, Cody heeded the beckoning of his friends Sheridan and Carr and came west. Upon arriving in Cheyenne Cody was met at the Union Pacific depot by First Lieutenant Charles King, Fifth Cavalry, who escorted him to the Fifth's camp west of town. Buffalo Bill was warmly welcomed as he rode among his old comrades. One soldier boasted to a newspaper back home that "all the old boys in the regiment upon seeing General Carr and Cody together, exchanged confidences, and expressed themselves to the effect that with such a leader and scout they could get away with all the Sitting Bulls and Crazy Horses in the Sioux tribe."[15]

Wesley Merritt had returned to Cheyenne on June 10, and while waiting for General Sheridan, he gave the Fifth Cavalry a thorough personal inspection. Merritt's interests were both professional and personal. He knew that the Fifth's colonel, William Helmsley Emory, was slated for retirement and that in all likelihood he would be promoted to Emory's command. This action was strongly endorsed by both Sheridan and Sherman, but as they awaited the slow processing of retirement papers, here was a chance to see the Fifth on the eve of its joining the campaign.[16]

Six companies of the Fifth Cavalry left Cheyenne on June 11 and enjoyed an effortless march to Fort Laramie, fishing and sightseeing along the way. Of the Chugwater valley, where there had been recent Indian raiding, one cavalryman wrote: "This valley is full of stockmen, their ranches stringing along its entire length, and only three or four miles apart. Hundreds of cattle could be seen grazing on the side hills."[17] Indians had run off over twenty horses from the valley just a few days earlier and had safely eluded Egan's pursuit. Now, as the troopers passed, Carr received telegraphed instructions from Lieutenant Colonel Robert Williams, assistant adjutant general for the Department of the Platte, to detach one of his companies at the Phillips ranch, where they were to await General Sheridan and then escort him to Fort Laramie.[18]

Sheridan was indeed coming. He arrived in Cheyenne on June 13 and conferred with Merritt on a number of matters. As for the situation at Red Cloud and Spotted Tail, Merritt reported that "the feeling among the Indians left at the agency is not good. The Fifth Cavalry is not here too soon." Sheridan did not grant interviews to the local newspapers, but they speculated that he was "not visiting the northern country for pleasure simply, but has business there of a most important character." Actually, Sheridan's travels to Fort Laramie and the agencies seem to be the result of a paranoia about the unseen rather than the unknown. The military hierarchy in Omaha and Chicago was receiving accurate and up-to-the-minute situational reports from these agencies, mostly from army commanders on the scene, not from the Indian agents whose veracity and support were questioned. Nothing substituted for a firsthand look at these troublesome areas, however, and when Sheridan arrived at Fort Laramie he received the customary courtesies paid to such an important officer, then attended to the continuation of his tour.[19]

Traveling with General Sheridan on this Wyoming trip were two trusted aides—his adjutant, Colonel James Barnet Fry, and his military secretary, Lieutenant Colonel James William Forsyth. Forsyth was a particularly close friend of Sheridan's and had served him since the Civil War. Both were part of a larger retinue of officers, including Sheridan's brother Michael and George Alexander Forsyth, who coordinated activities in the Military Division of the Missouri. While at Laramie Sheridan conferred with Eugene Carr and undoubtedly discussed a strategy for deploying the Fifth Cavalry in the campaign. But the general was eager to investigate the agencies, and at 5:00 A.M. on June 15 he crossed the new army bridge and proceeded to Camp Robinson. Accompanying him were his aides, his old friend Bill Cody, whom he had borrowed from the Fifth Cavalry, and a seventeen-man escort from Company F, Ninth Infantry, in the charge of a "reliable sergeant."[20]

Despite the stepped-up pace of troop movements and visits by such distinguished soldiers as General Sheridan, Major Townsend contended with a continually expanding routine that drew unrelentingly upon his ample administrative talents. Of late, for instance, the post had experienced maintenance problems on the telegraph line extending to Fort Fetterman. This was a critical link, and it was imperative that it remain open. Captain James Gilliss, chief quartermaster at the Cheyenne Depot, had queried Townsend on June 10 about rebuilding the line. To this came the response that as many as one pole out of ten needed replacing, and the nearest sources of timber were Laramie Peak or the head of Horse Shoe Creek. In the meantime Townsend and Captain Edwin Mortimer Coates, Fourth Infantry, commanding Fort Fetterman, agreed that each post would service its own half of the line. Seldom did this work out to mutual satisfaction, however, and the needed reconstruction remained months away.[21]

Lieutenant Morton, the post quartermaster, ultimately played a role in maintaining the telegraph, particularly when soldier details came to him for transportation and supplies. But now he was also deeply involved in the annual solicitation of bids for various contracts. The post relied on civilian contractors to provide baled and stacked hay as well as cordwood, and the quartermaster department routinely drew up agreements with independent freighters to haul the same broad assortment of quartermaster and commissary stores carried by government teams and wagons. Lieutenant Regan, post commissary, was also involved with bid work, particularly as he sought live beef cattle to meet coming needs. Solicitations appeared in virtually every newspaper in the Department of the Platte, including Cheyenne's *Sun* and *Daily Leader*. Ultimately, the Department of the Platte's chief quartermaster, Major Ludington, and chief commissary of subsistence, Major John P. Hawkins, awarded contracts to John F. Coad of Cheyenne to supply three thousand cords of wood as well as baled and stacked hay. These contractors often also supplied essentials to other posts in the department and like Murrin, who was a liquor wholesaler in Cheyenne, usually owned or operated other year-round businesses. Occasionally bulky items like hay and wood were bought on the open market, outside the bidding process. Trader John S. Collins, for instance, delivered five hundred cords of wood to the post in June at the prevailing rate of $7.27 per cord.[22]

After growing substantially in February, Morton's quartermaster employee rolls remained fairly static through June. Sixty-eight citizens, mostly teamsters, were accounted for at the end of April, but a number of these were transferred to Crook's campaign in May. In June Morton oversaw forty-three employees at the fort, including a carpenter and a mason who were working on a new post guardhouse. The last entry on the June roll was for the fort's neighbor and general entrepreneur Jules Ecoffey, who was signed up to supply six six-mule teams to ease the drain on quartermaster transportation.[23]

For other citizens at Fort Laramie, the campaign and gold rush continued to dominate discussions and provided abundant related activities as well. The *Cheyenne Daily Leader* ran an occasional column datelined Fort Laramie. This newsy report chronicled the comings and goings of the garrison, listed the many military and social dignitaries visiting the post, and generally served as a monitor for those who

While her husband, Thaddeus, campaigned with General Crook, Cynthia Capron endured Fort Laramie and the Sioux War of 1876 with fortitude. (Archives, American Heritage Center, University of Wyoming)

would not see official army communications. The author of this always entertaining column is not known, but it could well have been any of the officers or even one of the wives. Cynthia Capron, indeed, served as a correspondent for the *Chicago Tribune,* providing in her lengthy letters a broad range of news, including items fresh from her husband Thaddeus, who marched with Crook. Also, John Collins's evaluation of the Black Hills goldfields for a June issue of the *Omaha*

Herald was widely reprinted, though his assessment that "these new gold fields [are] the richest in placer mines that this country has ever known" seems more self-serving than a statement of fact.[24]

Many of the post families were entertained by the arrival of figures like Sheridan, Cody, "Wild Bill" Hickok, who passed through at the end of June, and Martha "Calamity Jane" Cannary. A coarse woman at best, Cannary was an occasional resident at Cuny and Ecoffey's roadhouse until her short-lived career as a teamster with the Big Horn and Yellowstone Expedition. She then drifted on to the Black Hills. Between other sordid adventures "Calamity" took a wild ride that, as reported in the *Daily Leader,* caused a considerable stir in proper Wyoming society. This is how the newspaper reported it:

CALAMITY JANE'S JAMBOREE

On Sunday, June 10th, that notorious female, Calamity Jane, greatly rejoiced over her release from durance vile, procured a horse and buggy from Jas. Abney's stable, ostensibly to drive to Fort Russell and back. By the time she had reached the Fort, however, indulgence in frequent and liberal potations completely befogged her not very clear brain, and she drove right by that place, never drawing rein until she reached the Chug, 50 miles distant. Continuing to imbibe bug-juice at close intervals and in large quantities throughout the night, she woke up the next morning with a vague idea that Fort Russell had been removed, but being still bent on finding it, she drove on, finally sighting Fort Laramie, 90 miles distant. Reaching there she discovered her mistake, but didn't show much disappointment. She turned her horse out to grass, ran the buggy into a corral, and began enjoying life in camp after her usual fashion. When Joe Rankin reached the Fort, several days later, she begged of him not to arrest her, and as he had no authority to do so, he merely took charge of the Abneys outfit, which was brought back to this city Sunday.[25]

Another notable visitor in June was the Brule Sioux chief Spotted Tail. On June 6 he paused at the fort while en route to see friends in Denver. By all accounts he was an imposing figure, and though fifty-three years old he walked erect and with enormous dignity. When he

Chief Spotted Tail, a powerful but moderate leader among the Brule Sioux. (State Historical Society of North Dakota)

returned about June 20 he collected the remains of his beloved daughter Mini-Aku, which since 1866 had reposed in a scaffold burial beyond the hospital. He had longed to bring her bones back to his agency on the White River, and he finally succeeded on this trip. There is a story that Fort Laramie's hospital steward, Theodore Brown, removed these bones just before Spotted Tail returned. Except for the quick reactions of Dr. Gray and Major Townsend, who saw to it that the remains were replaced, a fragmented skeleton and the incalculable wrath of a prestigious Brule could have resulted.[26]

Sheridan returned to Fort Laramie from his agency inspection on

Indian scaffold graves near Fort Laramie, 1876. D. S. Mitchell photograph. (Nebraska State Historical Society)

June 18. He collected very little new intelligence but confirmed the reports given him previously about the rather precarious state of affairs there. Even more important, however, he formed a visual image of the land, which would undoubtedly prove useful as new wide-sweeping movements were planned. Sheridan met with Captain Jordan, commanding Camp Robinson, as well as others and once more impressed upon them the importance of their duties. Back at Fort Laramie Sheridan saw Carr and Townsend. To Carr he gave orders to march his eight companies of Fifth Cavalrymen up the Black Hills road to the intersection of the Powder River trail and from there proceed westward, scouting as long as supplies allowed. Sheridan anticipated that the actions of Generals Terry and Crook, who were operating on the lower Powder River and south fork of the Tongue River, respectively, could well drive the Indians toward the Fifth Cavalry, and Carr "may have a good opportunity to strike them, or if not, at least your demonstration may be advantageous to Generals Terry and Crook."[27]

On June 18 Sheridan sent a long letter to Crook reporting that all was quiet at the Red Cloud Agency and that he was dispatching the Fifth northward to the Powder River trail. "I think that this will stir things up," he noted, "and prove advantageous in the settlement of the Indian question." Sheridan then added a series of briefs updating Crook's knowledge on other matters. Governor Rutherford Hayes had been nominated for president, and William A. Wheeler of New York for vice president, he wrote, "which is what we wanted." Colonel Emory had been retired, and Merritt would come to the Fifth Cavalry, possibly in time to take command of Carr's column. And it was necessary, he found, to revive the District of the Black Hills, with headquarters in the field under Carr. Crook had abolished the administrative District of the Black Hills on May 2, but as reestablished and redefined it embraced parts of western Nebraska and Dakota along with eastern Wyoming to, but not including, Fort Fetterman.[28]

Orders given to Major Townsend on June 18 were much more far-reaching, though the impact seemed less combat- or campaign-related than relevant to protecting routes to the Black Hills. First, Sheridan wanted Captain Gerald Russell's Company K, Third Cavalry, positioned on the Sidney–Red Cloud Agency road, patrolling as far south as Clarke's Bridge across the North Platte River. This new toll bridge built by Henry R. Clarke spanned the North Platte about three miles west of present-day Bridgeport, Nebraska. Opened on May 10, 1876, it gave new significance and impetus to the Sidney–Black Hills route. Russell's Third Cavalrymen, until this time, had been patrolling north of Camp Robinson toward the Black Hills.[29]

Sheridan then directed that Captain Michael Fitzgerald's Company D, Ninth Infantry, which had been encamped on the Niobrara River protecting the Laramie-Robinson road, be redistributed. Six men and a noncommissioned officer were to guard the Sidney–Black

Clarke's Bridge, Nebraska. Spanning the North Platte River in May 1876, this bridge and the Sidney–Black Hills road rivaled Cheyenne and Fort Laramie as an avenue to the goldfields. (South Dakota State Historical Society)

Hills stage station at the Niobrara River crossing, while the rest of the company was removed to a new camp in the White River canyon nearer to Camp Robinson. Meanwhile, Captain Egan's Second Cavalry company was to be broken up, with ten men under a good sergeant to take station and frequently patrol the Chugwater valley, while the captain and the rest of his company would continue to patrol the Custer City road north of Fort Laramie.[30]

By these deployments Sheridan was hoping to bolster an area of operations that was growing in significance with each passing day. Whether he viewed the military developments in southeastern Wyoming and western Nebraska as equivalent to the campaigning by Crook, Terry, and Gibbon is speculative. Clearly, however, the Red Cloud Agency, and to a lesser extent its neighbor the Spotted Tail Agency, figured strongly in his consciousness and planning. At the least this area was a sanctuary for the northern roamers, and increasingly there were suspicions that war matériel was being trafficked on the Powder River trail. Thus it was that the Fifth Cavalry was to be planted directly on that route. Meanwhile, the addition of these eight new cavalry companies released Russell's Third Cavalrymen, Egan's Second Cavalrymen, and other infantrymen to better protect not only the Cheyenne–Black Hills road but also now the Sidney–Black Hills road.

All these matters worried Sheridan. He was anxious about Crook, with whom he had had little communication since the Big Horn and

Yellowstone Expedition left Fort Fetterman in late May. Perhaps the Sioux could outflank him from the southeast. Sheridan hoped not, and he was doing his best to prevent it.[31]

Sheridan left Fort Laramie on June 19, accompanied by Major Townsend, who traveled with him as far as Cheyenne. In Townsend's absence Captain Pollock commanded the post. Over the next several days the broad orders given by Sheridan were translated into specific directives for the commands affected. Special order 131 on June 22, for instance, sent one "reliable sergeant and 10 privates, of Company K Second Cavalry, mounted, equipped, and furnished with 100 rounds of ammunition per man, with rations for 13 days" on detached service along the Cheyenne road. These men would form a permanent patrol to scout up and down the Chugwater valley, and the detachment would return to Fort Laramie only to resupply. The post commander meanwhile sent a harried note to headquarters, Department of the Platte, requesting that additional transportation be made available to the post: "Fort Laramie has been designated as the Depot of Supplies for the troops in the field under command of Lieut. Col. E A Carr 5th Cavalry. In addition thereto, I am obliged to furnish supplies to the Infantry camps on Sage Creek, and mouth of Red Canon, on the Black Hills road, and to parties repairing the telegraph lines, and to officers for various purposes between here and the agencies and to Fort Fetterman." Relief, unfortunately, was a long time coming, since there was very little uncommitted transport left in the department.[32]

At the Fifth Cavalry camp along the Laramie River one mile east of the post, officers and men alike were tending to last-minute details before departing for the field. Carr had his instructions from Sheridan, and the rest of his command, Companies C and G, arrived from Cheyenne on June 20. Carr also learned that thirty thousand rounds of carbine ammunition and ten thousand rounds of pistol ammunition had been sent from Omaha and the Rock Island Arsenal in Illinois and would soon reach the command. As the new commander of the District of the Black Hills, Carr's authority superseded Townsend's concerning operations at Camps Robinson and Sheridan and the surrounding territory, and his order 1 from the district made it clear that servicing his command would become one of Townsend's foremost responsibilities. He particularly wanted supplies "thrown forward" to the camp at Sage Creek, to be ready for the return of the regiment from the scout ordered by General Sheridan.[33]

As Carr attended to administrative details, his soldiers divided their time between drills, packing their escort wagons, and visits to the garrison. John Collins's store was a popular stop, since it offered a variety of sutler goods that would be unobtainable once the command headed north. For the most part, however, the Fifth Cavalrymen found Fort Laramie a very lonely post. Besides, they were eager for, as one soldier put it, the "warpath." Some in the Fort Laramie garrison welcomed their presence, however. "We feel perfectly safe . . . now for . . . companies of the 5th Cav. are camped near," Cynthia Capron wrote to her mother-in-law.[34] The garrison was probably equally charmed by certain of the Fifth Cavalry officers, who paid social calls as their schedules allowed.

The Fifth indeed included a significant number of prominent officers. Lieutenant Colonel Eugene A. Carr, for instance, was an 1850 graduate of the United States Military Academy, had served in the Regiment of Mounted Riflemen and on the frontier in the 1850s, was breveted repeatedly during the Civil War, including achieving the grade of major general, had served with distinction on the plains after the war, and eventually was awarded the Medal of Honor for gallantry at the Battle of Pea Ridge, Arkansas. Among other officers present were Major John J. Upham and Captains Robert Hugh Montgomery, Samuel Storrow Sumner, Edward Mortimer Hayes, Sanford Cobb Kellogg, and Julius Wilmot Mason. Each of these men had served in the Civil War, and Mason had commanded the official escort for Lieutenant General Ulysses S. Grant after he assumed command of the Armies of the Union in March 1864. Most had also seen field service on the Republican River Expedition and elsewhere against Arapahoes and Cheyennes in 1868–69 and in the Apache wars in Arizona during the early 1870s. One junior officer, First Lieutenant Charles King, probably caused few ripples as he went dutifully about his chores. But this soldier, seriously wounded in an Apache fight in 1874, would soon leave the regular army as a result of this wound and would become a writer of international acclaim. Among his future chronicles were numerous stories about the Fifth Cavalry

First Lieutenant Charles King, Fifth U.S. Cavalry, seen here as a captain in 1879. Like John Bourke, King was an important chronicler of the events of 1876. (Paul L. Hedren)

in 1876, a novel featuring social intrigue at Fort Laramie in that same eventful year, and many other important historical and fictional works.[35]

Dr. J. L. Powell, acting assistant surgeon, traveled as medical officer when the Fifth departed on its scout. As so many field doctors had done before him, Powell outfitted with stores collected at the hospital.[36] Dr. Gray there attended to Powell's needs and also treated William G. Felton, the sole survivor of the Red Canyon "massacre" on April 16. The *Daily Leader* of June 21 acknowledged receipt of a letter from Felton, who, as he said, had nearly recovered from the four wounds he received in "escaping from the red fiends." Felton planned to return to the Black Hills, and "he swears that he will have revenge for the blood he spilled in Red Canon."

All but one of the Fifth Cavalry companies left Fort Laramie early on June 22. The column totaled over 350 effectives. If these troops were bent on "stirring things up," as Sheridan had hoped, they did not have long to wait. On June 23 came news from the north that General Crook had engaged the Sioux on Rosebud Creek. Although he claimed a victory, other communications and orders led many to question the nature of this battlefield success. Since leaving Fort Fetterman on May 29, General Crook had angled northwestward, crossing and scouting various branches of the Powder and Tongue rivers until mid-June. On the sixteenth he cut loose from his supply train and marched down Rosebud Creek. There, a few miles into Montana, on June 17 the Sioux struck him as his men prepared morning coffee. For over six hours one of the largest Indian battles in the American West was waged over broken terrain, completely unsuited to the standard unit tactics in which the soldiers were trained. Still, the troops acquitted themselves well on a battle line that stretched nearly three miles. Eventually the Sioux and their allies disengaged. Crook held the field and immediately claimed a victory. Casualties, Indian and white alike, were light considering the numbers involved. But Crook, rather than pressing his advantage, promptly retired to his base camp in Wyoming, and in this light his victory turned to defeat. "In this retreat, rather than the casualties," notes military historian Robert M. Utley, "lay the full measure of the defeat, for it neutralized him at the most important juncture of the campaign."[37]

Crook's communication to Sheridan dated June 19 and transmitted via Fort Fetterman on June 23 reported on the fight at the Rosebud. This lengthy telegram concluded by saying that Crook was withdrawing to his base camp to care properly for his wounded. Furthermore, he was ordering five additional infantry companies to join him and would make no extended movements until they arrived.[38] Orders following up on Crook's request for more troops came in a flurry of telegrams originating at department headquarters in Omaha on June 23. First it was ordered that two infantry companies should come from Fort Laramie and three others from Camp Douglas, Utah. Omaha routinely transmitted this information to Chicago, but General Sheridan quickly countermanded the orders. It was not prudent, he wrote to Lieutenant Colonel Williams in Omaha, to take companies from Laramie, since there were only two there. Nor should infantry come from Camp Robinson. Instead, Sheridan suggested that four companies be sent from Camp Douglas and one from Fort Sanders. Telegrams authorizing these changes were promptly sent from Omaha. Townsend too was asked about his supplies of reserve ammunition, and Sheridan sent a warning to Carr via Fort Laramie to watch closely the movement of Indians in the direction of the Red Cloud Agency.[39]

More specific news of the Battle of the Rosebud came into the post on June 24. Cynthia Capron recalled that John Ford, the telegraph operator, hand-carried copies of newspaper dispatches and other reports to friends in the garrison. "He went to Mrs. Burt's first and she brought him in so that he could read them to us both at once," she recalled. The *Daily Leader*'s first reports appeared in the June 24 paper under the headline "Fighting the Fiends. A Pitched Battle between Crook's Command and Sitting Bull's Scalpers." Then followed two different accounts, one running nearly a column and a half, giving an accurate eyewitness report of the fight. Of greatest importance to the local garrison were the lists of casualties. Each of the four companies from Fort Laramie was engaged in the battle, but no casualties were reported in Captain Munson's Company C, Burrowes's Company G, or Burt's Company H. Only in Noyes's Company I, Second Cavalry, was there a wounded soldier, First Sergeant Thomas Meagher. Most of the heavy casualties were sustained by the fourteen other cavalry companies. Only one officer was wounded, Captain Guy Vernor Henry, but it was serious—a gunshot wound in the face.[40]

Other reports of the fight on Rosebud Creek followed almost daily in the local papers, including varied accounts by each of the newspaper reporters marching with Crook. John Finerty's dispatch to the *Chicago Times,* for instance, appeared in the June 27 *Daily Leader.* His was a fairly straightforward account of the action, but it concluded that the troops were generally reluctant to countermarch back into Wyoming. These were "brave men," he noted, and "would charge the Sioux to the gates of hell had they been allowed."

Elsewhere in Wyoming the Fifth Cavalry had advanced north on the Black Hills road and was halted on the Powder River trail. Carr had received additional instructions from Sheridan to remain in that area until further intelligence came from Crook and Terry. Carr meanwhile attempted to establish an express service between Fort Laramie and his command, but this brought a lengthy response from Major Townsend. "I will endeavour if possible to hire expressmen for that service but I have no troops available for that duty," he wrote. In continuing he reported that Egan's company was already divided and that the captain's personal force numbered only twenty men. As to transport, he would do his best to move supplies, and he had already directed Lieutenant Morton to reengage Ecoffey's wagon train for that purpose. Townsend concluded on a somber but frank note: "This post is stripped. I will forward to you your supplies as fast as transportation can be procured but I have none of my own and we must depend on what can be hired in the country round about."[41]

While Morton scrambled to arrange transportation, Townsend contended with reports of Indian harassment on the stage road. In the previous several weeks two stage stations north of Fort Laramie had been burned, including most recently J. W. Dear's ranch on Rawhide Creek. In the midst of this heightened depredation, in part attributed to the Indian prowess on the Rosebud, stage service north of the post had been reduced to an intermittent schedule. But on June 24 Luke Voorhees, superintendent of the stage company, announced that they would commence once-weekly service to Custer and Deadwood immediately and begin a triweekly line as soon as the road was clear of Indians so that "station keepers and stock will be safe on the route."[42]

Other traffic between Cheyenne and the Black Hills continued unchecked, despite persistent threats of hostilities. One party drawing greater than normal attention was that of stage actor Jack Langrishe. For nearly two decades Langrishe's troupe of actors had graced the stages of the West's mining camps, providing serious drama of high quality, giving pioneers "a touch of the culture they had left home." Although generally headquartered in Denver, most recently Langrishe's thespians had performed in Cheyenne. Attracted as he was to gold rushes and mining camps, on June 21 his fourteen performers left Cheyenne in a four-wagon caravan. They passed through Fort Laramie on June 25, spending a night, then continued north, ultimately reaching Deadwood, where they built several theaters and remained for nearly three years.[43]

Following Langrishe into the fort was Wesley Merritt, who arrived on June 27 on his way to assume command of the Fifth Cavalry Regiment. His long-awaited promotion to colonel was nearly official. The aged Colonel William H. Emory was formally retired by act of Congress on June 26, to date from July 1, 1876. Merritt's promotion would be effective that same date, but in the meantime General Sheridan was eager to get him into the field as quickly as possible and had dispatched him from Chicago on the twenty-third, the same day he learned of Crook's fight on the Rosebud. At Fort Laramie Merritt was provided with an escort consisting of the "available men and officers of Company K, Second Cavalry," and at 1:00 P.M. on June 28 they marched out to join the Fifth Cavalry at the South Cheyenne River.[44]

Arriving at the post that same day, to the surprise of his wife, children, and friends, was First Lieutenant Thaddeus Capron and three Ninth Infantry enlisted men from Company C, fresh from the Big Horn and Yellowstone Expedition. After the Battle of the Rosebud and Crook's retirement to his base camp along Goose Creek, the general elected to evacuate his wounded and gather additional supplies from Fort Fetterman. Escorting the wounded south were Company C, Ninth Infantry, with Munson and Capron, and Company F, Fourth Infantry, with Captain Gerhard L. Luhn and First Lieutenant Henry

First Lieutenant Thaddeus H. Capron, Company C, Ninth U.S. Infantry. (Fort Laramie National Historic Site)

Seton. Major Alexander Chambers commanded the small expedition of mercy, and Crook's chief quartermaster, Captain John Vincent Furey, along with several others, also returned to conduct assorted business. Capron had not yet received word about the death of his son Henry, so the selection of his company to join the escort was providential.[45]

The evacuation of wounded from Goose Creek began early on June 21. On the twenty-second, after the command had established camp for the night, couriers from Fetterman came upon them, and only then did Capron receive letters from his wife, Dr. Gray, and Major Townsend telling in wrenching detail of Henry's death. "The blow is terrible, and oh how I shall miss the dear little one," Capron confided in his diary. For five more days the little command marched on toward Fetterman, arriving there finally at midday on June 27. After ferrying the wounded across the North Platte and carrying them up the bluffs to the post hospital, Capron secured permission to ride to Fort Laramie, which he reached at 2:30 P.M. on June 28. Despite the Caprons' recent tragedy, their reunion was a joyous one, though much too short.[46]

As the month of July rushed upon the small Fort Laramie garrison attention shifted, at least briefly, to the coming hundredth anniversary of the founding of the nation, on Tuesday, July 4. Beginning two weeks before, the *Cheyenne Daily Leader* had been running a daily half-column announcement on the celebration planned for their community and reported, as well, on celebrations begun or anticipated in other cities across the land. At Fort Laramie's neighboring Three Mile Ranch, Jules Ecoffey planned a celebration too, but when he formally requested an artillery piece from Fort Laramie to use at the ranch, Adjutant Hay responded offering the commanding officer's regrets and noting that all field pieces would be employed at the post on the fourth.[47] Indeed, Fort Laramie was planning a grand celebration that would follow a general scheme outlined by the War Department a month earlier. In recognition of the "one hundredth Anniversary of the Independence of the United States," Fort Laramie orders directed that "all labor and military duty except necessary fatigues guard duty and roll calls will be suspended" and, further, Second Lieutenant William Norris, E Company, Ninth Infantry, would command the firing of three artillery salutes at prescribed times throughout the day.[48]

On July 2 the *Daily Leader* also noted that a traveler, Herman Haas, had just arrived in Cheyenne from Fort Laramie carrying news that had circulated around the post June 30 about a big fight between Sitting Bull's main village and either Terry's or Gibbon's troops, not Crook's. This intelligence had come from Indian runners to the Red Cloud Agency. At the moment still unknown to the larger world, Custer's Seventh Cavalry had engaged hostile Sioux and Cheyennes on the Little Bighorn River in Montana on June 25, and possibly the

Second Lieutenant William Foster Norris, Company E, Ninth U.S. Infantry, at the time of his graduation from West Point in 1872. (U.S. Military Academy Library)

reference, garbled as it had become in translation, referred to that encounter. If this assumption was true, Red Cloud Agency, Fort Laramie, and Cheyenne shared the joint distinction of announcing to the world early if not first news of that terrible fight, beating by at least one whole day similar "moccasin telegraph" news passed around Indian homes at Mendota, near Fort Snelling, Minnesota, on July 3 and official detailed announcements that appeared in newspapers beginning July 4.[49]

Thaddeus Capron left Fort Laramie early on July 2, concluding his short visit with family and friends. During his stay, news from the battlefields and reports about the ever-present Indian threat continued to dominate conversation. Locally, Luke Voorhees of the Cheyenne and Black Hills Stage Company had asked Major Townsend about the relative safety of the road between Fort Laramie northeast to Red Cloud, and to this came a reply that "at no time" was the route safe for one man, but that with the deployment of Captain Fitzgerald's Ninth Infantry company in the White River Canyon, it was "as safe as it ever is in Indian Country."[50]

Townsend was doing his best to juggle varied administrative responsibilities. After its return from escorting Wesley Merritt to the Fifth Cavalry's camp, Company K, Second Cavalry, refitted and was promptly returned to the field for continued scouting. Townsend faithfully shuttled important communications forward, including one to department headquarters requesting a course of action in the case of a man named Boucher, who lived near the Spotted Tail Agency. Boucher was known to be trafficking arms and ammunition to the Indians.[51] The major also grappled with the need, coming fast, to protect the advance of the telegraph line from his post to the Hills.

Construction of a telegraph extension to the goldfields had been anticipated for some time. All along, Fort Laramie had provided cooperative maintenance services for the telegraph line south to Cheyenne and northwest to Fort Fetterman, and even as the Black Hills extension was commencing, 575 poles were received at the Chug station to put the line in order between the Hunton ranch and the fort.[52] Actual construction north to the Black Hills of this "electric star of empire," as the *Daily Leader* called it, would be in charge of W. H. Hibbard, superintendent of the Western Union Telegraph Company in Salt Lake City. Hibbard left Cheyenne on July 3 with a corps of workmen and upon arriving at Fort Laramie he conferred with Townsend. The major then dutifully dispatched couriers north to Colonel Merritt and to the commanders of the Sage Creek and Red Canyon military camps, again advising them that he and they were obliged by the Department of the Platte to furnish escorts for this work party. Townsend cautioned Merritt that he was unable to do more because of the depleted state of his garrison.[53]

Most attention on July 4 was directed to celebrating the nation's one hundredth birthday. As previously ordered, nonessential military functions were suspended, and officers and enlisted men alike enjoyed a relatively leisure-filled day. Social courtesies were exchanged among the commissioned staff and their families, and later nearly all the officers, wives, and children went on a picnic south of the fort on Deer Creek. The War Department had prescribed a uniform series of artillery salutes for each of the nation's military posts, and at Fort Laramie Lieutenant Norris oversaw the discharge of thirteen guns at dawn, a national salute of thirty-eight guns at noon, and another thirteen guns at sunset.[54]

Before the cheer of the centennial faded on July 5 there came shattering news. Custer had been wiped out on the Little Bighorn. The *Cheyenne Daily Leader* bordered the front page of its July 6 edition in black and repeatedly mourned this "terrible slaughter" at the hands of Sitting Bull's "fiends." How long will such murder be tolerated? the paper cried. At Fort Laramie the discussions centered as much on Custer's motives as on the obvious nature of the tragedy where so many soldiers were killed. "Everyone seems to think that Custer made the attack prematurely to get glory for himself and his regiment," wrote Cynthia Capron to her husband. The continued prowess shown by the Sioux and Cheyennes had other implications for the small garrison. "I wake up in the night and often suffer very much from fear," she continued, for "the Indians could very easily take the post."[55]

Major Townsend reassured Mrs. Capron and other wives that the post was in no danger from Indians, but he indeed did command a severely depleted garrison, and this may have been the root of their alarm. Of his available command, Company F, Ninth Infantry, in the charge of First Lieutenant William Rogers, left the post on July 6 to escort supplies to Sage Creek and Red Canyon for use by the various commands in the field. Company K, Second Cavalry, departed on July 8 to scout after "hostile Indians" observed in the direction of Cottonwood Creek and Chugwater Creek, and with several smaller parties off on other duties only elements of Captain Pollock's Company E, Ninth Infantry, remained to secure the fort.[56] Cynthia Capron wrote to Thaddeus that after the departure of these various companies and details, only thirteen men were available for duty one morning, and of those six went on guard.[57]

Meager garrisons were relatively commonplace elsewhere in the Department of the Platte during these early summer months. In June only one sergeant, one corporal, and eight privates performed essential duties at Fort McPherson, Nebraska, and a similar skeleton detachment presided over North Platte Station.[58] Fort Laramie's serious depletion lasted only two days, and the return of Egan's cavalry company on July 11 strengthened the garrison base.[59]

During the first weeks of July there had been fairly consistent Indian activity on the Black Hills road north of Fort Laramie. A party of fifteen or twenty warriors chased two cattle herders into the Red Canyon camp on one occasion. And the Fifth Cavalry column detailed to patrol the Powder River Trail repeatedly sighted small parties of Indians and offered a spirited though nonproductive chase of one group on July 3. By July 6 the Fifth had moved into a camp adjacent to Lieutenant Taylor's Sage Creek infantry cantonment, and it was there on the seventh that they received word of the Custer disaster. The announcement was a shock there, as it had been in army circles everywhere. In the Fifth's case, however, the news was seen as a sure indication that they would soon be transferred from eastern Wyoming to the very front lines with General Crook.[60]

Crook, it seems, had been bargaining for just that. After his ill-fated Battle of the Rosebud he immediately called for five additional infantry companies to join him, and as he awaited their arrival in early July, General Sheridan offered Crook the Fifth Cavalry. Crook was delighted by this news, and on July 12 he issued orders for Merritt to advance on Camp Cloud Peak, as the base for the Big Horn and Yellowstone Expedition was being called. Merritt was further advised that if he marched via Forts Laramie and Fetterman, he should bring extra ammunition, horses, horse equipment, and full forage. With eight companies of the Fifth Cavalry in his command, plus additional infantry support, Crook was sure he could "end the campaign with one crushing blow."[61]

Merritt marched immediately, intending to travel by way of Fort Laramie, where he would collect his own supplies as well as horses and equipment for Crook. Sage Creek to Fort Laramie was normally a two-day ride, but on Merritt's second day he detoured slightly eastward to intersect the Laramie-Robinson road. Alarming information had just been received from Captain William Jordan at Camp Robinson that Cheyennes were about to bolt from the Red Cloud Agency. Merritt's obvious duty was to check this flight, and he dallied little in assessing and responding to an emergency.

At the Red Cloud Agency affairs had been deteriorating for weeks, particularly since the Custer debacle. Captain Jordan, who watched over the agency from his adjacent military post, had telegraphed Omaha on July 12 that conditions were uncertain owing both to the news about Custer and to the failure of the Interior Department to furnish beef due the Indians. To safeguard his own position, Jordan brought home the infantry company scouting south on the Sidney road, and he planned to recall Fitzgerald's company from White River Canyon if danger became imminent. Then came Jordan's communication dated July 14. "I have just received reliable information that about 800 Northern Cheyennes / men women and children / containing about 150 fighting men, and a good many Sioux all belonging to Red Cloud Agency are to leave here tomorrow for the north."[62]

A flurry of telegrams followed Jordan's dispatch. He notified Major Townsend, for instance, that a "threatening state of affairs now exists at Red Cloud agency demanding the presence of more troops," and he indeed withdrew Company D, Ninth Infantry, from White River Canyon. Omaha wished to know exactly how many Indians had left the agency to join the northern roamers and had sent that request via Fort Laramie to both Jordan and the commanding officer at Camp Sheridan.[63] Meanwhile, Merritt's Fifth Cavalry companies were gallantly marching north toward the Sage Creek camp. As their mission unfolded, it became clear that they would have to backtrack and position themselves in front of the fleeing Indians. In the next thirty-one hours the Fifth traveled eighty-five miles. Only brief halts were allowed, including one at Lieutenant Taylor's cantonment. There the available troops of Company H, Twenty-third Infantry, were added to the command as an armed escort for Merritt's supply train. By dawn on July 17, seven companies were secreted along the steep cutbanks of Warbonnet Creek, Nebraska, thirty miles east of the Sage Creek camp. The Cheyennes had not yet reached that location.[64]

The brief dawn encounter on July 17 between Cheyennes and the Fifth Cavalry, soon to be known as the Skirmish at Warbonnet Creek, was over almost as fast as it began. A dozen or more warriors had advanced ahead of the main Cheyenne camp, seven miles or so away, and were attacked by elements from Merritt's command. The greatest glory was Buffalo Bill Cody's. In the fight he personally led a charge on the advancing war party and with a deft shot produced the only casualty. Cody, by then a fairly accomplished actor, probably recognized a dramatic opportunity, and with considerable aplomb he neatly scalped the dead warrior, Yellow Hair, and waving the bloody trophy at the passing troops, declared it the "first scalp for Custer." Merritt's soldiers then chased these warriors and the rest of their village back to the Red Cloud Agency, a pursuit that took the rest of the day.[65]

Although by the standards of 1876 the encounter at Warbonnet Creek was small, the fight had considerable press quality. Beginning at Camp Robinson that night, the ranking officers of the Fifth Cavalry prepared official reports on their successful forced march and clash. These were telegraphed to division headquarters. Both of Cheyenne's newspapers picked up the story, and the *Daily Leader* printed Merritt's entire report, offering a rather typical aside that "it is a pity that only 'one good Indian' is the result of this campaign." Militarily the little fight did have numerous positive ramifications. Henceforth the army was finally able to boost a battlefield success after three pitiful failures. Also, Merritt's cavalry had quickly and professionally responded to an emergency. In a test of stamina and training they forced marched, blocked the Powder River trail, clashed with an advance party of warriors, and sent the whole Cheyenne camp scurrying back to the Red Cloud Agency.[66]

While the Fifth Cavalry was chasing Cheyennes, a band of thirty Indians was spotted on July 19 twelve miles down the Platte from Fort Laramie. Captain Egan and Company K, Second Cavalry, were immediately dispatched to chase these marauders, but as had become the pattern in so many previous cases, the sortie was fruitless.[67] That same day the officers at Fort Laramie debated a contemptuous newspaper report originating in Helena, Montana, that had just been received at the fort. The column asserted that the officers at Laramie had publicly branded General Crook a coward for retreating from the Rosebud Creek battlefield. Despite any personal feelings on the matter—and surely there were some—such a dangerous public statement was totally uncharacteristic of any officer. Moreover, as Major

Townsend pointed out in a public rebuttal, no such telegram had been sent from Fort Laramie, nor could a letter dated June 25 have reached Helena by June 30, when the assertion appeared in print. All the officers discussed the libel and then adopted a resolution denouncing what they saw as a "gross falsehood." They wanted an apology. At the least, when the *Cheyenne Daily Leader* and the *Army and Navy Journal* published their letter, they were accorded equal time.[68]

Wesley Merritt resumed his march from Camp Robinson to Fort Laramie on July 18, arriving there on the twenty-first to find surplus horses and equipment awaiting him. The Fifth spent all of July 22 preparing to resume their march to join Crook. Those who could escaped briefly to the garrison, where they exchanged courtesies and stopped at John Collins's store. Bill Cody and Lieutenant Charles King paused at the telegraph office, and the young officer hurriedly drafted a release for the *New York Herald* that described the recent fight with the Cheyennes. When it appeared in the July 23 Sunday paper, Cody's daring as the slayer of the Cheyenne Yellow Hair became a matter of public record. Cody too stopped at the post office, behind the three-company infantry barracks midway between the trader's store and the Laramie River, and mailed a box containing Yellow Hair's feather bonnet, shield, weapons, and scalp—trophies from the fight on the Warbonnet.[69]

While at Laramie, Merritt learned of other troop movements either pending or under way. The four remaining companies of his own regiment, E, F, H, and L, would proceed via Fort Laramie for duty at Camp Robinson.[70] Merritt also learned that Colonel Nelson Appleton Miles and six Fifth Infantry companies had been called from Kansas, while six companies of the Twenty-second U.S. Infantry under the command of Lieutenant Colonel Elwell Stephens Otis were en route from Michigan, all to join General Terry's expedition. Colonel Merritt undoubtedly also learned that the void left by the departure of his eight companies from the Black Hills road to the north would be filled by six companies of Fourth Cavalry. General Sheridan made that official on July 20 when he notified General Pope that the Fourth should be transferred promptly and that if Colonel Ranald S. Mackenzie, commanding the regiment, could be spared he should come as well, "as he is the very man [Sheridan wanted] at the Red Cloud Agency for the next two months."[71]

These are midsummer 1876 troop replacements camped at Fort Fetterman and bound for the Big Horn and Yellowstone Expedition. After the Battle of the Rosebud numerous additional infantry and cavalry companies gathered at Fetterman before continuing north to Crook's camp along the Big Horn Mountains. Photograph attributed to D. S. Mitchell. (National Archives and Records Service)

Merritt's eight companies of Fifth Cavalrymen broke camp early on July 23. As the chronicler Lieutenant King described it, the trumpets sounded "the General," which was the universal army signal to strike tents and march away. The white canvas was folded into the wagons, and soon the column of horse was off on the long-anticipated march to join General Crook. As the troops filed out of their camp and over the iron bridge, Captain Egan and Lieutenant Allison of Laramie's gallant gray horse troop came down to wish them "godspeed."[72] Also leaving Fort Laramie on the twenty-third was First Lieutenant George Taylor and Company H, Twenty-third Infantry, along with acting assistant surgeon A. P. Frick. Taylor's soldiers had remained with the Fifth Cavalry's wagon train, ultimately logging 241 miles from the time of their detail at Sage Creek until they returned. Dr. Frick had come to Fort Laramie at midmonth and was henceforth assigned to the Camp on Sage Creek for duty with this infantry company.[73]

Fort Fetterman continued to be the springboard for General Crook's operations in the north. An important partner to this strategic post was Medicine Bow, eighty-five miles south on the Union Pacific Railroad. This was the nearest transfer to the northern campaign, and since spring when the Fetterman–Medicine Bow road dried out, thousands of pounds of war matériel and, of late, hundreds of soldiers were moving north through the station. Shipment of government supplies, in fact, had become the hamlet's leading enterprise. "Munitions of war"—cartridges, shells, guns, commissary stores—were routinely on hand and caught press attention. The *Cheyenne Daily Leader* observed on July 15, for instance, the passing of eight tons of ammunition to Medicine Bow for General Crook and added a typical quip: "It is hoped that his gallant command will kill not eight, but eight hundred tons of Sioux with this great quantity of ammunition." Provisions, forage, and other campaign essentials were also moving forward. Captain Edwin Coates, Fourth Infantry, commanding Fort Fetterman, estimated that over 1,300,000 pounds of supplies and equipment were received at his post in July and August alone, with half as much received earlier.[74]

A revealing profile of Merritt's cavalry at Fort Fetterman was written by newspaperman Cuthbert Mills of the *New York Times,* who had just arrived from the east. The regiment campaigned for a month beyond Fort Laramie, he wrote, but the soldiers were still a "pretty sight" as they filed into the fort, forded the North Platte River, and moved into camp on the opposite bank. "They came along in thorough fighting trim," Mills notes, "flanking parties out, and videttes, too." But

> to a fastidious eye, or to one overnice in military etiquettes there was something quite shocking in the disregard of regulation uniform, and the mud-bespattered appearance of the men; but it was a pleasure to see how full of vim, of spirit, and emphatically, of fight the fellows looked. They had just done four weeks of hard marching, scouting and riding, with a little fighting thrown in, and both men and horses looked as if they were willing and eager for any amount of tough work. A gentlemen who stood watching the regiment pass told me he has seen English, French, Prussian and Russian cavalry in the field, and though the soldiers of those nations excelled ours in neatness and uniformity of appearance and dress, yet they, none of them, presented such a thorough fighting look as this Fifth Regiment. They were, perhaps, a little flushed with the way they had scattered the Indians who were leaving the agencies, and I can only add my wish that they may come back as flushed and as confident from their future encounters with the Sioux.[75]

Newspapermen and literary figures were not uncommon visitors in the Fort Laramie area at this time. The *Daily Leader,* for instance, noted the arrival in Cheyenne on July 18 of Leander P. Richardson.

This correspondent for the Springfield, Massachusetts, *Republican* was bound for the Black Hills, and he declared that "he will swim a river of Sioux blood but he will get to Deadwood." Richardson took the stage to Fort Laramie and there joined seven others who were also headed to the Hills. A chronicle of Richardson's trip appeared a year later in a monthly magazine, and the account neatly and accurately describes the route north of the fort, several of the stops, the soldier camp at Sage Creek, which at the moment was garrisoned by only six men— the rest were still scouting with Colonel Merritt—and a host of related observations. But Richardson and his Black Hills exploration proved enigmatic, even something of a folly, at least as the *Daily Leader* viewed it. Richardson's memorandum book allegedly was discovered in the coat pocket of a badly mutilated corpse found on the trail. For days the local paper carried melodramatic installments noting that Richardson had been seen here or heard from there, and it doubted all along that he had been murdered. Indeed, he had not met a sinister fate at all, but it was a month or more before the whole tale came out. His notebook had been stolen.[76]

Even as the Richardson drama was unfolding, the frontiersman and correspondent Captain Jack Crawford passed through Cheyenne en route to Medicine Bow and Fort Fetterman, where he planned to join Merritt and the campaign. Crawford had come out of the Hills through Fort Laramie earlier in the month on his way to Omaha and Chicago. While in Chicago he met with General Sheridan and exhibited a large collection of Black Hills ore, reportedly the first substantial evidence of gold-bearing quartz that Sheridan had seen.[77]

The local newspapers also reported a surge of Indian harassment on the Black Hills road in late July. In one instance three miners coming down from Custer were attacked in the Sage Creek valley, and Herman Ganzio of Milwaukee, Wisconsin, was seriously wounded in the knee, shoulder, and back and then half-scalped—his hair was not completely torn away before his attackers were chased off by his companions. Fortunately the small party successfully arrived at Fort Laramie, where the post's doctors, Gray and Petteys, provided every attention possible.[78] This stepped-up hostility also forced W. H. Hibbard of Western Union to withdraw temporarily from active work on the telegraph line, since his infantry escort was "compelled to fight Indians so much as to interfere with the work."[79]

Hibbard indeed had problems with his infantry escort, and they with him. On July 15 Lieutenant Taylor at Sage Creek queried Major Townsend about his proper duty as far as this construction was concerned. A response on July 18 reaffirmed that Company H, Twenty-third Infantry, must escort Hibbard's telegraph party as far as the Red Canyon camp, but Taylor was not obligated to detail working parties from the troops. Taylor, in the meantime, departed with the Fifth Cavalry to chase Cheyennes, leaving only a handful of soldiers to garrison Sage Creek and protect the telegraph. Townsend was also grappling with the reconstruction of the telegraph line from the Hunton ranch to the post, but this would be accomplished by a soldier work detail from Company F, Ninth Infantry, when they returned from the north after transporting supplies to Sage Creek and Red Canyon.[80]

Despite these responsibilities for the telegraph, along with necessary oversight given to the agencies, the constant movement on the Black Hills road, and dozens of other details, Indian trouble continued to be the major issue confronting the beleaguered Fort Laramie garrison in the waning days of July. There certainly was no letup in the overt harassment of civilian traffic north of the post, where Indian sightings were common, attacks frequent, and deaths a mounting concern. Cynthia Capron attributed these increased hostilities to the departure of Colonel Merritt's cavalry. They were "out of the way," she wrote, allowing these "cunning Indians" to get supplies from isolated ranches and poorly guarded wagon trains.[81] While this raiding had heretofore been generally characterized as the actions of small, independent war parties who probably left the safety of the agencies for the sheer thrill of the chase, a string of attacks beginning on August 1 allowed everyone the impression that Sitting Bull's war had truly invaded from the north.

The first incident occurred in the late evening of August 1 three miles south of Captain William Collier's camp in Red Canyon. As Collier reported it, sentries sounded an alarm after they heard continuous firing from a nearby ranch. Collier immediately formed his company, exclusive of the guard, and double-timed it to the scene, where he engaged twenty Indians in a lively skirmish. Collier's men repulsed the attack and the Indians fled, taking two "American" horses. One Indian was believed killed or wounded.[82]

These Indians were alleged to have stolen other horses and mules from the area earlier that day. And they were probably the same assailants who on the evening of August 2 attacked the down stage en route from Custer to Fort Laramie, north of the Sage Creek camp. According to one account, it consisted of a running fight between the stage and Indians that lasted for twelve miles. Eventually the coach was wrecked. One of the four stage passengers was wounded, but all eventually made it safely to Taylor's camp. While Dr. Frick tended the wounded man, the lieutenant immediately dispatched a wagon and soldiers to the scene. These infantrymen found that the Indians had run off the horses, cut up the harness and wagon top, and torn open the mail sacks. Most of the mail was recovered, but one piece lost, it was later discovered, was Captain Collier's report of the Red Canyon fight. He subsequently filed a duplicate on August 6.[83] Also on August 2 Indians attacked two hay cutters working on the Running Water or Niobrara River about forty miles northeast of Fort Laramie. In this instance one white man was killed but the other escaped.[84]

Elsewhere on August 2 a string of supply wagons owned by A. H. "Heck" Reel and under contract to the army was making its way toward Fort Fetterman. This was a sizable train, with nine or more wagons each loaded to capacity with government freight. In the charge of George Throstle, a crew of sixteen men, including "a few Mexicans and 'long-haired Missourians,'" tended the caravan as it slowly labored along the "cutoff" road. At a point on Elkhorn Creek thirty miles south of Fetterman, thirty Indians attacked the train. The fight lasted the rest of the day. Wagon boss Throstle was killed, mutilated, and scalped; a teamster was wounded; four horses and ten oxen were killed; and three wagons were burned before the Indians abandoned the attack that night. The train went on toward Fort Fetterman the next day and finally reached that post on August 5. Word of the attack preceded them and was telegraphed to Omaha on August 3.[85]

Since Fort Fetterman was without a cavalry company, orders from department headquarters for a response to this emergency came to Fort Laramie. Townsend was to dispatch Egan's company to relieve the wagon train and punish the Indians. The major probably only rolled his eyes at the directive, since he was receiving news of vigorous and widespread hostilities from all points north. Fort Fetterman had also dispatched a small infantry escort and an ambulance to convey Captain W. S. Stanton, chief engineer of the Department of the

Platte, to Fort Laramie, and now this escort too was overdue and the soldiers were feared dead. Townsend dutifully ordered Company K, Second Cavalry, to meet Stanton and trace the escort. The officer and his accompaniment were promptly located and advanced to their destinations. Egan's company then found and followed the trail of the roamers north of the Platte River. They had, by his estimation, a thirty-six-hour head start, so he did not overtake them. Still, littering their trail were army saddles and equipment that Egan reported had been taken from the casualties of his own company in the March 17 fight on the Powder River. Major Townsend sent these details to Omaha, and also news just received that eighty head of cattle bound for the agencies had been run off by white men and that he was now following up on this incident.[86]

Even before the widespread nature of this raiding was analyzed and could be attended came news that on August 4 other Indians had attacked ranches twenty-five miles south of Fort Laramie on the Cheyenne road. At least three related incidents were reported, including attacks on the Owen and Carrington ranches and the Baker and Davis freight train bound for Cheyenne. Stock was run off in each instance, but there were no casualties. With these attacks, along with alleged Indian sightings on nearby Sabille and Horse creeks and as close as four miles north of Cheyenne, a general excitement and alarm spread throughout the ranch country. Cynthia Capron commented on the army's futile predicament. The Indians "were very rarely punished, for before a call for the one cavalry company left between Cheyenne and Gen. Crook, could reach them, and the cavalry start out, they were gone beyond hope of catching them—Captain Egan's company was always going on these disappointing trips. There was no use saying nothing could be done even when every one knew it."[87]

Retaliation, however, was occurring. On August 4 stockmen surprised a camp of fifteen Indians near the old Bridger ferry site on the North Platte forty miles northwest of Fort Laramie. An Indian and two ponies were killed in the attack and fourteen horses were captured (or recaptured, as Fort Fetterman reported it). And for several weeks beginning August 4, editions of the *Cheyenne Daily Leader* reported on the arrival of Fourth U.S. Cavalry companies and other troops fresh for duty against "General Napoleon Sitting Bull."[88]

The arrival of Colonel Ranald Mackenzie's Fourth Cavalry marked a transitional phase in the broad military campaign against the Sioux, as it was being played out in southeastern Wyoming. General Sheridan was implementing new procedures for handling the Indians. He had long advocated placing troops permanently in the Sioux hunting grounds where, from military posts along the Yellowstone River and in the Big Horn country, troops could continually harass the Indians and ultimately force them out of fear and hunger to come in to the agencies. With military control of the agencies coming about as well, the returning Indians would be disarmed and unhorsed on arrival. Although the August 1 *Daily Leader* reported the implementation of this new policy at several of the Missouri River agencies, in Nebraska and Wyoming all was not yet fixed for such changes.[89]

At Fort Laramie Townsend, in fact, faced more routine matters. In mid-July he had employed John Baptiste Provost as a post guide and courier, but demands on this courier service increased so dramatically by the end of the month that he requested permission to hire another rider to bear letters to Fetterman and the agencies. When Sheridan, with his broader plans in mind, on August 4 ordered Townsend to establish a daily dispatch line to the agencies, not one but three additional couriers were entered on the quartermaster rolls. Sheridan further ordered that incoming dispatches to Fort Laramie be telegraphed directly to Chicago without delay and that informational copies be sent by mail to department headquarters in Omaha.[90]

When most of the supply activities related to General Crook's campaign shifted to the Medicine Bow–Fort Fetterman route in June, Lieutenant Morton's quartermaster employee rolls declined significantly. From a high of sixty-eight engineers, blacksmiths, wagonmasters, and teamsters in April as Crook organized his second campaign, Morton had only twenty-four civilians on his work force at the end of July and twenty-eight in August. Most of the discharged civilians were teamsters who probably drifted on to the goldfields or similar employment at Fort Fetterman. Morton also administered several of the quartermaster contracts that were awarded in June. Two of these were fraught with difficulties. Luke Murrin of Cheyenne reneged on his contract to deliver hay to Fort Laramie, but a Mr. Colin Hunter volunteered to deliver three hundred tons of baled hay provided he could use the government's baling press at Fort Laramie. Hunter planned to cut hay on the old Fort Mitchell reservation thirty-five miles down the North Platte. The department's chief quartermaster, Major Marshall Ludington, deferred the decision to Major Townsend, who readily approved, knowing how badly hay was needed at the post. Within several days of this action John Coad, also of Cheyenne, announced that he could not deliver baled hay as in his contract but would deliver stacked hay at a lesser price. This decision too passed through the channels, and Ludington approved the contract revision.[91]

Coincidental to the startup of the army's courier service from Fort Laramie to Fetterman and the agencies was a similar service originated by Deadwood businessmen Dick Seymour and Charlie Utter, called the "Pioneer Pony Express." A rider was leaving Fort Laramie every Wednesday bound for Deadwood with mail and light express matter. Short-lived competition came in early August when a man named Clippinger offered a similar service. The two companies even raced in a publicity scheme hatched on August 2 to see who could travel the 202 miles from Fort Laramie to Deadwood faster. The *Cheyenne Daily Leader* abetted the racers. The Cheyenne–Black Hills Stage, the paper announced, carried one hundred copies of its August 2 edition to Fort Laramie. There passengers would see the riders sort the mail, each taking fifty copies of the newspaper, pack their small pouches, and "ride away like balls shot from the cannon's mouth." Barring the failure of horse or rider, the mail would reach Deadwood in only two days; the paper would be but three days old.[92]

Unfortunately the publicity potential of the race was never realized, lost as it was in the larger news coming from Deadwood of the killing of James Butler "Wild Bill" Hickok on August 2. Hickok, a widely known scout, law officer, and gunman, had come to Deadwood only weeks before and was murdered there by a frustrated third-rate gambler named Jack McCall. Reports of the killing traveled to Fort Laramie, where they were relayed south on the telegraph beginning August 11. The first accounts erroneously said that a man named Bill Sutherland had killed Hickok. Regardless, the reports intimated that the killer "would not leave the town alive."[93]

In early August the *Daily Leader* carried other news of general interest to the Fort Laramie garrison. Their plucky Fourth Infantry comrades at Red Canyon, for instance, had taken measures to improve their small station. They were camped on a shadeless brow of a low hill but had recently cut evergreens from the nearby mountains and set them out in close ranks around their tents. "Though they have an abundance of cool, pure spring water at hand, there is no natural shade there," lamented the paper. Common in the paper were reports about Crook and Terry, the Custer fight, and the Black Hills. Most came as dispatches from newspaper correspondents on the scene or, in the case of the growing curiosity following the Battle of the Little Bighorn, transcriptions of official reports filed by officers engaged in the fight. Occasionally speculative and sometimes purely erroneous news made the headlines, as on August 16, when readers learned "'RELIABLE REDSKINS' SAY CROOK HAS WHIPPED SITTING BULL." This news about a great battle in which nearly all of Sitting Bull's force was killed came by way of Sioux City, Iowa, and Chicago. Remarkably, it neatly corroborated two local reports, one from Camp Robinson's post trader J. W. Dear and the other from Fort Laramie's own Major Townsend, each of whom declared he had learned about a major fight. Dear, however, stated that his Indian informants said it was Crook who defeated the Sioux, while Townsend relayed news via the Spotted Tail Agency that it had been General Terry who "met and whipped the Indians." Sadly, all were wrong.[94]

The *Daily Leader* continued to push the Black Hills, though that was hardly needed any longer, aside from any verifiable news value. The city and its papers had so successfully sold the nation on "its" route to the Hills that traffic via Sidney and all the various Missouri River communities may not have equaled, even in sum, what rolled north from Wyoming's "magic city of the plains." Yet the paper found occasion to publish, as on August 7, nearly half a page under the banner "THE LAND OF GOLD—THE BLACK HILLS—HOW TO REACH THEM," offering abundant details on gold-mining techniques, the geography of the Hills, and the related mineral potential of the region. The paper, too, fondly reported on the quantity of Black Hills gold shipped via the city. Common were the one-liners like "Stebbins, Post & Co. purchased twelve pounds of Black Hills gold," and "$1800 in Deadwood dust," or "Fourteen thousand dollars worth of gold was brought in from the Hills by stage last evening." The Laramie inhabitants probably delighted too in reading about their neighbors, as when the paper noted "E. H. Merrill, manager of G. H. & J. S. Collins' harness establishment, received yesterday a handsome gold brick valued at $1146, which was run from Black Hills gold purchased by J. S. Collins, post-trader at Fort Laramie."[95]

In the midst of other traffic, most of which was north- or southbound, there came on August 12 a Justice Department surveying party that had been investigating the old military road from Fort Leavenworth, Kansas, to Salt Lake City, Utah, in response to certain claims filed against the United States government. Guarding the civilians conducting the survey was a small military escort under the command of Second Lieutenant Christian Cyrus Hewitt, Nineteenth Infantry, with nine enlisted men from the Fifth Infantry. Hewitt maintained a daily diary of this expedition. As the party entered Sioux country, their vigilance increased. They saw that the Indians were burning off the prairie lands, particularly along the North Platte south of the Red Cloud and Spotted Tail agencies, and they encountered large haying camps along the river in the last few days before reaching Fort Laramie.[96]

Hewitt's party spent three and one-half weeks at the fort lounging, fishing, and hunting while they awaited further orders regarding their mission. The lieutenant attended a guard mount one morning, where he "heard very good music" from the Ninth Infantry's regimental band and saw "fair drill." He also noted many outfits going to the Black Hills gold country. They were a "miserable mob. Every man has either a gun & 2 revolvers straped to him or a revolver & knife—all go well fixed for any emergency." The infantry officer saw Captain Egan's cavalry company too. "It was a hard looking mob," he noted, "and with no fuss & feathers but look like business." On August 15 Hewitt received a telegram advising him to stop work at Fort Laramie and return to Fort Leavenworth. While he coordinated the close of the survey and the return of his small corps, he visited Cheyenne. Hewitt and his traveling companions kept a "sharp lookout" for Indians on the way to the city, and Hewitt did see what he "thought was two Indians away on a bluff watching us come to a ranch." Moreover, they passed cavalry companies en route to the Red Cloud Agency "to help disarm and take the ponies away from the Indians."[97]

Indian sightings and harassment remained fairly constant through the first two weeks of August. On the eighth Samuel Wagner, one of the government couriers, was jumped by six Indians on the Niobrara River. His horse was wounded, and the Indians chased him for twenty miles until his mount gave out; then Wagner hid in a gully till nightfall and after dark arrived safely at Fort Laramie.[98] Elsewhere the trail of another marauding band was spotted south of the fort between Chug Springs and the Eagle's Nest, and Egan's Company K was promptly dispatched to scout after these Indians.[99] "This garrison is too small," lamented a correspondent to the *Daily Leader* writing from Fort Laramie. "Too much escort-duty has to be done," continued the letter, "to spare the cavalry more than a few days at a time. What we need is a large force to scout continually, and follow up Indian trails whenever found. While General Merritt was scouting toward the Black Hills, depredations were very rare. One of the five companies of the Fourth Cavalry ordered to this Department has passed through to Red Cloud [August 8], and another is expected in a few days. It is hoped that, when all arrive at the agencies, orders can be enforced."[100]

The arrival and consolidation at Fort Laramie and Camp Robinson of Mackenzie's Fourth Cavalry companies dispatched from Texas and the Indian Territory was a significant development in the evolving pattern of the campaign. Actually it was two companies of Fifth Cavalry, H and L, that were the first supplementary troops to arrive on the scene, but this small battalion, under the command of Major George A. Gordon, paused at Fort Laramie only briefly on July 26–28 before advancing to Camp Robinson for duty.[101] The first of the Fourth Cavalry, Company I, commanded by Captain William C. Hemphill, passed through Cheyenne on August 3, arrived at Fort Laramie on the eighth, and departed for Camp Robinson the next day. Similarly, Company E, in the charge of Second Lieutenant Hobart Bellas, came into Fort Laramie on the tenth and left on the eleventh. Colonel Ranald Slidell Mackenzie, commanding the regiment, arrived at Fort Laramie on August 12 and promptly met with Major Townsend at headquarters. The colonel undoubtedly had at least a superficial understanding of the tasks ahead of him, although correspondence and soon a personal visit from General Sheridan would clarify his role at the agencies.[102]

Colonel Ranald Slidell Mackenzie, Fourth U.S. Cavalry. Mackenzie commanded the District of the Black Hills in the summer and fall of 1876. Although head-quartered at Camp Robinson, Nebraska, he regularly visited Fort Laramie during the Sioux War. (Fort Sill Museum)

Mackenzie, regarded by Sheridan and others as the finest cavalry commander in the service, had already received instructions to revitalize the District of the Black Hills. This on-again, off-again administrative unit of the Department of the Platte functioned little under Wesley Merritt's direction and apparently not at all after the Fifth Cavalry departed from Fort Laramie on July 23. Field order 1, dated August 13, 1876, announced Mackenzie's assumption of district

Two hundred of Colonel Ranald Mackenzie's Fourth Cavalrymen posed near the Eagle's Nest, southwest of Fort Laramie. D. S. Mitchell photograph. (Jim Crain)

command. Headquarters would be established at Camp Robinson. Thereafter the commanding officers at Laramie, Robinson, and Sheridan would submit to Mackenzie monthly troop reports and any information of special interest regarding the Indians. Other normal business could still be conducted through customary channels. Before departing for Camp Robinson with newly arrived Company B, commanded by Captain Clarence Mauck, the colonel queried department headquarters on the availability of two twelve pounder artillery pieces, with ammunition for those guns and the varied small arms in his assembling command. Omaha only passed the request for additional artillery on to Chicago, since there were no guns available in the department, but it was declared that there were .50 caliber and one-inch Gatling guns already at Robinson, along with a twelve pounder mountain howitzer, and that Camp Sheridan had another .50 caliber Gatling. And the department's ordnance officer promptly shipped 25,000 carbine cartridges, 25,000 rifle cartridges, and 30,000 pistol rounds via Sidney, Nebraska.[103]

Mackenzie departed for Robinson on August 14. The next day Townsend ordered Captain Pollock and Company E, Ninth Infantry, outfitted for fifteen days, to transport supplies and rations to the Sage Creek and Red Canyon army camps. Dr. C. V. Petteys would accompany the movement.[104] And in the midst of that preparation came reports of other troop transfers, some to destinations in Wyoming and Nebraska. To fill the void left in the Department of the Missouri after Mackenzie's cavalry was moved north, Sheridan gave General Pope four Second Artillery batteries. Sheridan also designated four Fourth Artillery batteries for duty in Nebraska. The units specifically assigned, C, F, H, and K, labeled by the *Daily Leader* as coming from the regiment "regarded as the flower of the artillery branch of our army," had been stationed until then at the Presidio of San Francisco, on Alcatraz Island, and at Point San Jose, California. Traveling in light order and equipped expressly for the field, the battalion arrived in Cheyenne by train on August 16. After a layover of two days, they marched slowly and deliberately to Fort Laramie, arriving on August 23. Accompanying these artillerymen was assistant surgeon Curtis Ethelbert Price.[105]

This battalion of Fourth Artillery was preceded into Fort Laramie on August 18 and 21 by Companies D, F, and M, Fourth Cavalry, accompanied by acting assistant surgeon Albert Chenoweth, and Companies D and G, Fourteenth U.S. Infantry, which had been transferred from Fort Cameron in southern Utah. Heretofore the three Fourteenth Infantry companies at Fort Cameron and two sister units at Camp Douglas, near Salt Lake City, had remained the only uncommitted troops in Crook's Department of the Platte. Virtually all the rest were either serving with him at the front, doing some form of escort duty, or acting as the usual one-company skeleton garrison at various military installations throughout the department. Concurrent with the dispatch of Companies D and G to Nebraska, however, was the movement of Company K, Fourteenth Infantry, from Camp Douglas to Medicine Bow for the purpose of conducting supply trains to Fort Fetterman. This five-company makeshift battalion of Fourth Cavalrymen and Fourteenth Infantrymen left Fort Laramie for Camp Robinson on August 23, just as the Fourth Artillery marched into the post. The artillerymen, in turn, departed for Camp Robinson on August 25.[106]

While a new scheme of operations was forming at Camp Rob-

Camp Robinson in 1876. Visible in the middle ground is "Camp Custer," a tent city belonging to Colonel Ranald Mackenzie's column of Fourth U.S. Cavalry after he had removed headquarters of the District of the Black Hills from Fort

Laramie to Robinson. The principal post structures dot the background; officers' row stretches across right center. D. S. Mitchell photograph. (U.S. Military
Academy Library)

inson, Major Townsend and the Fort Laramie garrison received other news of interest. Full details of a sad incident involving Captain Michael J. Fitzgerald, Ninth Infantry, appeared in consecutive issues of the *Daily Leader* to confirm earlier telegrams. He and some fellow officers and friends from Camp Robinson and the Red Cloud Agency had assembled at a target range for a shooting match. Between rounds, while the captain and two others were inspecting a target, a weapon in the hands of Second Lieutenant John A. Baldwin, of Fitzgerald's own company, accidently discharged. The bullet lodged in the captain's leg, which required amputation.[107]

On August 22, as the Fitzgerald story unfolded, the Adjutant General's Office published general orders officially reducing the size of Fort Laramie's military reservation. A major extension in 1872 had added thousands of acres along the North Platte well into Nebraska. This was land admirably suited for settlement, but since it was an official addition to the post it required an act of Congress to effect a change. Congress passed such legislation in 1876 and, as confirmed by army orders, the law effectively reduced the post's administrative landholdings to its pre-1872 size of fifty-four square miles.[108]

Despite virtually constant troop movement by now on all roads radiating from Fort Laramie, reports of Indian sightings were still being made. On August 22, for instance, Lieutenant Taylor, Twenty-third Infantry, dispatched the first sergeant and thirteen men from his company at Sage Creek to relieve a besieged freight train on Indian Creek, ten miles beyond his station. First Sergeant Thomas McClane's relief party reached the wagon train that same day and found two horses killed, three others run off, and seven mules wounded. No more than five or six Indians opposed fourteen "well-armed" men. The soldiers concluded that these civilians had done little to defend themselves during the attack but still dutifully escorted them to Sage Creek.[109]

Fortunately, in the waning days of August considerable progress was reported on the telegraph extension north of the post. Through the month W. H. Hibbard's crews had finished setting poles as far north as Sage Creek and were now stringing wire. All anticipated that this communications link between Fort Laramie and the Camp on Sage Creek and adjacent stage station would be opened shortly.[110] Evidently the line south of Fort Laramie was also upgraded satisfactorily, but on August 22 a letter came from Major Ludington, chief quartermaster in Omaha, about a related matter. Since last winter, he wrote, he had been attempting to thoroughly repair the telegraph line between Forts Laramie and Fetterman. Just the past July he had sent ten teams and wagons to Fort Laramie for hauling and placing poles, but Colonel Merritt had commandeered them all to haul supplies. Could Townsend therefore spare transportation and a limited force of civilian employees to cut and place poles? A party of six men and two wagons could do the job in one month, and a civilian repairer would be hired to supervise the work, Ludington wrote reassuringly. Townsend apparently avoided or ignored the request, since no reply is found in the post's letters or telegrams.[111]

With such diversions as the telegraph serving as a nagging reminder of the more mundane aspects of soldiering, it may have been easy for Townsend and his Fort Laramie garrison to grow oblivious to the larger aspects of the Sioux War of 1876. Yet as August drew to a close, the rise in retaliatory tactics at the Sioux agencies must surely have seemed a glimmer of hope for ending these hostilities. The army had suffered unprecedented setbacks at Powder River, Rosebud Creek, and the Little Bighorn River, and even in southeastern Wyoming the soldiers had endured a full measure of Indian raids, futile pursuits, and dusty marches. These local encounters were never full-blown battles, but they were unquestionably related to this widespread Indian war. Townsend's men surely anticipated future action. Everyone understood that Crook was again on the trail, but no one knew where he might emerge. Would there be another campaign? Would negotiations with the Sioux about the Black Hills, which were soon to start again, bring results? And would the massing of troops at the Red Cloud and Spotted Tail agencies have salutary effects? As was obvious to everyone, the war had not yet run its course.

Chapter Six

Victory at the Agencies:
September–October 1876

For months General Sheridan had advocated implementing new controls over the Sioux. As early as May he had urged that administration of the agencies and the warring Indians be turned over fully to the army so that it might carry out a strict policy of arresting, disarming, and dismounting those roamers who reappeared at the various stations. When he repeated his petition in July after Crook's ill-fated fight at Rosebud Creek and the costly Custer debacle, it received a far warmer reception. By July 22 Sheridan learned that the Interior Department was finally prepared to relinquish control of the Sioux. Sheridan moved swiftly, and on July 26 he sent telegrams to the commanding officers at Camps Robinson and Sheridan ordering them to designate carefully selected officers as agents for the Red Cloud and Spotted Tail agencies. Elsewhere, military control was effected at the Missouri River agencies with equal haste.[1]

Military rule was only the first phase of Sheridan's policy. He next planned the arrest and disarming of the agency Indians as well as the free roamers. Sheridan knew that at midsummer troop strength at Red Cloud and Spotted Tail was insufficient to impose such strictures. But after the coming of Mackenzie's Fourth Cavalry and other infantry and cavalry from elsewhere in the Department of the Platte and his Military Division of the Missouri, he could soon move forcefully. In the meantime his military agents attempted to keep their charges reasonably content by feeding them as liberally as possible.[2]

The agency Sioux were not particularly impressed by the military takeover. Ignoring the fact that they were known to be providing succor to their warring kinsmen and that many were openly sympathetic to their cause, they resented being treated as bad people when they were so plainly at the agencies and not among the defectors. One of the agency chiefs saw the transparency of Sheridan's plans and expressed it this way: "this was a war the whites had started, and having failed to defeat the wild Sioux, they were now going to treat the agency Sioux as conquered people and force them to give up the Black Hills and the hunting lands in the Powder River and Bighorn country."[3] Indeed, that had become the government's objective—Washington wanted a formal relinquishment of the Hills, a cessation of all hostilities, and the removal of the entire Sioux barrier, agency Indians and free roamers alike.

One of the first accomplishments after military takeover was a census. At Red Cloud 4,760 Sioux were tallied as they reported for rations; of those, 280 were grown men. The agent heretofore had certified 12,873 Indian residents. At the Red Cloud Agency, only 600 to 700 Northern Cheyennes were counted from a reported population of 1,200. At the nearby Spotted Tail Agency the census showed equally alarming results. Of 9,170 claimed on the rolls, only 4,775 were present. Results were similar at the various Missouri River stations. In explaining the gross discrepancies, suggestions of fraud from overcounting cropped up. More easily came the conclusion that as many as half of the Sioux had simply defected to the north to hunt and wage war. While the Cheyennes certainly allied with their friends the Sioux and warred hard all summer, their motivation was as much the fear of removal to the Indian Territory as any empathy with Sioux problems.[4]

In Washington, Congress was acting with an equally firm hand. As part of its annual Indian appropriation, legislation came on August 15 directing the president to appoint a commission to deliver the Sioux an ultimatum. This edict, known as the Agreement of August 15, 1876, contained eleven articles, several of which redefined terms of the now-famous 1868 Fort Laramie Treaty. Article 1, for instance, defined the Sioux reservation to exclude the land between the South Fork of the Cheyenne River and the North Fork of that stream. Between these branches lay the entire Black Hills. Article 1 also ceded to the United States all territory lying outside the reservation, and it terminated hunting privileges, thus abrogating article 16 of the 1868 treaty, which had specifically allowed hunting on traditional lands to the west and south. Among other conditions, the Sioux were to permit three wagon roads to be built across their reservation from the Missouri River to the Black Hills and would consider removal to the Indian Territory, "where they might live like white men." On the condition that the Sioux accept the reduced reservation, cede the hunting lands, and quit fighting, the government would provide schools, subsistence, and other necessities of life, but it threatened to terminate these concessions if the Sioux resisted.[5]

A well-stocked presidential commission appointed on August 24, including George W. Manypenny, Henry C. Bullis, Newton Edmonds, Bishop Henry B. Whipple, Albert G. Boone, A. S. Gaylord, and Jared W. Daniels, carried this ultimatum to the Sioux. Samuel D. Hinman, the veteran intermediary with the Sioux, would serve as official interpreter. Like Hinman, each of the commissioners had lengthy experience in Indian affairs. Manypenny, soon elected to chair the council, was a former commissioner of Indian affairs. Whipple was a respected missionary to the Minnesota Sioux. Edmonds, former governor of the Dakota Territory, had negotiated treaties in 1865; both Boone and Daniels were former Indian agents. After an organizational meeting in Omaha on August 28, the commissioners boarded a westbound Union Pacific train for their first stop, the Red Cloud Agency.[6]

Detailed descriptions of the Sioux commission and its task appeared in consecutive issues of the *Cheyenne Daily Leader* beginning August 23. Naturally the paper championed this final removal of the Black Hills from Indian domain, but it is doubtful that the commissioners had really been instructed to tell the Sioux to stop leaving the reservation, stop depredations on Black Hills miners, "or submit to extermination," as the paper told it.[7]

At Fort Laramie, Major Townsend had stood ready to receive the commissioners for several weeks. On August 23 the department had

Reverend Samuel D. Hinman, a respected missionary among the Sioux and an important visitor to Fort Laramie in 1876. (A. F. Burnham, Minnesota Historical Society)

advised him of their coming and had further directed him to provide transportation as well as Captain Egan's Company K, Second Cavalry, for escort to Red Cloud. The commissioners paused at Fort Laramie on September 3. Bishop Whipple stayed with Captain Pollock that evening, and the rest boarded at John Collins's Rustic Hotel. While at the post Whipple and Samuel Hinman conducted Sunday church services for members of the garrison, and later that afternoon the Bishop baptized the child of Lieutenant and Mrs. Morton. On

Monday, September 4, these men continued north on their mission. Townsend also provided the commissioners with six army wall tents from his post stocks, and these were subsequently replaced by the depot quartermaster.[8]

Colonel Ranald Mackenzie greeted the Indian commissioners when they arrived at Camp Robinson on September 6. Within a day negotiations began with Red Cloud's Oglalas. Approximately 150 Indians gathered for this initial meeting to hear the stern language of the "Agreement of August 15." As one historian described the package, it was "little more than a rehash of the conventional Indian Bureau program for the Sioux, through which, it was hoped, they would be led to ways of industry, education, and morality."[9] The Commissioners also issued a firm warning declaring that the Sioux would have to obey if they were to continue receiving rations and annuities. Perhaps the most serious obstacles were the articles of removal. At the least, Congress specified that the Sioux must agree to receive all annuities on the reservation in the vicinity of the Missouri River. These Oglalas and neighboring Brules had successfully avoided this same condition in the early 1870s after signing the 1868 treaty. Moreover, the government also wanted the Sioux to consider permanent removal to Indian Territory. The Sioux leaders agreed to consider these terms but then broke off the talks and left for Chadron Creek to council among themselves. Although talks were scheduled to reconvene on September 13, none of the chiefs appeared. The headmen also failed to show up on the fifteenth, though they did finally return on the nineteenth.[10]

Although the commissioners garnered substantial attention in the regional and national press, at the same time considerable coverage was being given to the actions of Generals Crook and Terry. After Crook's fight on June 17 he had retired to northern Wyoming to regroup, tend his wounded, and strengthen his command. Considerably annoyed by the delay of the Fifth Cavalry in joining him, despite their own calculated and productive activities north of Fort Laramie in July, he waited inactive for nearly seven weeks before finally resuming his campaign. Terry had not actively pursued Indians during much of the midsummer either, but considerable time and effort had been required to clean up the slaughter on the Custer battlefield, move dozens of wounded Seventh Cavalrymen to river transport, and restore order to his decimated column. The two commands finally joined on August 10 in the Rosebud River valley, north of where Crook had engaged Sioux and Cheyennes two months earlier.[11]

After their juncture, the combined forces of the Dakota Column and the Big Horn and Yellowstone Expedition lumbered eastward for several weeks in a futile attempt to encounter the now well-scattered warriors. Accomplishments were few, and after some direction from General Sheridan, the two commands again separated. Terry was ordered to deploy newly arrived troops at winter cantonments on the Yellowstone and then return the companies of his own command to their home stations. Crook, meanwhile, followed a relatively recent Indian trail eastward into the Dakota Territory, still hoping to close with the enemy.[12]

General Crook's route carried him within a four- or five-day ride of Fort Abraham Lincoln. At the head of the Heart River in what is today western North Dakota, however, he made a crucial decision to turn south toward the Black Hills, following what his aide Lieutenant John Bourke described as a "hot trail." Of fifteen days rations carried by the Big Horn and Yellowstone Expedition when they left the Yellowstone, only a two-day supply now remained in the packs and haversacks. Before commencing his southbound march on September 5, Crook composed a long telegram to General Sheridan. As well as providing an update on his actions to this point and assurances that he could still close with the warring Indians, he requested that 200,000 pounds of grain be sent to Custer City, along with twenty days' full rations of vegetables for the men. Crook clearly indicated that Custer City would function as his base of operations, even though it lay in the southern Black Hills. For immediate supply he must already have contemplated purchases on the miners' market in Deadwood and other northern Hills communities. Crook also asked Sheridan to advance two companies of cavalry from Red Cloud to his former base camp in northern Wyoming and from there to escort his wagon train to Deadwood.[13]

Before they separated General Terry had lent Crook some Arikara Indian scouts, since they were knowledgeable about the western Dakota Territory. These Rees carried Crook's urgent telegram to Fort

Lincoln. Bourke confided in his diary that the scouts had promised they would reach the fort on the morning of September 8. True to their word they did, because on that day a flurry of telegrams hummed over the wires throughout the Military Division of the Missouri.[14]

Sheridan and his division staff had a rather sketchy understanding of the supply condition at the forward military posts in the Department of the Platte, but what Chicago incompletely comprehended Omaha made abundantly clear in messages on September 8. Omaha reported, for instance, that only Fort Fetterman had stockpiles in the amounts Crook needed, but that orders were being issued to consolidate supplies from Fort Laramie and Camp Robinson so that issues would be in Custer City on time. Although Omaha had begun to inventory wagon transport before the September 8 barrage, Chicago was advised that teams and wagons could pose a substantial problem, implying that though the necessary supplies might be found, carrying them might be a more formidable matter.

While the headquarters offices sparred over administrative matters, Major Townsend and Colonel Mackenzie received their initial instructions. From Camp Robinson Mackenzie was to send north at once 50,000 pounds of grain and another 50,000 pounds of rations and other supplies. He was to use any contract train that was available, and it was to go under suitable escort. Townsend meanwhile was to begin forwarding dispatches and mail to Crook "wherever he may be found," and if necessary he was to hire a special courier for the job. Among correspondence now in Townsend's charge was bag upon bag of backlogged summer mail being held at Fort Fetterman for Crook's soldiers. Coates was told to get all of this to Fort Laramie promptly. Townsend was also told that Crook would ultimately bring the Big Horn and Yellowstone Expedition to his post and that ample supplies of clothing, grain, and subsistence supplies would be delivered before he came in.[15]

In another message sent via the Fort Laramie telegraph office Townsend learned of other major developments concerning both the coming winter operation and Sheridan's and Crook's more immediate plans. Sheridan wired Crook that he was to establish a thousand-man cantonment at old Fort Reno in northern Wyoming. The Powder River country could not be abandoned, he cautioned, or the

Indians would go right back there instead of surrendering. Crook was to bring his command into Fort Laramie, and from there his tired companies could go home and fresh troops would man the new cantonment. Finally, Sheridan requested that Crook come to Fort Laramie as quickly as possible ahead of the troops so that the two generals might plan the next movements of the Great Sioux War.[16]

All the commotion beginning September 8 may well have come as a jolt at Fort Laramie. For a brief period during the last of August and early September the official post records contain little of note. The heightened Indian raiding in early August had fairly well subsided. Even the shuffling of troops to the agencies had come to a halt after the departure of the Fourth Artillery companies on August 25. Despite some continued carping from W. H. Hibbard, who was extending the new telegraph line north of Sage Creek, the garrison had a moment to relax.

Cynthia Capron's daily routine may have typified these tranquil weeks. Tending children, particularly her oldest, Hazen, was her never-ending chore. Hazen enjoyed the boundless summer freedom of the garrison, much to his mother's dismay. Still, his antics at the cavalry stables, braiding the manes and tails of Egan's horses, or in the nearby Laramie River catching turtles or fishing for trout were merely innocent youthful fun. Birthdays nearly always were occasions for parties. Two-year-old Reynolds Burt celebrated his on August 2 in the midst of children from the post, and Jimmie Regan observed his on August 24. Social calls remained common, and members of the garrison enjoyed an occasional ride into the countryside as well. On September 1, for instance, Cynthia, Hazen, and Dr. Petteys took an evening horseback ride west toward the Ecoffey ranch. On their return they paused briefly at the "squaw camp" across the Laramie River, where an old woman gave Hazen a paper of buffalo berries. "He has been over there several times," Cynthia noted in her journal. Upon their return to the post after dark the riders discovered friends in one of the yards, still playing croquet by moonlight.[17]

This sense of nearness and sociability was an important grace at frontier posts like Fort Laramie, and it helped temper a larger anxiety expressed by Elizabeth Burt. "We at Fort Laramie were a profoundly depressed collection of women," she wrote. "Letters were

Government supply train crossing the Pine Ridge north of Fort Laramie. In the fall of 1876 wagon trains like this carried war materials to Crook's weary Big Horn and Yellowstone Expedition. D. S. Mitchell photograph. (Nebraska State Historical Society)

seldom received and those of the most meager details. Just brief and hurriedly written notes. You can well imagine how hard and sorrow-breeding it was to sit and think and think and imagine all kinds of disasters. Truly, wives of soldiers and sailors have mixed with their happiness, very many anxieties unknown to other wives."[18]

In the several days following September 8, the bombardment of orders and directives concerning Crook's operation and supply continued without letup. Crook wanted his wagon train sent from Wyoming, but rather than dispatch cavalry companies from Camp Robinson to effect this move, Omaha ordered Captain John Vincent Furey, chief quartermaster for the Big Horn and Yellowstone Expedition, to move his train without delay via Fort Fetterman. For the past month Furey's wagons, some 160 all told, had been corralled on Goose Creek under a loose guard of 200 well-armed drivers, discharged soldiers, and hangers-on.[19] On September 10 the department ordered Townsend to expedite shipment from his storehouses 25,000 pounds of grain and another 25,000 pounds of rations, plus thirty head of beef cattle. All this was to be sent under proper escort to Custer City. Omaha advised that if Egan's company was available, it should go as the guard, and if too few wagons were available in the local quartermaster pool, civilian transport should be hired.[20]

Townsend's response was commendably prompt. Special order 191 detailed Captain Egan's cavalry company as the required escort. They had just returned on the ninth after taking the Indian commissioners to the Red Cloud Agency. The same order relieved the eleven-man detachment from Company K, which heretofore had been posted to the Chugwater valley as a patrol on the Cheyenne road. This detail was to rejoin Egan immediately. Meanwhile, Lieutenants Morton and Regan supervised the loading of the assorted commissary goods, and on September 11 an overloaded shipment trudged north to Custer City.[21] Similar shipments were departing from Camp Robinson at this same time.

Morton had also hired special couriers on September 9 and 11 to carry "important dispatches to Department Commander." These men, George Stover and L. Fisher, were each paid $100 per trip to carry telegrams to Crook. A message of September 11 was particularly important. Sheridan advised Crook that he would be at Fort Laramie on the seventeenth and that they must talk personally. Whether or not Crook knew it yet, the summer operations had come under sharp attack in many influential newspapers, and Sheridan counseled him not to be discouraged by the newspaper attacks; he had done as well as could be expected and would have faithful support and supply.[22]

As if the near pandemonium of the recent several days were not enough to remind Townsend's garrison that a war was being waged against the Sioux, post headquarters received a message on September 10 from George Stover, the newly hired courier, that he had been attacked by a party of Indians nine or ten miles north of the Hat Creek ranch and was forced to retire to Taylor's army camp. Although shots had been exchanged, he had escaped unharmed and would try to get north again tomorrow.[23]

Townsend was again reminded of the vicissitudes of army service on September 10 he received when telegraphed instructions from the Military Division of the Missouri in Chicago to provide transportation and a suitable escort for three high-ranking foreign guests of the United States government. Accordingly, Townsend issued special order 192 the next day assigning Captain Pollock, First Lieutenant Christopher Hall, a Second Cavalry officer who had just returned from leave, and a detail of twelve men from Company E, Ninth Infantry, to accompany M. Notu, Y. Fukushima, and S. Tashro of Japan to the Red Cloud Agency. Notu was commander-in-chief of the royal army of Japan, and he and two of his top generals were in the midst of an American tour, examining this country's military institutions. They were eager to observe methods of Indian warfare, and next on their agenda in the West was a visit to Fort Laramie, Camp Robinson and its adjacent agency, and Fort Fetterman.[24]

Other supplies destined for Crook's command began appearing regularly at Fort Laramie. But with Townsend's lone cavalry company already traveling north with one train, a detachment of infantry now escorting Japanese army officers to Robinson, and after September 13 another nine-man detachment from Company F, Ninth Infantry, ordered to the Chug valley to replace the departed cavalry patrol, coordinating necessary escorts for the general's grain and rations became a joint effort between Fort Laramie and Colonel Mackenzie. Omaha had arranged this coordination, and over the next several weeks Townsend would usher trains north with what limited troops he could provide. The trains, in turn, would be met by a Third or Fourth Cavalry company or a dismounted battery of Fourth Artillerymen assigned from Camp Robinson, and these soldiers would escort the wagons to their destinations.[25]

Recruits bound for companies at Fort Laramie, Camp Robinson, and Camp Sheridan or on duty with Crook's field command began arriving regularly at this same time. Usually the enlisted men were billeted in one of the vacant barracks during their short stay at the post, and the accompanying officers might stay overnight with friends on officers' row or in the Rustic Hotel. But one newly minted young Fifth Cavalry officer from the United States Military Academy, Second Lieutenant Eben Swift, apparently not having any acquaintances on the wild frontier, recalled his arrival at Fort Laramie one evening after dark and told how he had slept with others on the sutler's store floor: "The place was filled with a half-drunken crowd. No soldiers, a lot of cattle men, and one fight."[26]

While the military posts in eastern Wyoming and western Nebraska bustled with activity resulting from Crook's call for rations and grain, the general's Big Horn and Yellowstone Expedition had its own moment of glory on September 9. An advance column of cavalry, not coincidentally ordered forward by Crook to the mining towns for food, discovered a Sioux village nestled in the Slim Buttes, seventy-five miles north of the Black Hills. In a dawn attack later supported by Crook's entire command, the soldiers routed the camp and captured valuable food. Sporadic firing continued into the next day. Before marching on, Crook destroyed the village and justly claimed a victory for his weary troops, who had indeed acquitted themselves well despite their debilitated condition.[27]

Of immediate interest to the Fort Laramie garrison were the reports of soldiers killed and wounded at Slim Buttes. The fight had been costly. On the official tally of casualties appeared Privates Robert Fitzhenry, Company H, Ninth Infantry, and J. W. Stephenson, Company I, Second Cavalry. Both had received severe gunshot wounds in the leg. Two other men from Company I, Privates Shanahan and Walsh, received slight wounds but did not make the official tally. Minor wounds counted for nothing during the Indian wars.[28]

The matter of food for Crook's soldiers had become critical. Although winter provisions captured in the Slim Buttes camp temporarily alleviated shortages, Crook's army before and after the fight had resorted to eating their own horses and mules to survive. The saga, known variously as the "mud," "horsemeat," or "starvation" march, is well chronicled by participants and later historians.[29] The travail finally came to an end on September 13 when the first supply wagons reached the starving army. These were not wagons led out from Camp Robinson or Fort Laramie, however, but the result of massive purchases by Crook's commissary in Deadwood, Crook City, and other northern Hills communities.

On September 10 Crook had ordered his guide and courier Frank Grouard to ride to the nearest telegraph line to transmit dispatches to Sheridan, including news of the previous day's fight. Grouard traveled with Captain John W. Budd's commissary party as far as the northern Hills and then continued south through the gulches and small towns dotting the goldfields to Custer. Riding with or near him always was Jack Crawford, the well-known Black Hills chronicler and, of late, scout for Crook. Crawford bore newspaper dispatches, and a literal race occurred between him and Grouard to see who could get the first news of Slim Buttes to civilization. At Custer City Grouard stopped and hired another courier to keep the official dispatches moving. When this rider reached Collier's Red Canyon soldier camp, the messages were turned over to that office to carry on, and the soldiers did so on September 14. Crawford, meanwhile, pushed on and reached the telegraph at Sage Creek only to discover that it was temporarily down. He left second copies of his dispatches there with instructions to relay them south as soon as the wire was open, and he then continued to Fort Laramie, reaching there on September 16. By then the news was already on the wire, allowing most of the nation's papers to carry stories about the Slim Buttes victory in their Sunday editions on September 17. Sheridan received his official reports on the sixteenth at Fort Laramie.[30]

Eager as he was to establish new controls at the various Sioux agencies and continue the broad but as yet marginally successful operation against the warring Indians, General Sheridan had been contemplating his western trip for weeks. When he passed through Cheyenne on September 15, newspaper reporters were not accorded a formal interview, so hurried was he to get north. But Sheridan's purposes quickly became a matter of public record. At Fort Laramie he would meet with Crook and "arrange for a lively campaign against the hostiles during this and the next month, as well as the establishment of a winter cantonment at some point north of Fort Fetterman."[31] Although a new winter camp in the midst of the Sioux hunting lands was by now a generally known objective, little so far had been announced in military communications or in the press about a major new offensive against the Indians. If it originated from Wyoming, this would be the third such campaign organized in the Department of the Platte.

At the time of Sheridan's arrival at the fort, Crook was still off somewhere in the northern Black Hills. In a letter sent by courier on the sixteenth Sheridan provided Crook with an update. All the rations and forage he requested had been sent and "must be in Custer." While noting that Crook should have everything else he wanted, he reiterated a more urgent desire: While your command is resting, I want to see you here! Major Townsend learned from Sheridan of other plans affecting both his Fort Laramie command and the larger continuation of the Sioux War. There was soon to be a general garrison reshuffling, for instance, suggesting that he and his Ninth Infantry comrades would soon have new residences. Meanwhile, as the lieutenant general awaited the arrival of Crook and Colonel Mackenzie, who was also requested, he proved himself a "No. 1 sportsman" by going fishing.[32]

Townsend's routine tasks during this interval were little changed from earlier months. Quartermaster supplies for Crook's soldiers and others were rapidly arriving at the post, in each instance requiring that a formal board of survey unload, inventory, receipt, and store clothing and uniforms, tents, and numerous pieces of related camp and garrison equipage.[33] Townsend also tended the advance of the telegraph, a nagging responsibility. On September 4 he and W. H. Hibbard discussed the issue of providing military escorts, especially now that the superintendent and his crew of twelve men would soon be working between Sage Creek and Collier's camp, on what was considered the most dangerous portion of the line. Although the major could not spare men from his own small command, he once again ordered Lieutenant Taylor and Captain Collier to furnish telegraph escorts from their camps.[34] On another matter, Lieutenant Taylor asked of Townsend whether his command would remain in the field during the coming winter. A reply dated September 17 was probably not what Taylor had hoped for: "In all likelihood your company will remain at its present camp during the coming winter and . . . you had better make preparations accordingly." Ditto to Captain Collier.[35]

On September 15 General Crook acknowledged Sheridan's re-

Deadwood, Dakota Territory, seen in the fall of 1876. D. S. Mitchell photograph. (Jim Crain)

quest that he come to Fort Laramie. In a hurried note he said that he would leave in the morning and travel thirty or forty miles a day until he reached there. That evening Crook and his staff sat around a huge log fire and drank toasts of champagne procured from Deadwood and served in tin army cups. In the morning he began his trek southward. Traveling with him was a sizable retinue of officers, including his aides-de-camp John Bourke, Walter S. Schuyler, and William P. Clark; his chief of scouts Captain George M. Randall; Majors Alexander Chambers and Thaddeus H. Stanton; and Fort Laramie's own Dr. Albert Hartsuff and Captain Andrew S. Burt. Four newspaper correspondents came with them as well, and the party was escorted by twenty troopers in the charge of Second Lieutenant Frederick W. Sibley, Second Cavalry. Colonel Wesley Merritt, the next senior officer pres-

Captain James Egan's Company K, Second U.S. Cavalry, with General Crook (*right front, wearing tan coat*) in Custer City on September 19, 1876. D. S. Mitchell photograph. (South Dakota State Historical Society)

ent, was placed in command of the Big Horn and Yellowstone Expedition during Crook's absence.[36]

The road through the Hills was dotted with mining communities. From the start each mayor or assembly of village notables expected Crook to receive ovations, which were often tumultuous, and to offer remarks, which he often did. Crook's entourage stopped in Deadwood on the first day out, and they were greeted warmly by its citizens. Midway between Deadwood and Custer City on the second day of their ride they encountered a trainload of government supplies bound for the expedition. In the charge of Captain Frank G. Smith, Fourth Artillery, this was the first of many such loads in the Hills as a result of Crook's plea and Sheridan's prompt action. The travelers made it as far as Custer City on the second day. Upon arrival there they found another train of supplies, this in the charge of Captain Egan, Lieutenant Allison, and Company K, Second Cavalry. As Bourke recorded in his diary, "We had quite a chat with them and then lay down to rest."[37]

On the morning of September 19, before Crook departed from Custer City, he posed for a photograph with Egan's "gallant grays." Often incorrectly attributed to the Yankton photographer Stanley J. Morrow, this small stereographic image of these proud, well-seasoned horsemen with their esteemed department commander was actually taken by D. S. Mitchell of Cheyenne, who happened to chance upon Crook and these soldiers as he photographed the towns and activities of the Black Hills gold rush. Before departing Egan generously exchanged the fresh horses belonging to his company for those being ridden by Crook and his party, and the officers were then quickly off for Camp Robinson, nearly one hundred miles farther south. Egan, meanwhile, was ordered to cache his trainload of supplies at Custer, with a small guard, take the empty wagons on to Colonel Merritt, and assist the expedition in transporting baggage back to that city.[38]

Crook was determined to make forced marches to Camp Robinson, and he directed that his escort and packs continue south at a more leisurely pace so as not to impede his run. Mounted on Egan's fresh horses, Crook and his intimates traveled the one hundred miles to Robinson in about twenty-four hours of almost non-stop riding. "How soul stirring it is to ride at full speed on a swift, strong horse after lumbering along for weeks on some jaded sorry hack," noted reporter Finerty. "It is like changing from a stage coach to a lighting express."[39] Crook was not long at Robinson. After accepting the greetings of the garrison and conferring briefly with members of the president's Sioux commission, who updated him on the slow and as yet fruitless deliberations with the Indians, he and an even smaller party continued in an ambulance for Fort Laramie, which they reached finally on Thursday, September 21.[40]

Crook's welcoming party was an august one, headed by General Sheridan and his staff, Colonel Ranald Mackenzie and his staff, who had arrived on September 18, plus Townsend and virtually all of the Fort Laramie garrison. Laramie also welcomed home two of her resident officers who had been off on campaign, Dr. Hartsuff and Captain Burt. But the pomp of the moment was short-lived, and almost immediately the ranking officers retired to post headquarters to get on with business. Sheridan led the discussions, providing Crook with details on his plans to occupy the Sioux hunting lands and control the agencies. Crook had hoped to operate out of the Black Hills during the coming winter, but Sheridan vetoed that plan, reiterating his intent to establish a major winter cantonment near old Fort Reno. Farther north in the Department of Dakota, General Terry was coordinating the development of another new camp at the confluence of the

Tongue and Yellowstone rivers, and he planned to construct a second one in the spring at or near the confluence of the Bighorn and Little Bighorn rivers within a few miles of the Custer battlefield.[41]

At the Missouri River Sioux agencies, the revitalized Seventh Cavalry would soon move in and begin disarming and unhorsing the natives. Crook and Mackenzie would do the same at the Nebraska agencies. For the local opener, Sheridan wanted Mackenzie to round up Red Cloud's followers and have them brought to their agency. Returning roamers would be disarmed and unhorsed as well. The Indian ponies would be sold and the proceeds used to buy cattle for the tribes. As for a winter campaign, the two generals discussed the probability that mass surrenders would end the present hostilities and concluded that a major offensive in loose unison with that planned by Colonel Nelson A. Miles, Fifth Infantry, in Montana was a surer means of reducing resistance. The specifics of such an operation would be Crook's to organize, but unquestionably Mackenzie would have a major role in the new campaign.[42]

This strategy conference lasted into September 22. Crook, with characteristic zeal, promptly began the careful organization of his fall operations and also tended to innumerable departmental papers that were delivered from Omaha by Captain Azor H. Nickerson, Twenty-third Infantry, and others. Two items were of immediate interest to Major Townsend. First, Captain Edwin Pollock's Company E, Ninth Infantry, was to be equipped for field service and transferred without delay to old Fort Reno. Pollock had learned from Crook that he was to take charge of the various troops being assigned to this forward cantonment. Townsend also learned more fully about plans to transfer the headquarters and other companies of the Ninth Infantry to new stations, and even discovered that the regiment's long-absent colonel, John H. King, was to be relieved of his recruiting assignment in New York City and returned to his troops at their eventual new headquarters station, Sidney Barracks, Nebraska.[43]

This "council of war," as one historian called it, adjourned later on the twenty-second, with Mackenzie departing for Camp Robinson and Sheridan and Crook entertaining the Japanese army officers who had just returned to Fort Laramie, while also making a round of social calls in the garrison. Sheridan, his staff, and the visiting foreign guests de-

Captain Edwin Pollock, Company E, Ninth U.S. Infantry, seen here in the mid-1860s. Pollock participated in Fort Laramie's varied summer duties, and in the fall of 1876 he commanded the force that established Cantonment Reno, Wyoming Territory. (U.S. Army Military History Institute)

parted for Cheyenne on September 23. Although there remained ample business for Crook, Cynthia Capron noted in a letter dated the twenty-fourth that he, John Collins, and Burt "have been out hunting or fishing everyday lately." Crook's propensity for mixing outdoor sporting activities with business was by now widely known.[44]

Crook's affinity for civilian dress was also widely understood in military circles but seems to have been barely known otherwise. Collins, the post trader, recalled an occasion in 1876 when a newspaper-man, freshly arrived on the Cheyenne stage, asked where he might find General Crook. The clerk directed him to the officers' club-rooms adjoining the back of the store, and when the reporter looked in he saw a few young officers but "not one who had the appearance of a general." Returning to the store, he inquired again and the clerk asked:

> "Did you see a large man with a full beard dressed in canvas hunting clothes and a slouch hat?"
>
> "Yes," replied the stranger, "I saw a seedy looking man dressed as you describe, but I am looking for General Crook."
>
> "That's him," said the clerk.
>
> "Well," said the reporter, "I took that man to be one of the bosses of a mule train."

Collins often chided Crook for this unsoldierly appearance, but the general remained unmoved.[45]

Crook was the guest of Andrew and Elizabeth Burt during his stay at Fort Laramie. He was "most agreeable," remembered Elizabeth, "adapting himself readily to any inconvenience that arose." But "he was not a great talker," she added.[46] Although Crook dominated the post's guest list after Sheridan departed, the arrival and departure of other officers received considerable attention too. The Big Horn and Yellowstone Expedition remained essentially an intact corps of sol-diers in the Black Hills, but certain of its staff and line officers were permitted leaves of absence. Many of Crook's immediate staff had left the expedition when he did on September 16, for instance, but had enjoyed a more leisurely pace getting to Fort Laramie. Crook's aide-de-camp and chief chronicler Lieutenant Bourke came into the fort on September 24 in the company of acting assistant surgeons Robert B. Grimes and E. P. LeCompte and several others from the general's staff. That day too Captain John Furey and the baggage train of the expedition arrived at the post from Goose Creek via Fort Fetterman. The wagons were hurriedly overhauled and then continued to the Black Hills.[47]

In most instances these officers merely passed through the post, pausing to pay respects as necessary or to deliver mail or messages to

Captain Andrew Sheridan Burt, Company H, Ninth U.S. Infantry, seen here as a lieutenant colonel in the late 1880s. (U.S. Army Military History Institute)

various inhabitants, but otherwise staying only long enough to catch the next southbound stage at the Rustic Hotel. Three newspaper correspondents, Reuben Davenport, *New York Herald*, Joe Wasson, writing for the *New York Tribune, San Francisco Alta California,* and *Philadelphia Press,* and John Finerty, *Chicago Times,* came through too. For the most part, the correspondents covering the campaign seem to have justly earned the soldiers' respect. "They proved excellent campaigners," remembered one officer, "and welcome, indeed genial associates." But twenty-nine-year-old Finerty, the "fighting Irish pencil pusher," as he was affectionately known, emerged above the rest as a tireless, balanced newsman, using pencil and carbine with equal facility—"the gem of the lot," said Charles King of the Fifth Cavalry.[48]

At the infantry barracks adjoining the parade ground, Pollock's Company E, Ninth Infantry, was tending to last-minute business before taking its turn in the field during the Great Sioux War of 1876. Although the company had had its share of vigorous exercise all year long as it tramped the Cheyenne, Custer City, and Camp Robinson roads protecting supplies and escorting travelers, until now it had also enjoyed the relative comforts of barracks life, with proper army meals, warm beds, clean uniforms, and the fellowship of the garrison. But soon it would join infantry companies from Fort Hartsuff, Nebraska, and Fort Bridger and Camp Brown, Wyoming, in the Indian country. The men marched northwest to Fort Fetterman on September 27. Although Lieutenant Regan had prepared to depart with his company, Townsend placed him on detached service at Fort Laramie just before they marched. He could ill afford to lose his commissary officer and post treasurer. As it was, his officer complement was stretched thin and his sole remaining Company, F Ninth Infantry, was being administered without the supervision of a commissioned officer. That company's captain had long been on detached duty in New Orleans; First Lieutenant William Rogers had been detached to Indianapolis for recruiting duty just two weeks earlier; and Second Lieutenant Rockefeller had been campaigning with Crook all summer. Fortunately Thomas Burrowes and Andrew Burt had returned from the expedition, though Burrowes was sick in quarters. And on September 29 Company K, Second Cavalry, returned from its jaunt to the Black Hills.[49]

By his own authority Townsend could keep Regan, but with the Ninth Infantry destined to be transferred soon to other posts, he petitioned Crook to allow First Lieutenant Thaddeus Capron to return to Fort Laramie from the field. With the departure of the headquarters detachment of the regiment, including regimental quartermaster Morton, and considering the huge volume of stores being received and forwarded, Townsend wanted Capron to "get the run of the business by the time Lieut. Morton leaves." Obviously never stated but undoubtedly a factor in Townsend's request was his friendship with Mrs. Capron. He called frequently at her home, and she had already had a difficult summer, exacerbated by the death of her youngest child. With the return of Captain Burt as an example of what could happen if the proper questions were asked, indeed Townsend tried.

Camp Sheridan, Nebraska, in 1876. This small military post protected operations at the nearby Spotted Tail Agency. D. S. Mitchell photograph. (U.S. Military Academy Library)

His request, in fact, was formalized in a letter that was hand delivered
to Crook. The general may have had a callous heart, but more than
likely he already knew that most of the Ninth Infantry officers would
not be much longer at Fort Laramie, so on that same day, September
25, he denied the request.[50]

The travel of other officers provided steady conversation at Fort
Laramie. Crook's quartermaster, Captain Furey, was detached from

his wagon train while it was being overhauled at the post and sent to Omaha on "public business." Departing with him on September 28 were Crook's aides Bourke and Schuyler. Also on that date oral instructions given surgeon Hartsuff on September 15 relieving him from duty with the Big Horn and Yellowstone Expedition were confirmed, and he was advised that he could begin a leave of absence immediately. Meanwhile a similar request for the use of leave by Dr. Petteys was denied. Crook would soon assign him to the new expedition to be formed against the Sioux and Cheyennes.[51]

In the midst of this other traffic and business came news from the

Red Cloud and Spotted Tail agencies that the Sioux commissioners had secured enough Indians' signatures on the congressional ultimatum of August 15 to conclude their stay there and were moving on to the Missouri River agencies to begin discussions. The previous report, while Crook and his staff were passing through Camp Robinson en route to Fort Laramie, was that negotiations had stalled. The commissioners, indeed, had delivered and explained the document, never denying or sidestepping its harsh terms. It was the discussion of several of the articles, particularly those requiring relocation, that had slowed progress, so that the Sioux finally moved off to parlay among themselves.

On September 19 Red Cloud and the other Oglala leaders and headmen returned to the meeting. They would give up the Black Hills. As for removal to the Indian Territory, though some young men would be sent to investigate that country, they seriously doubted that they would go there. Other Oglala leaders including Young Man Afraid of His Horses and Sitting Bull (not the Hunkpapa medicine man with the same name) made impassioned speeches declaring their desire to remain in the north country. Bishop Whipple reminded the chiefs that the president would have them go to a new Missouri River agency if they did not move south, but on that point the September 19 talks broke off. The next day, however, all the leaders except Sitting Bull returned to sign the document.[52]

The actual signing ceremony was a somber affair. Most of the leaders placed their marks only after offering statements suggesting that they either did not understand the terms or would not abide by them. The commissioners, at this point, seem to have done little to correct misunderstandings or soothe frayed feelings, preferring instead to finish their distasteful labors and move on. At the Spotted Tail Agency signatures were collected on September 23. A distinct feeling of duress pervaded this ceremony, just as at Red Cloud. Standing Elk, a progressive Brule chief, remarked to Commissioner Gaylord: "My friend, your words are like a man knocking me in the head with a club. By your speech you have put great fear upon us. Whatever the white people ask of us, wherever we go, we always say *Yes—yes—yes!* Whenever we don't agree to what is asked of us in council, you always reply: *You won't get anything to eat!—You won't get anything to eat!*"[53]

Finished with their business in Nebraska, the commissioners moved on to Standing Rock and the other Missouri River agencies, where they began collecting signatures on October 11. These Oglalas, Brules, and other Sioux knew the consequences of their actions, despite statements to the contrary. As one historian described it, these agency Indians were desperate. "Caught between the Army on one side and the hostiles on the other, they knew that they had no choice but to make the best of life at the agencies, and when representatives of the Great Father came with a paper which they must sign or have their rations cut off, they signed."[54] Article 12 of the 1868 treaty, which required that three-fourths of all adult male Sioux approve any reservation land cessions, was conveniently ignored, and some of the chiefs and representatives were allowed to sign for all their people. The Black Hills question was settled, at least on paper.[55]

At Fort Laramie Townsend continued to send out supplies, mail, horses, and other materials to the Big Horn and Yellowstone Expedition. The paymaster, Major William Arthur, made rounds at Fort Laramie, Sage Creek, Red Canyon and Camps Robinson and Sheridan paying the troops, and he then paid the men of the expedition.[56] All of this mail, clothing, rations, baggage, and pay was warmly received by the soldiers in the Black Hills. Since September 16, when General Crook left the command, these troops had been inching their way south, bivouacking in the broad, grassy meadows along Whitewood, Box Elder, and Rapid creeks. Recuperation was everyone's foremost thought. While they were camped along Box Elder Creek on September 29, the first wagons sent from the south reached them, and Charles King noted that "for the first time in four long weeks, small measures of oats and corn were dealt out to our emaciated animals."[57]

The intense gold extraction tempted many of the soldiers as they traveled south. Diaries and journals mention how the officers and men "wandered off to visit the mining gulches" and "watched them washing gold." Near Custer City, one of the expedition's doctors, Bennett A. Clements, joined Eugene A. Carr and Lieutenant William C. Forbush, both of the Fifth Cavalry, at a particularly prosperous claim, and each washed a pan of dirt, with Clements recovering 50¢ in gold dust, Carr 75¢, and Forbush $2. According to a detailed account, the own-

Laramie Peak in 1876. Although forty-five miles distant, this prominent land-mark is visible on Fort Laramie's western horizon. D. S. Mitchell photograph. (Nebraska State Historical Society)

ers of this claim were recovering $800 daily.[58] The mining commu-nities offered other diversions too, but for the most part the men of the expedition enjoyed what King called "dull work." There was plenty to eat, there were no drills, vocalists and yarn spinners performed at the evening campfires, and at last, letters came from home.[59]

Crook, meanwhile, was enjoying a leisurely escape of his own. On October 3 he departed with John Collins, "Teddy" Egan, and an aide, Lieutenant William P. Clark, on a hunting trip to Laramie Peak. Twenty men from Egan's company served as an escort, though the special orders detailing them described the outing in more evasive terms as a "scout toward Laramie Peak." Collins wrote at length about the trip in his memoirs, telling how the men rambled over the north-east side of the mountain killing deer, elk, and mountain sheep and how he discovered a recently used Indian lookout high on a ledge from which one could plainly see the valley of the Platte, the Laramie, and the surrounding country for fifty miles or more. On another occasion, one morning Egan and his troopers came upon a burning campfire. Freshly killed elk meat was hanging from a nearby tree, and moccasin tracks were plainly visible in the dust. Undaunted, the hunters cooked their breakfast over the same fire and continued their hunt. Many other recent Indian signs were observed before the trip was over. Returning to Fort Laramie, Crook and his party delivered sixty-four deer, four elk, four mountain sheep, and one cinnamon bear to the garrison.[60]

Word of Crook's pleasure trip to Laramie Peak reached his Black Hills troops about the time he returned to Fort Laramie. In an exceedingly critical tone, Charles King expressed in a private letter home the sentiments of at least some officers with the expedition. "Crook is enjoying himself two hundred miles away hunting & picnicing around Laramie Peak, his detractors say to dodge the *New York Herald,* and while our horses are starving for sufficient grass, we have no grain, and becoming weaker every day." The *New York Herald* was indeed publishing intensely critical articles, with its correspondent Reuben Davenport filing charges that Crook should be court-martialed for his conduct of the campaign and that the whole affair might be likened to Napoleon's retreat from Moscow. Some of King's assertions about the condition of the stock are borne out in a letter from Merritt to Crook dated October 8. However good the grass may have been earlier in the season, it was now very poor, he wrote. The grass is of a type "which seems to suffer great injury from the frost," and although he was changing camp often he could not report that the "cavalry horses have improved greatly in flesh."[61]

Fort Laramie, meanwhile, continued to receive shipments of ammunition, rations, and most recently, winter uniforms and clothing such as buffalo overshoes, sealskin gauntlets and caps, and woolen mittens. These replenished the post's own depleted stores and formed the necessary stocks for the pending third campaign against the roamers.[62] Of slightly greater interest to at least some of the post's inhabitants was the return of the Cheyenne photographer D. S. Mitchell. Mitchell had traveled to the Black Hills the previous spring to photograph the gold rush, and among dozens of views he took in the popular stereographic format were towns, claim sites, and prospecting activities. He photographed soldiers too, though unlike his contemporary, Stanley J. Morrow, who specifically photographed Crook's troops in the Black Hills, Mitchell documented various movements of Mackenzie's Fourth Cavalry, government trains bearing supplies to Crook, the view of Egan's cavalry with General Crook mentioned earlier, and even one of the Lieutenant Taylor's military camp at Sage Creek. Mitchell paused long enough on this trip to climb the bluffs southeast of the fort and take the one known photograph of Fort Laramie in 1876, which showed the stark reality of the post in unvarnished detail (see p. 36). Unfortunately, aside from this general view, few Mitchell photographs are known today.[63]

In early October one of Fort Laramie's most reliable soldiers, Ordnance Sergeant Leodegar Schnyder, approached Major Townsend regarding a transfer. He explained that he had served faithfully at the fort for over twenty-seven years. Now, with five children and a wife to support, he wanted to move to a post nearer the railroad, where he could live more cheaply. The major, with respect for a soldier of such steady caliber, relayed Schnyder's wishes to the adjutant general of the army on October 2, adding his own endorsement. As can happen to well-intentioned but perhaps ill-timed requests, however, no response was forthcoming, at least through official channels.[64]

After his hunting foray to Laramie Peak, Crook returned to the business of the Big Horn and Yellowstone Expedition, attending to personnel moves and the column's slow but calculated march to the agencies as a part of the disarming and unhorsing work anticipated there. Crook expected to mass these soldiers at the Red Cloud and Spotted Tail agencies alongside Mackenzie's combined cavalry and artillery. Townsend, meanwhile, saw his local routine interrupted on October 10 when the body of a civilian named Rhodes was brought into the fort for burial. Rhodes had been herding cattle on Horseshoe Creek forty miles northwest of the fort when he was jumped by Indians on the ninth. The post's doctors examined the body at the hospital deadhouse before interment and noted that a small piece of scalp had been taken and an arrow was pushed up the anus. The *Daily Leader* claimed that the ears had been cut off.[65]

No sooner had Rhodes been placed in the cemetery than another body was delivered to the hospital. Upon examination, the doctors noted that in this case eight wounds had been inflicted and a full scalp taken. That it occurred at about the same time as the Rhodes incident seems to tie the killings together.[66] Perhaps the attackers were the same Indians whose signs were so plentiful around Laramie Peak when Crook, Collins, and Egan were there.

Indian raiders, described as twenty-five to thirty in number, next appeared in the Chug valley stealing horses. Word of repeated sightings and stock losses was carried quickly to the eleven-man detachment of Second Cavalrymen stationed in the valley. Second Cavalry troopers had just returned to this watch after having been spelled briefly by Ninth Infantrymen so these mounted soldiers under Egan could escort supplies to the Hills. Sergeant Joseph Parker commanded these cavalrymen, and they promptly chased the Indians. In a sharp fight on Richard Creek, fifteen miles southwest of the Hunton ranch on the evening of October 14, the soldiers and some ranchmen cornered the raiders. In the exchange one soldier, Private Warren C. Tasker, was killed, receiving a fatal wound above the left eyebrow. During the fight Parker found his initial position too widely exposed, so before dark he withdrew one hundred yards to a more defensible location. Tasker was left behind where he fell.[67]

Sometime after dark the raiders withdrew, and in the morning the Second Cavalrymen recovered Tasker's body. He was not mutilated, but he had been stripped except for his socks. Elsewhere in the Indian positions Parker found evidence of the excellent armaments these raiders carried; a Spencer carbine had been left behind, and empty cartridge packages and shell casings for Sharps improved rifles littered the ground. Tasker's body was removed to the Hunton ranch and was then carried to Fort Laramie, where he was buried on October 17. Present at the ceremony were Mrs. Capron and Mrs. Egan. With the killing of a private in the Powder River battle on March 17 and the accidental drowning of their first sergeant in May while hunting a deserter, this was the third service-related fatality that year in Company K, Second Cavalry.[68]

In the midst of this raiding and bloodshed west of the fort, there came news of similar but apparently unrelated attacks northeast of Fort Laramie beginning on October 10. A party of four Indians identified as Cheyennes killed a herder named Jack Monroe at the Pratt and Ferris ranch on Rawhide Creek, then took some horses and continued south to Nick Janis's ranch on the North Platte. From there they made away with twenty-five more horses. Some of Janis's ranch hands took after the raiders but, though giving lively chase, could not catch them. While the small detachment of Second Cavalrymen investigated matters west of the fort, the raiding to the east prompted Townsend to dispatch Egan's available cavalrymen on yet another chase. As it so routinely turned out, the scout was profitless.[69]

In sum, these had been costly raids, resulting in one pitched fight, one soldier and at least three civilians killed, and approximately 120 horses taken. As a rancher put it, "Send more guns and ammunition. . . . The country around here is full of Indians." Naturally the *Cheyenne Daily Leader* seized the occasion to call Crook to attention, and also to share some advice with travelers. "As men who recently arrived here from the Hills have asked us how they are to tell whether the Indians mentioned are or are not hostile," the paper replied that "the only certain and safe way of gathering this information is by shooting all Indians at sight, and then examining their pockets. If they have passes from agents and traders they are hostile; if not, they are probably returning from a 'visit' to friends in Sitting Bull's camp, and should be shot for luck."[70]

Crook by now was inured to harangues from papers like the *Daily Leader,* but he had every intent of moving against the Indians, and on several fronts. He had been carefully monitoring the movements of the Big Horn and Yellowstone Expedition to Camp Robinson, and on October 14 he headed there from Fort Laramie. Chief Red Cloud continued to bother the military authorities. After signing the Black Hills Agreement he and his followers had moved thirty miles or so east of the agencies to a camp on Chadron Creek. The army felt sure he was in constant communication with the roamers and demanded that he move back to the agency where he could be more easily watched. He was told that if he did not cooperate his rations would be cut off and troops would move him back forcibly. Red Cloud replied defiantly that he would be fed on Chadron Creek.[71]

With this to set the stage, Crook waited only for Merritt to bolster troop strength at the agency. As it was, there were already four companies in the permanent Camp Robinson garrison and two at Camp Sheridan. Mackenzie commanded another force of fourteen companies at his camp near Robinson. Merritt, meanwhile, led the Big Horn and Yellowstone Expedition, composed of thirty-five companies of soldiers. The general plan for unhorsing and disarming these Indians would have Merritt's force blocking escapes to the north while Mackenzie approached from the south to surround and search the camps. This long-anticipated action was scheduled for October 24.[72]

Nervous that Red Cloud and his many followers might move farther away or even join the warring Indians, Crook had Mackenzie leave under cover of darkness on October 22 with eight companies of Fourth and Fifth Cavalry. En route he was joined by Major Frank North and his detachment of Pawnee Scouts, who had been brought in for this action and the next campaign. At dawn Mackenzie deployed his troops, with half advancing on Red Cloud's camp and the other half moving on the nearby village belonging to Red Leaf, a close ally of Red Cloud. Completely surrounded, both Red Cloud and Red Leaf surrendered quietly. The tipis were searched, and an insignificant lot of firearms and ammunition was recovered. Major North did capture 722 ponies, and these were led off. Although a few old men were allowed to ride and the women were given some horses to pack the camp, almost everyone walked to the agency.[73]

Before the full impact of the surrender was felt, on October 23 Crook struck one final blow by announcing that from that time forward Red Cloud and Red Leaf would no longer be chiefs of the Oglalas; Spotted Tail was to be chief of both his own people and also everyone residing at Red Cloud Agency. It was a clear insult. Crook might remove a title, but he could hardly take away influence. And although Red Cloud could not understand such base treatment, he boasted that his people would continue to follow him and that Spotted Tail would be a chief of the Oglalas in name only. That seems to have been the result. Historian James Olson concluded that Crook's action might even have strengthened Red Cloud's influence. Spotted Tail never acted for the Oglalas, and soon Red Cloud "resumed his position of leadership, in name as well as fact."[74]

Crook did not move against Spotted Tail's Brules or the Cheyennes and the other visiting tribes, but he was immensely proud of his

General Crook, facing right in this Stanley J. Morrow photograph, oversees the installation on October 24, 1876, of Spotted Tail as chief of the Brule and Oglala Sioux. This clear insult scarcely diminished Red Cloud's enormous influence among the Sioux. (U.S. Military Academy Library)

actions against the Oglalas. In a letter to Sheridan on October 23 he recapped the efforts of the previous two days. The surrenders had been effected without a shot, he declared, and thus the "line of the hostiles and peaceably disposed is now plainly drawn and we shall have our enemies in the front only. . . . This is the first gleam of daylight we have had in the business."[75] Sheridan was pleased by the initial news from Red Cloud, but when Crook did not subject Spotted Tail and the others to like measures, his praise quickly turned to condemnation. Crook had not "performed what he promised and what was expected of him."[76]

At the Missouri River agencies, meanwhile, the disarmings and unhorsings were accomplished without incident. In all, some valuable arms and ammunition and thousands of ponies were confiscated. Those horses taken on the Missouri were trailed east to Fort Abercrombie or to Fort Abraham Lincoln and then sent to St. Paul, Minnesota, for sale at public auction. Hundreds, however, died from disease, exposure, or drowning or were lost through sheer negligence.[77]

The 722 ponies taken from Red Cloud's and Red Leaf's people were trailed to Fort Laramie by Frank North and twenty Pawnee Scouts. Lieutenant Morton received the horses on October 25 and turned them into the quartermaster corrals. On October 27 a small advertisement appeared on the local news page of the *Daily Leader* announcing the "Auction Sale of Indian Ponies." More than 400 ponies and a number of firearms, the advertisement declared, would be sold at public auction on November 2 at Fort Laramie. Terms would be cash at the time of sale.[78]

Crook, flushed with his achievements over Red Cloud, immediately turned his attention to disbanding the Big Horn and Yellowstone Expedition and forming a new command that soon would take the field against the northern roamers. Many of Crook's weary soldiers had been in the field nearly five months; some of the Second and Third Cavalrymen had also participated in the Big Horn Expedition the previous March. Before releasing the command, Crook issued a final congratulatory order. The men had evinced a high order of discipline and courage, he noted, with wonderful powers of endurance, patience, and fortitude as they dealt with deprivation and hardship. Though serving without incentive to promotion and without favor or hope of reward, "you may," he praised, "congratulate yourselves that, in the performance of your military duty, you have been on the side of the weak against the strong, and that the few people there are on the frontier will remember your efforts with gratitude."[79]

Then came the welcome order to go into winter quarters. The distribution of the thirty-five companies of the expedition did not correspond to precampaign points of origin. Although these troops would indeed sit out the next movement against the warring Indians, Crook had every intent of placing his field-hardened regulars in strategic posts at the agencies, near the Powder River country, or on the

Indian camp near Red Cloud Agency, 1876. Dozens of villages like this dotted the environs of the Red Cloud and Spotted Tail agencies of Nebraska during the

railroad within an easy commute. Fort Sanders at Laramie City, for instance, would receive Companies A, B, D, and E, Second Cavalry, while Fort D. A. Russell would have the headquarters and Companies A, B, F, and I, Fifth Cavalry, and I, Second Cavalry. Nebraska's railroad posts would receive Fifth Cavalry Companies C, E, G, and M at Fort McPherson, and D and K, Fifth Cavalry, and H, Ninth Infantry, at Sidney Barracks. Fetterman would have Companies I, Third Cavalry, and F, Fourth Infantry, while to Camp Sheridan went Company M, Third Cavalry. Camp Robinson was soon to become the most heavily garrisoned post in the Department of the Platte, with ten companies ordered there, including B, C, and L, Third Cavalry, D and G, Fourth Infantry, G, Ninth Infantry, and B, C, F, and I, Fourteenth Infantry. Fort Laramie would soon emerge with the next largest garrison when Major Andrew Wallace Evans arrived with Third Cavalry regimental headquarters and band, Companies A, D, E, F, and G of that regiment, and Company C, Ninth Infantry.[80]

These changes of station required considerable effort. Company property had to be transferred from precampaign posts to new ones, and existing summer garrisons in many cases had first to be redeployed, these troops destined either for the next campaign or for their own new stations. At Fort Laramie, as an example, Companies C and

centennial campaign. Photograph attributed to D. S. Mitchell. (National Archives and Records Service)

H, Ninth Infantry, and I, Second Cavalry, returned to the comforts of their old post on October 27 and 28.[81] But the foot soldiers of H and the horsemen of I immediately began packing. Such moves were an accepted part of military life, and while the chore was much easier for a private, who probably had no more personal belongings than could fit in a satchel or two, transferring the possessions and furnishings of a commissioned officer and his family was considerably more of an undertaking. Packing and transferring company and regimental property was equally taxing.

Meanwhile, other troops from the late expedition continued to arrive, headed south or to Fort Laramie itself. Crook and a number of senior officers, including Colonel Merritt and Lieutenant Colonel William Royall, Third Cavalry, preceded everyone into the fort on October 26, but then came virtually all of the returning cavalry, including the five new Third Cavalry companies ordered to Fort Laramie plus the Second and Fifth Cavalry companies en route for Fort D. A. Russell or Fort Sanders. To ease the travel between Camp Robinson and Fort Laramie, Crook arranged to have 20,000 pounds of forage from Fort Laramie delivered to the Rawhide Creek crossing. Lieutenant Allison and four enlisted men from Company K conducted this special train and then returned with the horsemen. These were ragged-looking soldiers as they arrived at Fort Laramie, most bearded, still only sketchily bathed, and in tattered uniforms. But they exhibited a cavalier jauntiness that could have come only from field conditioning. Luther North particularly remembered the infantrymen as they came into the post. "They were in the finest kind of condition," he wrote. "They marched from Ft. Robinson to Ft. Laramie in three days, a distance of ninety miles, and didn't seem to mind it at all. They could outwalk my horses." The men had indeed outwalked horses at the last of the campaign and had eaten a few of them, too.[82]

General Crook continued to use Fort Laramie as department headquarters "in the field" while he prepared for the next movement against the Sioux. In an order from there dated October 27 he clarified the placement of certain Ninth Infantry personnel stationed at Laramie. The regimental staff, noncommissioned staff, records, band, and Company H of the regiment were to proceed without delay to Sidney Barracks. This movement had been intimated a month before when Sheridan and Crook held their strategy council at the fort.[83]

While supervising the packing of regimental property along with his own family's possessions and welcoming the transient officers and troops coming through Fort Laramie, Townsend tended to routine details as well. Reports of Indian raiding continued to dominate day-to-day news, though for the first time all summer cavalry other than Egan's company was responding. The occasion was the sighting of Indians on Horse Creek north of Cheyenne. Sent after them was Second Lieutenant George Francis Chase, Third Cavalry, and 110 men assembled from the Fort D. A. Russell garrison. Chase had only recently returned from the summer campaign, but he had "been anxious to make a trip of the kind for a week past," announced the *Daily Leader*. Numerous other sightings were reported too, and horses were stolen from ranches on Bear and Horse creeks. After ten days on the trail, Chase never closed with the raiders, and at best he received a taste of the futile campaigning that had marked Captain Egan's service throughout the summer.[84]

For Egan this was not an occasion to relax, because on October 27 T. A. Kent, a rancher near the F. M. Phillips place west of the fort, asked if Townsend could send a "few men to help us run the Indians out of the country"; twenty-five had just been seen fifteen miles from the ranch. Townsend dispatched the captain and sixteen men from his company, plus fifteen Pawnee Scouts from North's detachment, to the Phillips ranch to investigate. The same special order that sent Egan west recalled the Second Cavalry patrol from the Chugwater valley. There would soon be plenty more mounted soldiers in the valley as the Fifth Cavalry continued to Fort D. A. Russell. More important, Crook had designs on Egan's valiant crew.[85]

From the north came news that the telegraph wire had been cut sixteen miles south of Red Canyon. Repairmen on the scene saw the tracks of some sixty Indians going west, and the band had their lodge poles.[86] This traffic on the Powder River trail and similar sightings in the weeks to come was most assuredly in response to the unhorsings and disarmings under way at the Nebraska agencies. This dramatic news from the Sioux agencies in October overshadowed the steady northward progress of the Cheyenne and Black Hills telegraph line. Early in the month the wire had reached Captain Collier's camp at Red Canyon, and at month's end it was within twenty-five miles of Custer City. Progress at the Hat Creek Ranch too was altering the appearance of this station, next to Taylor's Twenty-third Infantry camp on Sage Creek. There Jack Bowman and Joe Walters, the latter a discharged sergeant late of Company E, Twenty-third Infantry, were developing what the *Daily Leader* described as a first-class hotel, soon to be complete with telegraph and post office, brewery, bakery, and butcher and blacksmith shops. Some of the amenities, particularly the brewery, were surely a source of discomfort to Lieutenant Taylor, though certainly that was mitigated by the arrival of a grocery source and other comforts.[87]

Both of these Fort Laramie subposts, Sage Creek and Red Canyon, were fitting up for the winter. Although Crook had first indicated that these specific companies of Fourth and Twenty-third Infantry would be in residence all fall and winter, he changed his mind on September 30. The camps would indeed remain open, but these companies would be moved. As they awaited orders to that effect, Collier and Taylor still began laying in supplies of clothing, tools, food, and hay. Many personal possessions these soldiers needed for the winter had been left behind at their permanent quarters, and on October 24 permission was granted to First Sergeant Thomas McClane,

Twenty-third Infantry, to travel to Omaha Barracks to retrieve his company's property and clothing. Collier undoubtedly did likewise for his men of Company K, Fourth Infantry, during a leave of absence granted October 7.[88]

At month's end Fort Laramie was in a state of metamorphosis. General Crook's summer war had officially ended, and his Big Horn and Yellowstone Expedition was disbanded. It had been an awesome season, with devastating battles in Montana, repeated Indian contacts nearer the forts and agencies, unrelenting traffic on the Black Hills road, and important progress with the agency Sioux. Thus, much of the coming campaign would be a virtual repeat of what the fort had seen twice before. But as the momentum grew for a third and perhaps final movement against these northern Sioux, the post itself changed. Soon the tested and proven summer guard, the Ninth Infantrymen and Second Cavalrymen, all under the capable leadership of Major Edwin Franklin Townsend, would be gone, called to other challenging assignments. Such, of course, was the nature of the military, with its relentless call to duty wherever needed. Yet surely this change had an impact on garrison survivors, Laramie's neighbors, and those who had served faithfully behind the battle lines of Rosebud Creek, the Yellowstone, and Slim Buttes. The stirring summer days of 1876, indeed, were over.

Chapter Seven

Winter Operations:
November 1876–January 1877

Mounting the Powder River Expedition, as General George Crook's third major campaign against the northern roamers was soon to be called, was considerably easier than mounting either of the two movements preceding it. A steady stream of war materials had been funneled to Crook's forward military posts all summer and fall, and diverting supplies from one need to another was easily arranged. By now Crook had complete and immediate mastery over the troops in his department, and on this occasion there were no lengthy trans- or interdepartmental movements. Virtually every company desired was already field equipped and within an easy ride of a point of assembly; selected for this campaign was Fort Laramie.

While logistically the Powder River Expedition was much easier to plan, Crook's functionaries still faced ample pressure as they attended to a multitude of tasks in the days before departure from Fort Laramie. Lieutenant Bourke, in fact, complained in his diary that the pressures at headquarters were such that he had to abandon daily entries and confine himself to describing "special moments" from "time to time." He did mention the bustle at the fort, "with troops moving in and troops moving out, officers running hither, thither and yon, changing quarters, drawing supplies or other duties."[1]

The Powder River Expedition would be smaller than the recently disbanded Big Horn and Yellowstone column, massing in sum eleven companies of cavalry under the command of Colonel Mackenzie, four companies of dismounted artillery and eleven companies of infantry in the charge of Lieutenant Colonel Richard I. Dodge, Twenty-third Infantry, plus scouts and other auxiliaries. General Crook, for the third consecutive time, would personally lead the troops. Fort Laramie's contribution to this winter movement was Company F, Ninth Infantry, commanded by Second Lieutenant Charles Mortimer Rockefeller, and Captain James Egan's Company K, Second Cavalry, along with Major Edwin Townsend, the second-ranking infantry officer on the new expedition and civilian physician Charles V. Petteys. Egan's Grays, one of Crook's favorite companies, was the only unit that had been on one of the previous campaigns. On this occasion the Grays would serve as provost guard at headquarters, supplying mounted couriers and mail carriers as needed, along with attendants for the wounded should that duty be necessary.[2]

Major Townsend had ceased functioning as Fort Laramie's post commander at midnight, October 31, and on November 1 the newly assigned companies of Third Cavalry officially joined the post. Officers of the Ninth Infantry had exercised control over Fort Laramie's operation since August 1874, but now Major Andrew W. Evans assumed that responsibility. With Evans came First Lieutenant Charles Morton, Third Cavalry, as new post adjutant succeeding Leonard Hay. And in a temporary move, Lieutenant Thaddeus Capron of the remaining Company C, Ninth Infantry, was appointed both post quartermaster and post commissary officer, replacing departing Alfred Morton and James Regan.[3]

Among other Third Cavalry officers either already present or en route to Fort Laramie were Captains Deane Monahan, Alexander Moore, and Joseph Lawson and Lieutenants John C. Thompson, Alexander D. B. Smead, Bainbridge Reynolds, and Francis H. Hardie. The recent field records of these new arrivals varied. Several, in fact, including Monahan and Hardie, had been on detached service or leave and had not campaigned in 1876. Moore, after incurring Crook's wrath at Powder River, did not go with the Big Horn and Yellowstone Expedition, but Evans, Morton, Lawson, and Reynolds—the last the son of the regiment's colonel—had been at Rosebud Creek and

Slim Buttes. Technically, with Fort Laramie now serving as regimental headquarters, Colonel Joseph J. Reynolds and Lieutenant Colonel William B. Royall were properly carried on its monthly rolls, but these officers never joined the post.[4]

One of Evans's first official actions was to relieve those Ninth Infantrymen reassigned to Sidney Barracks, and on November 3 these men marched south. Departing officers included Hay and Morton, Captain Andrew S. Burt, and Second Lieutenant Edgar Robertson of Company H, along with the sixty-one men of that company, plus the regimental noncommissioned staff and the band. Although on detached service, the regiment's senior officers Colonel John H. King and Lieutenant Colonel Luther P. Bradley would now be carried on the Sidney Barracks rolls. And so too was Townsend, who did not march south but joined the new Powder River Expedition effective the third. On November 4 Company I, Second Cavalry, departed for its new station, Fort D. A. Russell. This sixty-two-man mounted unit led by Captain Henry Noyes and Lieutenants Christopher Hall and Frederick Kingsbury, had been at the post more than a year.[5]

As these infantry and cavalry soldiers were making their final preparations on November 2 before departure, there was considerable commotion at the quartermaster corrals, where the recently surrendered Sioux ponies were being auctioned off. Of the 722 brought into the fort on October 25, many of the finest had already been siphoned off for varied official uses. Crook, for instance, had the North brothers and their hundred-man Pawnee Scout detachment each select a horse from the corrals, and then 70 more were taken from the herd as a campaign reserve. About 150 ponies were diverted to mounting other scouts, guides, and friendly Indians, and on the appointed sale day the 405 remaining horses were sold to the public. Bourke remembered paying forty dollars for a perfectly matched and well suited but unbroken span of beautiful dark bays, but most horses sold for a little over five dollars each to traders, cattlemen, and miners. The proceeds from this and several other auctions were to have been used to buy cattle for the agency Sioux. Apparently, however, the cattle were never purchased, nor was the money ever properly accounted for.[6]

Crook, meanwhile, had been concentrating on enlisting Indian scouts from the Nebraska agencies. His attempts at that the previous May had failed, but his appeals were now being met with much greater favor. He used these enlistments, in fact, to refute criticism from Sheridan for not expanding the disarming and unhorsing at the agencies. These were basically loyal Indians, he explained, and to take away their guns and horses would only alienate them further. Instead, he would give them an opportunity to prove their loyalty by serving as scouts in his forthcoming campaign against Crazy Horse. Certainly too he remembered his old Arizona lesson that the best way to track and corner warring Indians was to employ recently converted kin.[7]

More than 150 Sioux, Cheyennes, and Arapahoes joined the expedition at Fort Laramie. Among that number were fighting men who had recently surrendered at the agencies after coming down from the northern camps. Many came mounted on their own ponies, demonstrating the half-heartedness of the unhorsings. Others were remounted on surrendered horses.[8] The core of the Powder River Expedition comprised those troops most recently committed to Mackenzie's use in the District of the Black Hills, headquartered since August at Camp Robinson. After regrouping from the actions against Red Cloud and Red Leaf, these Fourth and Fifth Cavalrymen, Fourth Artillerymen, and Fourteenth Infantrymen left their summer station on November 1 and came into Fort Laramie on the fourth.

The Powder River Expedition, nearly 1,500 men strong and with another 430 scouts, packers, and teamsters, marched from Fort Laramie on November 5. Bourke considered it the best-equipped and best-officered of any force in his experience. The troops had been liberally supplied, particularly with winter gear. With sealskin caps and gauntlets, fur leggings, felt boots, and three blankets per soldier besides tents and overcoats, these men must have been the envy of those Fort Laramie veterans who remembered so well Crook's opening Big Horn Expedition the previous March. Most of Crook's command marched via the south river road, but the general and some of his headquarters attendants traveled the north bank or "hill" route. Curiously, no newspaper correspondent joined the column at Fort Laramie, but a reporter from the *New York Herald*, Jerry Roche, did catch the troops as they were pushing out from Fort Fetterman.[9]

Other military traffic remained fairly steady on the various roads to and from Fort Laramie. Captain Michael Fitzgerald, for instance, had recently passed through from Camp Robinson to Cheyenne. After being seriously wounded in a shooting accident the previous August, he had been confined to quarters. Although he did not lose his leg, as first reported, recovery was a long and painful ordeal. Then, to compound his agony, Fitzgerald's wife died two weeks after the shooting, the strain of his accident apparently more than she could bear. Now, with the captain's company off with Crook, he was embarking for Boston on a much-needed leave of absence.[10] Coming into the post too, soon after the expedition had departed, were a detachment of Third Cavalry recruits, plus laundresses and families of that regiment that until now had been assigned to Fort D. A. Russell. The laundresses quickly settled into the small apartments provided for them in the former cavalry barracks on the east bank of the Laramie River or in "adobe row" adjacent to the quartermaster corrals. And on November 11 the Third Cavalry Regimental Band arrived from D. A. Russell.[11]

Competing for interest with the formation and departure of Crook's latest expedition against the Sioux and Cheyennes were the elections coming on Tuesday, November 7. The *Daily Leader* had been giving the various national, territorial, and local campaigns increased attention for weeks and had unabashedly endorsed a straight Republican ticket for months, even though voters in the territory were not entitled to vote for president. Laramie County, which in 1876 was a fifty-mile-wide north-south tier stretching from Colorado to Montana, was divided into eleven voting precincts. Locally, eligible voters could cast their ballots at the Maxwell ranch in the Chugwater precinct or at the Cuny and Ecoffey ranch in the Fort Laramie precinct. Judging the Fort Laramie polls would be Isaac Bettleyoun, George E. Breckenridge, and J. J. Hanoff. Rancher Bettleyoun had been prominent in the Fort Laramie area for years, and members of his family had married Indians and traders from the post's earliest days. Breckenridge too was a Fort Laramie native, and throughout 1876 he appeared on the monthly quartermaster employee rolls as a wagonmaster.[12]

On election day, just over two hundred votes were cast in the local precinct. The county gave a majority of its votes to the Republican candidate for Congress, William W. Corlett, though Fort Laramie voters gave a strong majority to the Democratic incumbent W. R. Steele. The election garnering the most local interest was for justice of the peace. Isaac Bettleyoun emerged fifth out of six candidates, and only the first two were seated.[13]

On November 8 Major Evans promulgated a general order revising the schedule of bugle calls to be sounded at Fort Laramie. This list is only slightly changed from the one that had governed the infantry regime at the fort for the previous four years. Evans did specify that each general call was to be sounded from his headquarters at the southwest corner of the parade ground.

Reveille First Call	Daylight
Reveille	Five minutes after
GUN FIRES AT FIRST NOTE OF REVEILLE	
Assembly	Five minutes later
Stable Call	Ten minutes after Reveille
Fatigue Call (Sundays excepted)	7:30 A.M.
Surgeon's Call	7:45
Guard Mounting First Call	8:50
Guard Mounting Assembly	8:55
Guard Mounting	9:00
Drill Call (Saturdays and Sundays excepted)	10:00
Recall from Drill	11:00
Water Call	11:00
First Sergeant's Call	11:30
Recall from Fatigue (Sundays excepted)	11:45
Mess Call	12:00 P.M.
Fatigue Call (Sundays excepted)	12:45
Fatigue Call (target practice days)	12:45
Recall from Fatigue (Sundays excepted)	4:00
Stable Call and Water Call	4:15
Call for Band (Saturdays excepted)	Not specified
Retreat	Sunset
Tattoo First Call	8:20
Tattoo	8:30

Taps	8:45
Dress Parade (when ordered)	Not specified
SUNDAYS	
Inspection First Call	8:50 A.M.
Inspection Assembly	8:55
Assembly Guard Detail	9:25
Guard Mounting	9:30
MONDAYS	
Target Practice	12:45 P.M.[14]

By mid-November several other Third Cavalry officers had joined the post. After the regiment's adjutant, First Lieutenant John Burgess Johnson, had properly settled into his new home, Evans appointed him post adjutant and returned Charles Morton to his company. The regimental quartermaster, First Lieutenant George Augustus Drew, came into the post on November 15, and by month's end he was detailed as post quartermaster replacing Thaddeus Capron, who had doubled as quartermaster and commissary officer through all of November. Dr. Albert Hartsuff returned from his leave of absence on the twenty-third and resumed his duty as post surgeon, relieving Dr. Gray of that assignment. By November 30, 12 officers and 2 doctors were officially present for duty, as were 450 enlisted men.[15]

As had Townsend before him, Major Evans quickly contended with the burden of telegraph maintenance. The Western Union line to the Black Hills had progressed nicely in the previous weeks, and on November 8 service was opened to Custer City. W. H. Hibbard's crews, meanwhile, were pushing the wire on to Deadwood. Indian presence remained ominous, however, particularly between Red Canyon and Sage Creek, and it was common for detachments from those stations to see the tracks of in- or outbound natives and to have to repair a deliberately cut telegraph wire where their trails and the line intersected.[16]

Perhaps more troublesome to Evans than this Black Hills line, which could be repaired by the infantrymen from the Sage Creek or Red Canyon subposts, was that connecting Laramie and Fetterman. This older wire had been a persistent headache all summer, and despite the Department of the Platte's best attempts to keep it in service, and Townsend's repeated Band-Aid remedies, breaks remained common so that small patrols were needed, such as the seven-man Third Cavalry detachment ordered out on November 20 to "place it in thorough order." Fort Fetterman's commanding officer shared the responsibility for the upkeep of this line, and in November he suggested that John Hunton, a well-known local rancher, be contracted to repair the line. That proposal was overruled by Omaha; the department, at the same time, contracted with Hibbard to work over the line. He could do it at lower rates than Hunton offered and, equally important to the department, had a corps of experienced repairers while Hunton had none.[17]

Other telegraph-related business came to Evans's attention on November 20, coincidental to the dispatch of repairers on the Laramie-Fetterman line. He learned then that the Western Union Telegraph Company was assuming the salary of the Fort Laramie operator, effective November 1, 1876. Since 1867 this operator had been a civilian employee of the Quartermaster Department. John W. Ford held the post in 1876, having been in continuous service at Fort Laramie since April 1874. The Quartermaster Department took on these operational expenses when Western Union's main line was rerouted through Denver in the mid-1860s. Before this it had come through Fort Laramie, but when Western Union proposed to abandon major sections of the old line in western Nebraska and eastern Wyoming, the army agreed to take responsibility for a connection between Cheyenne and Fort Laramie as well as for that piece of original line between Laramie and Fort Fetterman. Until now the army had correctly assumed that commercial business over this wire could not sustain expenses without military subsidy. But now, with Western Union serving the Black Hills, profitability had changed and the Quartermaster Department asked the company to assume the upkeep and expenses of this important north-south line. Western Union readily concurred.[18]

On November 22 a small caravan of soldiers came into the fort from the Black Hills escorting the seriously injured First Lieutenant Adolphus H. Von Luettwitz and Private Charles Foster, both of the Third Cavalry. These soldiers had received wounds at the battle of Slim Buttes, Von Luettwitz taking a bullet through the right knee, while Foster suffered a shattered left hip and right hand. These men had

had their legs amputated and were left in the care of attendants at Crook City when the Big Horn and Yellowstone Expedition reached that point on September 17. Dr. Charles Stephens had been detailed from the expedition to attend these cavalrymen while they recovered sufficiently to leave the Hills. Meanwhile Stephens and the Big Horn and Yellowstone Expedition's chief medical officer, Major Bennett A. Clements, arranged for travel. Evans assigned the escort from Fort Laramie, and on November 1 Second Lieutenant Julius H. Pardee, Twenty-third Infantry, was ordered north to Crook City with twelve Third Cavalrymen to bring down these soldiers. Pardee was properly assigned to Sage Creek but had been detached to Wesley Merritt's command since mid-July. Clements wanted this party well equipped, and indeed it was, with a horse for Pardee, two ambulances, three six-mule wagons, camp equipment, twenty days' grain for the animals, tents for the escort, and a Sibley tent, stove, and pipe for a nighttime hospital.[19]

Private Foster's Company K, Third Cavalry, took station meanwhile at Fort Laramie, and when he arrived there Dr. Gray immediately admitted him to the hospital. Gray then examined Lieutenant Von Luettwitz and strongly recommended to headquarters that he not travel farther without the continuing services of a doctor. Evans queried Omaha on this matter, and on November 23 the department authorized travel for Dr. Stephens and one attendant as escort for Von Luettwitz. On the twenty-fifth these three men continued south for Fort D. A. Russell, pausing overnight at John Hunton's ranch at Bordeaux.[20]

Foster was not the only combat casualty bedridden in the Fort Laramie hospital, for on November 26 Private John H. Terry, Company D, Fourth Infantry, was transferred from Fort Fetterman. Terry had received a gunshot wound in the leg at the Battle of the Rosebud on June 17 and was now slowly making his way back to his company, which was stationed for the winter at Camp Robinson. Terry left the post on December 8. Foster, meanwhile, remained confined to the hospital until the following March 19, 1877, when he was discharged from the army on a surgeon's certificate of disability.[21]

On November 26 Fort Laramie learned of the death of her neighbor Jules Ecoffey at the Three Mile Ranch. This reportedly resulted from a beating in Cheyenne three months previously by a "worthless bummer known as 'Stonewall.'" Ecoffey was one of those stalwart Fort Laramie entrepreneurs from the post's early days. A confidant of Red Cloud, he had traveled to Washington with him after the 1868 treaty negotiations and had been a trader among the Oglala Sioux in the early 1870s. The *Cheyenne Daily Leader* said he had come to the territory in the 1840s when the American Fur Company was still a force in the region's economy. The revered pioneer was buried in Cheyenne on December 1.[22]

News of a different sort broke on Wednesday, November 29, when the post learned that Crook's Powder River Expedition had engaged Cheyenne Indians in northern Wyoming on November 25, capturing a major village and many horses. After leaving Fort Fetterman on November 14 this well-equipped force had traveled the now well-worn road north to the new, remote supply outpost known as Cantonment Reno. There they discovered, much to Crook's pleasure, that Captain Pollock, late of Fort Laramie, and his four-company infantry battalion were established in adequate though thoroughly unpretentious quarters. Bourke described these improvements as dugouts in the ground, palisaded with cottonwood logs and roofed over with dirt. Despite makeshift conditions, Pollock's men graciously welcomed the expedition and generally exhibited the positive outlook so common among regulars. "The officers and soldiers of the garrison were taking things philosophically," remarked Bourke, "and there was no growling or complaint of any kind."[23]

Crook's force weathered a blizzard before marching north from the cantonment on November 22. His scouts had captured a young Cheyenne warrior several days earlier and had learned from him that Crazy Horse was camped on Rosebud Creek near the battleground of June 17 and that another smaller village of Cheyennes, which the informant had come from, was situated on the upper Powder River. Then on November 23 Crook learned of yet another larger Cheyenne village in a canyon of the Big Horn Mountains on Crazy Woman's Fork of the Powder River, the very stream his command was now on. Crook immediately ordered Mackenzie to take the entire cavalry force except Egan's company, plus all the Indian scouts, and find this village.[24]

These ruins of Fort Reno (1866–68) served as an important landmark for troops campaigning in northern Wyoming. Nearby in the fall of 1876 General Sheridan established Cantonment Reno. D. S. Mitchell photograph. (U.S. Military Academy Library)

Mackenzie's force, 1,100 strong, pushed a short distance up Crazy Woman's Fork on November 24 but passed most of the day hidden in the foothills. After the moon came up that night the soldiers went on, and in the early dawn of the twenty-fifth they approached a camp containing more than 175 lodges and nearly 1,500 Indians, all of whom followed Dull Knife, an important Cheyenne leader. The attack that morning was a complete surprise, with cavalrymen and Pawnees bursting upon the village and other scouts sharpshooting from the surrounding high bluffs and cutting off the easy avenues of escape. Most Cheyennes retreated to the mountainside beyond the camp, but not before the troops had captured their pony herd and all of the village. It was a rich prize; each lodge, wrote Bourke, was "a magazine of ammunition, fixed and loose, and a depot of supplies of

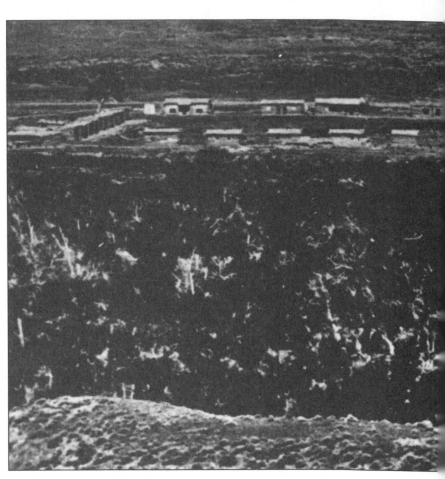

Cantonment Reno, late in 1876. This outpost, soon to be relocated and renamed Fort McKinney, represented a purposeful garrisoning of troops in the midst of

every mentionable kind." In destroying the lodges the soldiers discovered innumerable war trophies, including Seventh Cavalry relics from the Little Bighorn fight and much from the Battle of the Rosebud. Among many army horses in the herd were two mounts belonging to Egan's Company K, Second Cavalry, which had been lost in the small fight on Richard Creek, Wyoming, just six weeks before.[25]

The soldiers carried on their labors of destruction all through the night and into the morning of November 26. Their thoroughness

the Powder River country. D. S. Mitchell photograph. (U.S. Military Academy Library)

could well have been motivated by retribution as well as by Bourke's declaration that a village half destroyed was scarcely injured at all. The full loss to the Cheyennes, however, was barely comprehended at the time, and only when they began surrendering at the Red Cloud Agency weeks later did white authorities learn of the widespread suffering that resulted from the battle. It turned bitterly cold that evening, nearly thirty degrees below zero by one account, and these people had been thrown to the elements without clothing, blankets, or provisions. Eleven Cheyenne babies froze to death that night; thirty Cheyennes had been killed outright in the fight. Soldier casualties included First Lieutenant John Augustine McKinney, Fourth Cavalry and six enlisted men killed, and twenty-six others wounded.[26]

Some of the Pawnees and other scouts trailed the Cheyennes into the mountains on the twenty-sixth and nearly fell into trap. They beat a hasty retreat but had seen enough to know that the Cheyennes were "badly cut up, almost naked, without blankets, moccasins or ammunition, and hauling many wounded." Mackenzie welcomed the news, but he chose to let "General Winter" finish the episode and began a gingerly withdrawal to Crook and the infantrymen. The two commands reunited on November 28. Crook immediately sent a courier to Fort Fetterman with a telegram for Sheridan, and it was this news taken from the wire that Evans and Fort Laramie received on November 29.[27]

The *Cheyenne Daily Leader* soon carried other reports of Mackenzie's fight with Dull Knife, and also some occasional news from Montana regarding the movements of Sitting Bull and his followers, who were being harried and harassed by troops garrisoning the new cantonments on the Yellowstone River. But Evans's command paid greater attention to the more routine tasks related to servicing Fort Laramie and its two small subposts in winter. Stocks of hay and grain were replenished after Crook's departure. A major shipment of heating and cooking stoves was distributed among his immediate garrison and to the camps at Sage Creek and Red Canyon, and these outposts also received doors and window sashes. Construction was begun at the fort of two new sets of stables, which were badly needed with the increase of the cavalry complement. And the guard moved into the new grout guardhouse that had just been completed at the northeast corner of the parade ground. Soon the old stone guardhouse would be refitted to serve as the post schoolhouse and library.[28]

Word of irrational bloodletting and death continued to shock the post, however, and not always were Indians to blame. The scout and frontiersman Moses E. Milner, known locally as "California Joe," was treacherously murdered at Camp Robinson late in the fall. And on November 1 Joe Walters was killed in a fight at Cuny's Three Mile Ranch. Walters was a discharged Twenty-third Infantryman, who until recently had been an employee at the Hat Creek Ranch adjacent to the Sage Creek cantonment and now was tending bar at Cuny's. Apparently he scuffled with a freighter named Charlie or Garsy Brown, had his own gun turned on him, and was shot through the bowels.[29]

Fortunately, not all of early December's news was so grim. On the first the Cheyenne and Black Hills Telegraph Line was completed to Deadwood, and a salvo of telegrams heralded the accomplishment. The mayors of Cheyenne and Deadwood exchanged congratulations, and Deadwood's newspaper, the *Pioneer*, sent greetings to the press of the United States to mark this milestone of progress. "God bless the telegraph!" they cried. Captain Richard I. Eskridge passed through in early December, too, en route to Company H, Twenty-third Infantry, at Sage Creek. Eskridge had managed to avoid summer field service with his company but now had been ordered to return. Undoubtedly he carried unofficial news that Company H was soon to be relieved from duty in Wyoming and in a short time would leave for Indian Territory. Virtually all of the Twenty-third Infantry, in fact, was to be relieved from service in the Department of the Platte and would soon garrison posts in General Pope's Department of the Missouri.[30]

Among other recent news received at Fort Laramie was notification from Camp Robinson's post commander, Major Julius W. Mason, Third Cavalry, that two hundred recently surrendered Indian ponies were being trailed to Cheyenne for sale. When the horses reached Fort Laramie, Mason wanted Evans to ensure their transfer to the quartermaster depot in Cheyenne. This was accomplished by a special order on December 5 detailing Second Lieutenant George F. Chase and fourteen men of Company F, Third Cavalry, as escort. Chase was assigned to Company A, but he had been in and out of Forts Laramie, D. A. Russell, and McPherson on regimental business all fall.[31] Evans too received an urgent telegram from the Department of the Platte on the fifth requesting that 50,000 pounds of grain be shipped to Fort Fetterman for Crook's troops. This was part of a larger requisition from Crook of 500,000 pounds of grain. Evans and Drew, the Fort Laramie quartermaster, could spare 40,000 pounds and this was dispatched on December 6, so quickly that Omaha thanked them for their promptness.[32]

The Cheyenne and Black Hills Stage Company issued a six-month travel statement early in December. Between April 1 and November 30 the company had made seventy-two trips between Cheyenne and the Hills, carrying 556 passengers from Cheyenne to Deadwood and 344 from Cheyenne to Fort Laramie. This averaged, according to the report, 12½ passengers in each coach between Cheyenne and the fort, and better than 7⅔ per coach from the fort to Deadwood.[33] Fort Laramie also read in the Cheyenne papers of the pending court-martial of Colonel Joseph J. Reynolds and its own Captain Alexander Moore, scheduled to convene in Cheyenne about December 15. An august court was to be assembled, to include Brigadier General John Pope and Colonels John H. King, John Gibbon, Jefferson C. Davis, John E. Smith, George Sykes, Franklin F. Flint, and Alfred Sully. Among six lieutenant colonels and majors also detailed was Luther P. Bradley, one of Fort Laramie's recent commanding officers.[34]

At Sage Creek Captain Eskridge attended to the assembly of his company and its removal from Wyoming. His orders were confirmed on December 5, and he had only to await the arrival of a replacement company. Omaha arranged the transfer of Company I, Fourteenth Infantry, from Camp Robinson to replace Company H. It was planned that Eskridge utilize the baggage wagons bringing the replacement company and that he march to the Union Pacific Railroad via Camp Robinson and Sidney. He vehemently protested that route, however, saying it was longer, lacked fuel, and was generally uncharted and difficult between his post and Robinson. Omaha relented on December 12 and directed Evans to allow Eskridge to move via Fort Laramie as long as he reached the railroad in the shortest time possible. Eskridge, unfortunately, did not receive this communication. Eskridge also asked that Evans and Drew intercept any freight bound for his company and have it shipped to Omaha Barracks, where it could be packed with the heavy baggage of the company, which was soon to be en route to Fort Gibson, Indian Territory.[35]

Company I, Fourteenth Infantry, arrived at the Sage Creek Cantonment on December 12. This was a severely depleted unit, mustering only twenty-nine enlisted men for duty and none of its officers. Company I had been on the recent Big Horn and Yellowstone Expedition and as yet had not received enough recruits to return it to proper strength. Commanding the unit in lieu of its regularly assigned officers, who were either on leave or on detached service, was

Hat Creek Stage Station, Wyoming, about 1877. This combination hostelry and stage stop stood adjacent to the Fort Laramie subpost of Camp on Sage Creek. (Archives, American Heritage Center, University of Wyoming)

The Hat Creek stage station of the mid-1880s, as photographed in 1985. Nearby stood the army's 1876 Camp on Sage Creek. (Paul L. Hedren)

First Lieutenant Charles Akers Johnson, Company F, Fourteenth Infantry.[36]

Johnson and Eskridge exchanged courtesies on the twelfth, and both officers sent formal letters to Major Evans on December 13, Johnson assuming command of the post and Eskridge announcing his departure. Curiously, both letters went under the dateline "Camp at Hat Creek." Until then this station had been officially known as "Camp on Sage Creek," but Eskridge's first communication from there on December 6 carried the heading "Hat Creek." Properly this military station was on Sage Creek, a lesser tributary of the South Fork of the Cheyenne River, and there was a Hat or Warbonnet Creek thirty miles east in Nebraska, but despite the army's attempt to maintain proper distinctions, the stage station constructed there quickly became known as the Hat Creek Ranch. The army relented altogether on December 16 when the Department of the Platte directed that this station henceforth be known as "Camp on Hat Creek."[37]

Richard Eskridge's Company H, Twenty-third Infantry, with First Lieutenant George Taylor and Second Lieutenant Julius Pardee, marched south via Camp Robinson. Permission to come through Fort Laramie and Cheyenne was received well after had they reached the railroad at Sidney. Like Fort Laramie's small summer garrison, these men of Company H had provided faithful, tireless service protecting travelers, guarding telegraph construction, and ensuring relative order on the Black Hills road. They were field hardened and had contributed in their own way to the larger new order on the northern plains.[38]

In addition to the Reynolds and Moore court-martial news emanating from Cheyenne, on December 14 a general court-martial was convened at Fort Laramie to try four enlisted men. Whereas garrison courts-martial to try soldiers for lesser infractions such as fighting or drunkenness on duty were staged at Fort Laramie almost weekly, a general court-martial occurred much less frequently. Both proceedings investigated offenses against martial law, or good order and military discipline, but the differences were of degree. The garrison court-martial of Private Hugh McLean, Company C, Ninth Infantry, on March 28, for example, found him drunk and disorderly in front of the post trader's store, in violation of the sixty-second article of war, and sentenced him to forfeit to the United States five dollars of his pay for one month.[39] In December's general court-martial the convening orders originated at headquarters, Department of the Platte, to try cases of serious breach of orders, desertion, and theft. John Redmond, Company H, Twenty-third Infantry, for example, had deserted his company, taking a Springfield rifle, a gun sling, and sixty cartridges. Found guilty, he was sentenced to be dishonorably discharged, to forfeit all pay and allowances due, and to be confined at hard labor for three and one-half years. Redmond was promptly transferred to the military prison at Fort Leavenworth, Kansas.[40]

On a merrier note, Major Evans dispatched Sergeant Patrick Flood and Private Fred Weber, both of Company K, Third Cavalry, to Cheyenne on December 16 to do the "marketing for this Post for Christmas." Flood and Weber were allowed one wagon for transportation and were rationed through December 24. In addition to purchasing special provisions for the various company messes, certainly these soldiers carried long shopping lists from officers and their enlisted comrades.[41]

With winter gradually settling over Fort Laramie, it might indeed have been possible to forget, at least occasionally, that an Indian war still went on beyond the reaches of the post. The last serious raiding south of the North Platte or along the Black Hills road had occurred nearly two months earlier, before the Third Cavalry came into the post. Mackenzie's decisive fight with Dull Knife was already "old news," and increasingly the Cheyenne papers indulged in winter banter—noting the first sleigh appearing on the streets of Custer, saying that "old Santa Claus" was headquartered at the post office news depot, and reporting that owing to heavy snows, mail bound for Fort Fetterman would be routed via Cheyenne and Fort Laramie rather than Medicine Bow. But then on December 20 came news of "the Indian Creek Butchery."[42]

On Tuesday, December 19, a small civilian wagon train tended by five teamsters was camped along Indian Creek, six miles east of Camp on Hat Creek. The men were asleep in their tents when, about 9:00 P.M., they were attacked by Indians. Although the party was well armed, two whites were killed and six of the eight horses were run off before a defense could be organized. The three survivors abandoned the camp and fled to the army cantonment at Sage Creek, where they arrived about 11:00 P.M. First Lieutenant Charles Johnson responded with a squad of infantrymen and recovered the dead, one a German known only as Fritz and the other B. C. Stephens from Salt Lake City. Both had been shot and then horribly mutilated with a butcher's cleaver taken from one of the wagons. Scattered about the camp were flour, corn, and other provisions. Many eatables were gone, as were all the flour sacks and the six horses. The attackers' trail led eastward toward the Red Cloud Agency but soon petered out, "the Indians evidently scattering."[43]

Johnson brought the bodies to Hat Creek for burial and dutifully filed several reports for Major Evans on December 20. In addition to the Indian trail he had followed east from the scene of the attack, he learned of others that had been spotted or crossed by recent travelers. And on the twenty-first Evans learned that the Hat Creek–Camp Robinson mail carrier had been fired upon and his horse wounded. On making his way to Hat Creek the carrier saw "plenty of trails" beside and across the one he traveled. How much of this traffic was related to action in the Powder and Yellowstone River country, where Crook's Powder River Expedition was still active and Nelson A. Miles continued his unrelenting pursuit of the roamers, certainly neither Johnson nor Evans was in a position to measure. But surrenders at the agencies remained fairly steady in late December and early January, particularly as scattered bands of Cheyennes came in, many of whom had recently been devastated by Mackenzie's troops at Crazy Woman's Fork.[44]

The Stephens and Fritz killings remained a subject of curiosity and discussion well beyond the relative significance of the event. Perhaps this was a slow period for news, but the *Daily Leader,* in one of its several reports of the incident, suggested that the recent butchery was not the outrage of Indians but had been perpetrated by horse thieves led by Persimmon Bill. Bill had been the scourge of the Black Hills road the previous spring but seemed to have dropped out of sight after that. A letter from Major Julius Mason at Camp Robinson, however, confirmed that twenty Cheyennes had indeed attacked the train and killed the men. At least one of the wagons from the scene was later exhibited at a corral in Cheyenne. A wagon might otherwise be hardly worthy of a thought, but as the *Daily Sun* expressed it, this one "contained the imprint of one hundred and sixty bullets."[45]

Christmas and New Year came and went with little, if any, fanfare at Fort Laramie. If any diarist recorded temperatures and the weather, fair or foul, as Luther P. Bradley had done a year earlier, none of this information seems to have survived. At the transition Evans commanded a garrison slightly larger than Bradley's—seven companies present for duty December 31, 1875, versus a December 31, 1876, tally of seven companies in post, one on the rolls but detached to Crook's Powder River Expedition, and two more companies garrisoning subposts on the Black Hills road. Certainly the complexion of the garrison had changed, from an infantry regimental headquarters post complete with five companies of foot to a cavalry regimental head-quarters station. This deployment, of course, better suited General Crook's desire to have mounted troops near troublesome areas like the Black Hills road and the Nebraska agencies.

The post's winter routine was little changed from the norm of many previous years. The frantic movement of supplies as part of Crook's campaign had subsided, but there was still traffic on the roads in and out of the fort. The telegraph required constant maintenance—at year's end both the Cheyenne and Fort Fetterman lines were down at the same time.[46] Word had come too that Crook's Powder River Expedition was returning by way of Fort Fetterman. Crazy Horse's Sioux had led Crook a lively chase, but the weather was simply too harsh to permit effective movement.

One minor problem that erupted early in January 1877 had nothing to do with the routine of the war, the telegraph, or the gold rush. The reduction of the post's official reservation the previous August had opened a question of boundary description, and on a tract along the left bank of the North Platte squatters had taken up residence. Particularly annoying was John J. McGinnis, who was settled well within what Evans considered the proper reservation. McGinnis, moreover, had opened a whiskey shop and prominently displayed a license issued by the U.S. Internal Revenue Collector for Wyoming to retail liquors and tobacco "one and one half miles from Fort Laramie." As Evans pointedly asked the assistant adjutant general in Omaha, what right did a United States official have to grant a license to trade on a military reservation?[47]

McGinnis proved a considerable thorn to Major Evans. He was brought into the post on January 1 on the charge of stealing government hay, but before the issue could be resolved the major received a clarification on the reservation question and at once dispatched Captain Deane Monahan, officer of the day, to remove the liquor-peddling squatter. Evans's order, in a letter dated January 6, 1877, is revealing:

Captain

You will proceed with a mounted detachment of one noncommissioned officer and eight (8) privates and with one or more wagons, to the hut recently erected upon the reservation of this Post by one

Maginnis—taking the said Maginnis with you under guard, and you will load all the effects of the squatter upon the wagons, using also his own wagon if there be one, and remove the effects and family beyond the limits of the reservation—upon the west side—you will be particular to see that all whiskies or other liquors are removed. You will seize all stolen public property you may find there, and then turn it over to the Quartermaster. You will arrest all enlisted men you may find there, without passes. You will effectually tear down the hut or house erected by the squatter, Maginnis, so as to render it impossible to occupy it as a residence, and should the material of which it is composed appear to have been cut on the reservation or stolen from the Post—you will not permit the removal of the same—but should such seem to be private property, it may be removed by the claimant.[48]

McGinnis was brought to Cheyenne on the hay charge, and a reporter for the *Daily Sun* assembled a damning report about the man. McGinnis apparently had run afoul of the law in Iowa and had served a term in the Fort Madison penitentiary. He was subsequently in and out of trouble in Omaha and then drifted on to Cheyenne early in 1876, where he crossed the law again, this time for his involvement with a stolen-property fencing operation. Although tried and convicted, he was acquitted in a retrial and next appeared on the Fort Laramie military reservation selling whiskey to soldiers. Evans handily resolved the problem, and Monahan followed his directive to the letter, removing McGinnis to Cottonwood Creek, where he eventually established the Ten Mile Ranch to serve Black Hills traffic. The stage stopped there only out of necessity, however. Meanwhile, McGinnis's young daughter Elizabeth attended school at Fort Laramie in 1876 and 1877. On the occasion of a return to the fort in 1950 she fondly remembered various building locations and such personalities as John Collins and Leodegar Schnyder among many others prominent at a later time. If she alluded to or even knew of her father's misdeeds, no mention appears in the interview.[49]

General Crook's Powder River Expedition came into Fort Fetterman on December 29, received assignments to various stations throughout the department and elsewhere, and then went on to Fort Laramie, where the troops arrived and encamped January 4, 1877.

The expedition formally disbanded at Fort Laramie, with Mackenzie's six Fourth Cavalry companies returning to Camp Robinson on
the seventh and most of the remaining troops continuing to Cheyenne. The special order dispersing the troops sent Egan's Company
K, Second Cavalry, to Fort Fred Steele, Major Edwin Townsend to
Omaha Barracks, and civilian physician Charles V. Petteys to Fort
D. A. Russell. The same order relieved the remaining Twenty-third
Infantry companies from duty in the Department of the Platte and
sent them to Kansas, and it also returned the battalion of Fourth
Artillerymen to San Francisco. When all was settled, Crook's department had effectively gained half a regiment of cavalry from its pre-
war strength. Crook also gained the mobility of another full regiment
of horse, the Fifth Cavalry, in exchange for the Twenty-third Infantry, which was sent to General Pope's Department of the Missouri.[50]

Crook, Mackenzie, and a number of the headquarters officers,
meanwhile, had left Fetterman for Cheyenne by the cutoff road. On
the way they saw a detachment of cavalry from Fort Laramie repairing the Fetterman-Laramie telegraph line, and they passed New Year's
Day struggling through heavy snowdrifts in the Chugwater valley. The
officers reached Cheyenne on January 3 flushed with the successes of
their recent campaign, "which commenced with surrounding Red
Cloud's Indians, and ended with giving the Cheyennes a disastrous
surprise."[51]

Crook's business in Cheyenne was varied. Although the prospect
of a renewed campaign in the spring seems to have been a consistent
thought, certainly there was a sense that the Great Sioux War was
coming to an end. As the *Daily Sun* reported it, "but a small force of
troops will be needed in the spring for this purpose, and it is even
doubted whether the hostiles will be able to muster another regular
campaign." Surrenders at the Nebraska agencies and along the Yellowstone and Missouri rivers continued with pronounced regularity.
And those Sioux and Cheyennes "still defiant toward the government were scattered in small bands, starving, harassed, and seeking
only to evade capture." In the last campaign, moreover, Crook had
successfully enlisted heretofore hostile Sioux and Cheyennes to fight
their brethren, and this unquestionably had a demoralizing effect on
the northern roamers.[52]

Beyond plotting the renewal and conclusion of the Sioux War,

Crook returned to participate in the Joseph J. Reynolds and Alexander Moore courts-martial, which were finally about to convene at Cheyenne's Inter-Ocean Hotel. Most of the trial officers and witnesses were rooming at the same hotel, and as they waited for the proceedings to begin they found ample occasion to exchange social courtesies throughout the community and at nearby Fort D. A. Russell and Cheyenne Depot. They were also able to view such curiosities as the latest delivery of Black Hills gold at the Stebbins, Post and Company bank, including one nugget weighing sixty-five ounces, and to enjoy specially arranged concerts by the Fifth Cavalry Regimental Band.[53]

The Reynolds and Moore courts-martial remained the last unfinished business from the very opening movements of the Sioux War of 1876. The Third Cavalry colonel faced a battery of charges ranging from disobeying orders, misbehavior before the enemy, and conduct to the prejudice of good order and military discipline through conduct unbecoming an officer and a gentleman. Testimony began January 8, and it was a bitter struggle throughout. Reynolds, confident of his innocence, engaged in cross-examination and in many acrimonious exchanges, including a stinging attack on General Crook for dividing the command and for failing to cooperate with him. Witnesses were heard in the morning, and the daily session usually adjourned early in the afternoon. At a break on January 13 the members of the court posed for a group photograph by D. S. Mitchell. Crook and his wife, who had come from Omaha, also sat for the photographer.[54]

During some long delays in the Reynolds trial owing to the unavailability of certain witnesses, testimony was begun January 16 in the Moore case. Moore faced two charges: disobeying orders and misbehavior before the enemy. Testimony for and against the captain, and final statements in the Reynolds trial, were heard through January 19, and then both cases were closed and the proceedings sealed pending the customary reviews. Reynolds was subsequently found guilty of all charges and was sentenced to be suspended from rank and command for one year. Moore likewise was found guilty of conduct to the prejudice of good order and military discipline, though he was acquitted on the charge of disobeying orders, and was sen-

Members of the general court-martial convened in Cheyenne on January 5, 1877, to try Joseph J. Reynolds and Alexander Moore for their failure at the Powder River fight on March 17, 1876. *Left to right, front row:* Colonel George Sykes, Twentieth Infantry; Colonel Jefferson C. Davis, Twenty-third Infantry; Colonel John H. King, Ninth Infantry; Brigadier General John Pope; Colonel John Gibbon, Seventh Infantry; Colonel John E. Smith, Fourteenth Infantry; Colonel Franklin F. Flint, Fourth Infantry. *Second row, left to right:* Major David G. Swain, judge advocate; Lieutenant Colonel David Huston, Sixth Infantry; Lieutenant Colonel Luther P. Bradley, Ninth Infantry; Lieutenant Colonel Pinkney Lugenbeel, First Infantry; Lieutenant Colonel Amos Beckwith, assistant commissary general of subsistence; Major George D. Ruggles, assistant adjutant general. D. S. Mitchell photograph. (Geo. V. Allen)

tenced to be suspended from command and confined to the limits of his post, Fort Laramie, for the same period. These sentences were later remitted by President Grant, but both officers were disgraced. Reynolds retired from the army on June 25, 1877, on account of disability; Moore never overcame the stigma and resigned his commission in 1879.[55]

This news from Cheyenne was a curious but temporary diversion from other matters pressing at Fort Laramie. On January 3, for instance, a "robbery" occurred at the post. Details of what might better have been called a theft or burglary are sketchy, but fourteen new Colt revolvers and fourteen sabers were taken from the post's ordnance storeroom. A prompt investigation headed by Captains Munson and Monahan and Lieutenant John C. Thompson suggested that these weapons were headed for the Black Hills, and Major Evans alerted the commanding officer at Red Canyon to search any suspicious vehicles passing that location.[56]

At nearly the same time Lieutenant Rufus Brown, then commanding the Red Canyon subpost, notified Evans that Dr. R. M. Reynolds was suffering greatly from delirium tremens, and the lieutenant was unsure that he would recover. Could Evans send a physician to help? Reynolds's difficulty with liquor was already a matter of record, and quickly Evans ordered Dr. A. P. Frick at Hat Creek to go north and investigate. He also applied to Omaha for a permanent replacement. Several days later acting assistant surgeon Albert Chenoweth, now at Camp Robinson, was ordered to Hat Creek for duty, and Lieutenant Brown was advised that upon Chenoweth's arrival Reynolds's contract was to be annulled for drunkenness.[57]

This medical concern at Red Canyon became a lesser issue compared with occurrences on the telegraph line between Forts Laramie and Fetterman. Evans had recently detailed two small squads of soldiers from the garrison to put various sections of the line in order, and he had another nine-man detachment from Company A, Third Cavalry, who had just escorted a trainload of supplies from the Phillips ranch to Fetterman, return along the line to make additional repairs. Corporal Charles A. Bessey commanded these troopers from Company A, and on Elkhorn Creek about fifty miles from Fort Laramie he discovered fresh traces of Indians. To avoid a surprise in camp, Bessey and three others made a reconnaissance, and about midnight they collided with a party of twenty raiders. A sharp fight ensued in the early hours of January 13. Bessey and Privates William Featherall and James Taggart were wounded and three army horses were killed before the Indians withdrew.[58]

News of the fight was rushed to Fort Laramie, and Evans immediately dispatched Captain Deane Monahan and every available trooper of Company G, Third Cavalry, in pursuit. Monahan took an ambulance as well, to remove the wounded soldiers to the care of Dr.

Hartsuff and Dr. Gray at the post hospital. Owing to a severe snowstorm no trail was found, but Monahan scouted the country to the mountains and returned to the post on January 17.[59]

An official report of the Elkhorn Creek fight was transmitted to Omaha and eventually came to General Crook's attention. He was much pleased by the bravery these cavalrymen had shown, and he publicly commended them in general orders published on March 16, 1877. The gallant fight on January 13 against a largely superior force of hostile Indians "is referred to as an example worthy of praise and imitation," he wrote. Notwithstanding the odds, and despite their wounds, the little band of soldiers had fought valiantly. Bessey and his complement were to be "thanked and commended for their behavior upon this trying occasion," the approbation concluded.[60]

The raiders, meanwhile, next appeared January 16 at several of the Chugwater ranches, where they stole thirty-one horses. Their trail led northwestward toward Laramie Peak. Another party, or perhaps a splinter from the larger band, was also observed on the Fort Laramie road on January 17. On January 23 raiders attacked the mail carrier working between Hat Creek and the Red Cloud Agency, but he escaped unharmed. Travelers also reported sighting other small parties of Indians on the road north of Sage Creek.[61]

This increase in Indian traffic annoyed Evans, but at least it had an answer. Repairing the telegraph line was even more irksome. Evans had to tolerate some of this, of course. He knew that portions of the line were aged and that routine servicing was a task no different from daily fatigues or escort service. Telegraph repair, however, was a duty shared with neighboring commands, and on January 13 he vented his anger at the lack of cooperation shown by the commanding officer at Fort Fetterman. He was "constantly compelled to put repair parties upon the telegraph line" to that post, Evans scolded, and "on at least three different occasions the 'break' has been found within 3 miles of Fort Fetterman; once at least within sight of the Post, and almost always on the Fetterman half of the line. I think it only fair that Fetterman should keep half the line in repair and indeed believe that there is a Dept. order to that effect."[62]

As for the increased Indian traffic, perhaps most was correctly attributed to the continuing surrenders of northern roamers at the Nebraska agencies. Several factors were involved. Certainly the recent field successes of Mackenzie and Nelson A. Miles had had a devastating impact on the warring camps. Dull Knife's Northern Cheyennes had suffered terribly before reaching Crazy Horse's camp in mid-December, and there was no safety with either Crazy Horse's or Sitting Bull's people. From the new Tongue River Cantonment Colonel Miles's Fifth Infantrymen had sparred with the Sioux and Cheyennes repeatedly in December and early January and had engaged in a pitched battle on January 8 in Montana's Wolf Mountains. Moderates in the northern camps pointed to this suffering as the inevitable consequence of prolonging the war.[63]

At the same time, authorities were carefully cultivating influential leaders among the agency Sioux to act as peace talkers. They hoped that these spokesmen, motivated by a deep concern for the welfare of their people, would travel to the warring camps, have extensive talks with the fighting chiefs, and persuade them to surrender. Several attempts from the Red Cloud Agency in October and November 1876 had been unsuccessful. But Camp Robinson's commander Major Julius Mason, Third Cavalry, had successfully befriended Spotted Tail, and by early January that Brule leader was prepared to locate Crazy Horse's camp and convince him to come in. This initiative, soon to be duplicated at other Sioux agencies, was clearly emerging as the leading alternative to further campaigning. As winter turned to spring, this struggle for supremacy and control over the northern plains had nearly run its course. And by hindsight one can appreciate the overwhelming success and speed with which the peace talkers closed this horrible war.[64]

Chapter Eight

War's End:
A Fort Laramie Perspective

When we compare the early months of 1877 with January, February, and March 1876, the difference of one year is astonishing. For most of the centennial year, and certainly at its start, the northern plains were the focus of national attention. The gold rush to the Black Hills had blossomed in the best tradition of an American bonanza. Newspapers carried multiple stories about the goldfields and the natural advantages of getting there by way of the West's "magic city," Cheyenne. Indeed, that community's boosterism had worked, and the greatest wave headed for the new El Dorado funneled directly through Cheyenne and on to Custer and Deadwood.

Simultaneously the great Indian war to determine final control of the whole northern plains had also captivated the nation. Locally the Fort Laramie garrison, like nearly every other military post in the entire Division of the Missouri, made plans to join the campaigns. But remarkably, twelve months later this dual-faceted fever of gold and war had almost disappeared. Travel to and from the Black Hills remained steady, but in 1877 it could better be characterized as civilized business traffic, not a boom-or-bust run. And the Sioux war too had nearly run its course. In early 1877 talk at Fort Laramie centered more on drills, finishing the new cavalry stables, the monotonous repairs to the telegraph, and almost incidentally, on mop-up activities related to various campaigns. Not all the northern roamers had surrendered, and raiders were still to be seen on the horizons. But the army was clearly not anticipating a second year of fighting, and for most of the issues still to be resolved in 1877, Camp Robinson was responsible, not Fort Fetterman or Fort Laramie.

Indeed, the Great Sioux War was nearly finished. Nelson Miles's Montana troops had borne the brunt of the war's final fury. Operating from a new cantonment at the confluence of the Tongue and Yellowstone rivers, his infantrymen had ruthlessly hounded Sitting Bull's and Crazy Horse's followers throughout the winter. At the same time parlays between the military and the free roamers became ever more common and peace factions within the warring camps grew steadily stronger. The strength of these villages continued to erode, and by spring bands large and small had surrendered to the army and were settled at the Sioux agencies. Sitting Bull's midwinter decision to quit the war and lead his Hunkpapas to Canada further reduced the roamers' numbers. Crazy Horse's Oglalas remained the last large group of Teton Sioux to be dealt with, and Spotted Tail, the widely respected Brule leader, would soon take on that charge, as would, ultimately, Red Cloud.[1]

After several unsuccessful attempts to talk the raiders' camps into surrender, by mid-January 1877 attention was diverted to Chief Spotted Tail, General Crook's proclaimed leader of all the Brule and Oglala Sioux and an uncle of Crazy Horse. Initially Spotted Tail would not undertake a mission to these warring camps. Although friendly to the whites, he was not a yes-man for the army, and he fretted about espousing the standard terms of unconditional surrender, knowing of the government's desire to relocate the Brules and Oglalas to new Missouri River agencies or even to the dreaded Indian Territory. General Crook himself traveled to the agencies in late January, principally to induce Spotted Tail to travel as a peace talker. The chief remained reluctant until February 9, when runners came to the agency bearing word that the roamers would surrender, but only if Spotted Tail would visit them as Crook's representative. Carrying the general's personal promise that he would do all in his power to get these Sioux an agency of their own in their own country, Spotted Tail led 250 Brule warriors north to find the war chiefs. Other peace talkers carried similar messages to the Cheyennes and smaller northern camps.[2]

Negotiations had finally supplanted fighting. Small parties from the north slipped into the agency camps with increasing frequency in February. In March several larger groups, including more than 260 impoverished Cheyennes, appeared at the Red Cloud Agency.[3] Crook, meanwhile, returned to the more commodious Fort Laramie to await the results of Spotted Tail's mission. There Bourke confided to his diary not about the war, but about Major Evans's devoting much of the winter to daily drills and other instruction and about how his troops had markedly improved.[4]

Bourke committed several diary pages to a description of Fort Laramie during this two-month stay. The daily routine was, all things considered, "rather monotonous." He and his department companions regularly attended guard mount, visited the headquarters stables at the old fortified quartermaster corral to see that their horses were properly cared for, and devoted several morning hours and most of the afternoons to departmental correspondence. The lieutenant and his friends were often enticed to afternoon open-air concerts presented by the Third Cavalry Regimental Band, and they enjoyed regular use of the post library as well as the book collections maintained by Company E, Third Cavalry, and Company C, Ninth Infantry. Bourke also made repeated mention of Evans's attempts to divert the Laramie River channel away from the fort. The river had been cutting dangerously close to the south and southeast corners of the original quadrangle, and Evans ordered construction of a diversionary dam using worn-out wagons filled with stone and scrap iron, tied together with logging chain.[5]

General Crook was in and out of the post during February, March, and April. For several days during the first part of March he traveled to Cheyenne to confer with General Sheridan, but by the eleventh he was back at Fort Laramie in time to depart with his aide Lieutenant Walter Schuyler, along with Colonel Mackenzie, Lieutenants Henry W. Lawton, Fourth Cavalry, and John C. Thompson, Third Cavalry, and John Collins, to hunt on Laramie Peak. Hunting remained Crook's favorite recreation.[6]

Crook had returned to the fort by April 4 when news from Spotted Tail was received from First Lieutenant Jesse M. Lee at the Spotted Tail Agency. The chief, returning from his mission to the north, reported that he had spoken with many influential war leaders and

First Lieutenant John G. Bourke, Crook's aide-de-camp, dressed in a unique scouting outfit for the winter operation of 1876–77. Practicality in clothing took precedence over parade-ground order during Indian campaigning. (U.S. Military Academy Library)

had convinced most of them to surrender. Some, in fact, returned with Spotted Tail, and other small groups began to arrive almost daily thereafter. Spotted Tail had not seen Crazy Horse, however, for he had refused to meet with his uncle face to face. Red Cloud, meanwhile, had opened his own discussions with First Lieutenant William P. Clark, Second Cavalry, Crook's emissary at Camp Robinson. Through the course of the Sioux War, Red Cloud had been the object of scorn and extreme caution. So questionable were his motives and loyalties that Crook had stripped him of all authority. Now, after Spotted Tail had failed to deliver Crazy Horse and had not even seen him but only conversed with his father, Red Cloud offered to find this last holdout and urge his surrender.[7]

Like Spotted Tail, Red Cloud was an uncle to Crazy Horse. Perhaps more important, he was an Oglala, not a Brule. Crook understood the nuances, and with northern Indians coming in regularly and Red Cloud now offering a reasonable prospect of bringing in Crazy Horse and his followers, this mission was promptly endorsed. Red Cloud set out with sixty-four well-equipped followers on April 11. Crook, meanwhile, headed for Camp Robinson on April 10, and for the next several weeks he and his staff paid careful heed to the surrenders taking place at the two agencies. Bourke at first gave them considerable detailed attention in his diary, but by late April he wrote "it has become so ordinary an occurrence, that I chronicle it as a matter of course and not as of special significance." Crook participated mostly as an observer, but he personally accepted the surrender of six Cheyenne chiefs when they came into Red Cloud in mid-April. These people had participated in the Dull Knife fight on November 25, and many showed the harsh effects of that clash. Finally on April 27 Crook received the heartening news that Red Cloud had spoken to Crazy Horse and that he too at last was coming in.[8]

General Crook, by a twist of fate, was called to Washington on April 28, reportedly to speak for Red Cloud and Spotted Tail on the relocation matter, and so he was not present for Crazy Horse's surrender. Crazy Horse, meanwhile, had moved to a small tributary of the South Cheyenne River, seventy-five or eighty miles northwest of the agency. His people were coming slowly down the Powder River Trail and would be at Red Cloud in eight or nine days. Red Cloud had reported that Crazy Horse's followers were starving, and a large issue of live beef and hardcrackers was dispatched to his camp, situated by then nearer the little Fort Laramie subpost on Sage Creek. Second Lieutenant J. Wesley Rosenquest, Fourth Cavalry, commanded this small relief party. On meeting the great Sioux leader Rosenquest shook his hand; he is alleged to be the first white man ever to do so.[9]

Crazy Horse announced that he would come into the Red Cloud Agency on Sunday, May 6. That morning Lieutenant Clark, who was again Crook's chosen representative at the agency, went out to meet the powerful leader. They smoked a pipe and shook hands. As a token of goodwill, Clark was presented with gifts. Then Crazy Horse and his people came into the agency. The procession was impressive. Crazy Horse and his chiefs Little Big Man, Little Hawk, He Dog, Old Hawk, and Big Road led the parade. Next came the various warrior societies, each man dressed in his best. Then came the old men, women, and children. All told, Crazy Horse's camp numbered 899 people, including 217 men, 312 women, 186 boys, and 184 girls. They set up 146 tipis. Clark and one other man led a search of the lodges that evening and netted 117 firearms. Thomas Moore, Crook's chief packer, seized the ponies and mules. Bourke thought they could not have numbered fewer than 2,200.[10]

The significance of Crazy Horse's surrender was quickly appreciated by the witnesses at Red Cloud Agency and Camp Robinson, but the symbolism was probably lost to everyone. By Bourke's reckoning nearly 4,500 Indians had surrendered at the two agencies since January. Of these, half belonged to Crazy Horse's extended camp and to the Miniconjous and Sans Arcs who had surrendered at Spotted Tail. The remaining 2,250 were Cheyennes and Sioux from other non-agency bands. Only fifty lodges belonging to the Miniconjou chief Lame Deer and the followers of the Hunkpapa medicine man Sitting Bull remained beyond government control. To all intents, Crazy Horse's surrender concluded the war. Just as important, his final triumphant entry on May 6 ended a proud, centuries-old life-style and marked the dawning of a new age.[11]

The Fort Laramie garrison did not participate in the Indian surrenders at the agencies. With the current disposition of troops leaving a much-strengthened complement at Camp Robinson, and with Mackenzie's Fourth Cavalry still camped nearby, Evans had only to attend to routine business. He had already grappled with a fiscal problem arising out of the 1876 campaigns. The Department of the Platte had a budgetary ceiling for army transportation expenses. Yet the costs of serving Crook's far-flung field commands, as well as a new cantonment in the Powder River country and a score of military posts like Fort Laramie that had to be maintained almost entirely by contract teams, collectively had driven charges well beyond the monthly allotments. Although Lieutenant Colonel Robert Williams, Crook's assistant adjutant general, petitioned General Sheridan to intercede on the department's behalf, the immediate outcome was a forced reduction of quartermaster employees throughout the Department.[12]

When the transportation crisis came to a head in mid-December 1876, Fort Laramie carried thirty-one quartermaster employees on its rolls at a cost of $1,285 per month, the second-highest monthly expense in the department, following only Camp Robinson, with forty-six quartermaster employees and a monthly expense of $1,875. The resolution at Fort Laramie was a directive to discharge one civilian blacksmith, one civilian saddler, one quartermaster agent, and all the civilian teamsters now employed at the post and to replace them with extra duty men assigned from the enlisted ranks. Thereafter, from January through December 1877, Fort Laramie's quartermaster rolls exceeded five employees only once.[13]

Major Evans also dealt with several field emergencies in February. The first was Indian-related but not of a customary kind. With Indian ponies being surrendered in considerable numbers at the Red Cloud and Spotted Tail agencies, they fell easy prey to horse thieves who were drawn to the White River country. Three such incorrigibles ran off thirty ponies from Red Cloud about February 1, and since their trail angled southwestward as if toward Cheyenne, Evans was ordered to intervene. On February 2 he dispatched Second Lieutenant Henry Rowan Lemly, Third Cavalry, and twenty-five cavalrymen to capture them. Lemly scouted down the North Platte River and intercepted the thieves. After a spirited chase he captured two, as well as twenty-four of the ponies, but the third raider managed to escape owing to the "superior fleetness of his horse." Lemly was duly complimented by Evans and later Crook for his "energy, zeal and efficiency" in the "suppression of a dangerous class of scoundrels who prey upon Indians and white men alike."[14]

Indian raiding parties were also seen twice more in February, though not thereafter. On February 9 First Lieutenant Alexander D. B. Smead and thirty-three Third Cavalrymen pursued Indians who had attacked a ranch on Horse Creek, thirty miles north of Cheyenne. On February 25 Second Lieutenants Bainbridge Reynolds and Francis A. Hardie led twenty cavalrymen after raiders sighted north of the fort on the Black Hills road. Both columns returned in due course without finding any Indians.[15]

In addition to these sorties, Evans maintained a small squad of soldiers at the Phillips ranch in the Chugwater valley. This detail, usually numbering ten to twelve soldiers, was the continuation of an assignment begun the previous summer when Major Townsend commanded the post, and it had originated in reaction to nearly continual Indian raids in this populated valley. During Evans's tenure Indian sightings had almost subsided, yet perhaps for mere psychological value, small Third Cavalry patrols were rotated to this ranch well into the spring.[16]

As the Indian situation wound down in early 1877, so too did the Black Hills gold rush, and transportation and travel patterns to the mines changed. As yet not every creek bottom in the Hills had been thoroughly prospected, but the easy wealth available to placer miners was giving way to capital-intensive hard-rock ventures underwritten by eastern investors. Black Hills towns, too, were maturing. Those built on the dreams of quick riches faded fast, but commercial centers like Custer City, Deadwood, and Rapid City, situated on main travel thoroughfares, steadily gained population.[17]

For another decade the Cheyenne to Deadwood road remained an important route to the Black Hills. Its natural advantages of railroad transportation to Cheyenne, the substantial iron bridge at Fort Laramie, and commercial stage service on the Cheyenne–Black Hills road made an unbeatable combination, rivaled at best by service out of Sidney, Nebraska, and to much lesser extent by connections along the Missouri River. In late March the Cheyenne and Black Hills Stage, Mail, and Express Company was making daily runs from the "magic city" to the gold towns. In April the company added regular night service and successfully negotiated for the government mail contract.[18]

Stage engineers, however, had laid out and were rapidly completing a shorter route from the Hat Creek station to Deadwood. Until now the road extended from Hat Creek northeast through Red Canyon and Pleasant Valley to Custer City, and from there north to Deadwood. In June 1877 this old route was abandoned in favor of a shorter trail that skirted the western Black Hills, passed through the site of the Jenney Stockade, a remnant of the 1875 government-sponsored exploration, and from there went northeast to Deadwood. By way of Custer City, the distance from Cheyenne to Deadwood was 311 miles; using the new route it was 266 miles. Travel time via the shortened route averaged from fifty to fifty-two hours; occasionally trips were made in as little as forty-seven hours.[19]

The abandonment of the Red Canyon stage route had major implications for the lone infantry company residing at the mouth of the canyon. In April General Crook had already asked Captain Collier, commanding the subpost, whether it should be maintained. Collier answered yes, suggesting it be continued at least through the coming summer.[20] By late May, however, the decision was made to abandon the subpost, and telegrams were sent from Fort Laramie in early June to orchestrate the removal of public stores and transfer Collier's Company K, Fourth Infantry, to Fort Bridger, where it had come from in June 1876. Over the winter of 1876–77 Camp Mouth of Red Canyon had taken on an air of permanence, with several log buildings replacing the canvas shelters protecting the soldiers and with two company laundresses and four children also taking up residence. Before the small garrison marched south in June these buildings were stripped of doors, windows, and reclaimable lumber, and that property, along with all quartermaster and commissary stores, was transferred to Camp on Hat Creek. The dismantling and packing went rapidly. By June 13 the station was officially abandoned, and Collier's company marched down the now familiar Cheyenne road, a highway they had helped establish and make safe.[21]

On June 17 Company K, Fourth Infantry, was officially dropped from Fort Laramie's "attached garrison." The men spent that night at the fort, and by June 25 they were encamped at Fort D. A. Russell. On the twenty-sixth they returned to their Fort Bridger barracks after an easy ride on the Union Pacific Railroad across Wyoming.[22]

The small army cantonment on Sage Creek, better known by the misleading name Camp on Hat Creek, did not experience the same abrupt loss of mission as had occurred at Red Canyon, at least not for another half-year. Hat Creek remained a pivotal location on the Black Hills road. Although the garrison no longer contended with warring Indians or telegraph construction, there was a midsummer upsurge in harassment of road agents. The army's effort to trap and capture highwaymen was predictable, and Major Evans went so far as to offer the stage company a guard of two infantrymen for every coach whenever asked.[23]

At the end of June 1877 Evans rotated the Hat Creek garrison. Company I, Fourteenth Infantry, commanded by First Lieutenant Frank Taylor, had been in residence for the previous six months. On June 22 First Lieutenant Smead and twenty men from Company F, Third Cavalry, were ordered north from Fort Laramie to replace Taylor, and on their arrival at the subpost the infantrymen proceeded to Camp Douglas, Utah Territory. The soldiers marched by way of Fort Laramie, passing through on June 30, and camped that evening at the Six Mile Ranch southwest of the post. The remaining men of Company F, led by their captain, Alexander Moore, joined Smead's detachment in mid-July and remained at Hat Creek into December, when that outpost too was officially and rather unceremoniously abandoned.[24]

The closing of the Red Canyon subpost, the redirection of attention at Hat Creek from warring Indians to stage robbers, the ceaseless two- and three-man sorties after breaks in the telegraph wire, and other relatively commonplace functions became, collectively, the ultimate indication that by summer Fort Laramie had shifted from the intensity of wartime service to the mundane predictability of household business, or what the army tended to call the "usual guard, garrison, and escort duties." There remained, in fact, but one more Sioux War episode to play out in Fort Laramie's world. This final tragedy unfolded not in the shadows of Laramie Peak, but seventy-three miles northeast at Camp Robinson.

Since surrendering in May, Crazy Horse and his Oglala Sioux followers had led a cautiously detached existence near the Red Cloud

Agency. In some measure the chief had grown reconciled to agency life, but more often his sullen disposition caused many to fear that he was plotting trouble. As the conqueror of Crook at the Rosebud and a leader against Custer at the Little Bighorn, Crazy Horse was easily the most glamorous leader in all the Sioux camps. But his widespread appeal among the young warriors was matched by an equally strong reserve shared by most Indian leaders, even those in Crazy Horse's own camp. Some even warned the whites that Crazy Horse was wholly unreconstructed and, if given a chance to resume his wild life in the north, would flee without hesitation. The army by this time was involved with the Nez Perce outbreak in the Northwest, and efforts were made in Nebraska to enlist Sioux scouts to chase these mountain people. Crazy Horse, however, was sure that these scouts would instead be used to hunt down Sitting Bull, and he demanded that the Sioux stay home. In the same breath he threatened to take his own followers and head north.[25]

Alarmed, Lieutenant Colonel Luther Bradley, now commanding at Camp Robinson, requested additional cavalry from Fort Laramie and queried General Sheridan about a course of action. During this exchange General Crook was traveling on a westbound Union Pacific train to the Nez Perce front. Sheridan intercepted Crook before he reached Sidney and ordered him to personally investigate the situation at Red Cloud. "The surrender or capture of 'Joseph' in that direction is but a small matter compared with what might happen to the frontier from a disturbance at Red Cloud," Sheridan admonished. Only a month earlier Ranald Mackenzie's six Fourth Cavalry companies had been relieved from their duty in Nebraska and returned to the Military Department of the Missouri, so Sheridan ordered Major Evans to dispatch two of his cavalry companies to bolster Bradley's command. Evans reacted quickly, and on September 1 Major Julius W. Mason, who had commanded Camp Robinson the previous winter but was now reassigned to Fort Laramie, marched immediately with Companies E and G, Third Cavalry, led by Second Lieutenant Lemly and by Captain Deane Monahan.[26]

At Camp Robinson Major Mason took charge of an eight-company cavalry battalion. Crook had concluded that Crazy Horse must be arrested, and he ordered Bradley to take him prisoner. He then dashed off for Cheyenne, content that "everything at the agency is perfectly quiet and will remain so." On the morning of September 4 Mason's soldiers and another four hundred Sioux, including Red Cloud, American Horse, and Little Wound, all in the charge of Lieutenant William P. Clark, approached Crazy Horse's village six or seven miles below the post. They found the camp broken up and the occupants mostly scattered. Crazy Horse had escaped alone and was headed for the Spotted Tail Agency. There friendly Indians arrested him on September 5, and he was brought under a loose military guard to Camp Robinson.[27]

Few at Camp Robinson knew that Crook intended for Crazy Horse to be immediately imprisoned at the post and then to be quickly and secretly removed to Cheyenne, where he was to be sent by train to Florida for incarceration. Not suspecting the gravity of his own situation, Crazy Horse, joined now by hundreds of his followers, was the center of attention as he rode through Camp Robinson. He still carried a pistol and two knives. When he and his escort pulled up before the adjutant's office, which stood adjacent to the camp guardhouse, they were met by the officer of the day, Captain James Kennington, Fourteenth Infantry. Thinking that he was secure and would soon meet with Lieutenant Colonel Bradley or a higher military authority, Crazy Horse went with Kennington into the guardhouse. Apparently only then did the great Oglala realize that he was to be imprisoned. In a mighty fury he drew one of his knives and stabbed at the captain. In the scuffle that ensued, a member of the guard, Private William Gentles, Company F, Fourteenth Infantry, mortally wounded Crazy Horse with a bayonet lunge.[28]

Crazy Horse died about midnight, September 5, 1877. John G. Bourke, one of the most astute chroniclers of these important times, offered perhaps the most poignant eulogy, as applicable to the war itself as to one of its leading characters: "As the grave of Custer marked the high-water mark of Sioux supremacy in the trans-Missouri region," he wrote, "so the grave of 'Crazy Horse,' a plain fence of pine slabs, marked the ebb."[29] As for the graceful old fort at the confluence of the Laramie and North Platte rivers, this Great Sioux War served as its own high-water mark in a long and illustrious history. This final stroke at nearby Camp Robinson also marked Fort Laramie's ebb. Never would the exhilaration return.

Epilogue

The conduct of the Great Sioux War of 1876–77 was almost a text-book operation. Certainly the United States Army had not yet re-duced Indian fighting to written narrative, but tactically General Sheridan orchestrated a campaign markedly similar to those he had waged against the southern plains tribes in the late 1860s and again in the Red River War of 1874–75. In each instance he deployed in-dependent commands from divergent military posts and relentlessly tracked down foes, his troops closing with the Indians in numerous pitched battles. A striking difference, however, between these earlier campaigns and the Great Sioux War was the multiplicity and intensity of the operations. When the hoped-for wintertime success against the Sioux eluded Crook, Terry, and Gibbon, these commanders waged a protracted summer and fall war, and Miles continued it into yet an-other winter. After combat embarrassments at Powder River and Rosebud Creek and the terrible annihilation at the Little Bighorn, the generals reorganized, pressed forward again, and ultimately col-lected major victories at Slim Buttes, on the Red Fork of the Powder River, and in several Montana winter engagements.

To effect permanent removal of this perceived Sioux barrier to northern plains settlement, by mid-1876 Sheridan organized a sec-ond military front when he located battalions of Fifth and Fourth

Cavalry in the very southern extremes of the Black Hills. These gold-fields had become a cause celebre for this war, and Merritt's and Mackenzie's cavalrymen offered a reassuring and politically valuable presence on the important southern routes to the Hills. At the same time, these soldiers watched over the Red Cloud and Spotted Tail agencies; they interfered with the supply of reinforcements to the northern roamers, posting a combat victory at Warbonnet Creek in the process; and they effected the debilitating unhorsings, disarmings, and surrenders at these agencies in the fall and winter of 1876–77.

This campaigning had not been without enormous expense. In December 1877, the United States Senate asked General William T. Sherman for information on the costs of the war, both in cash and in casualties among the rank and file. These figures were not immediately at hand, but Sherman quickly obtained pertinent data from his supply departments, the adjutant general, and Generals Terry and Crook. Terry estimated the total costs of the Sioux War in his department at $992,808. Crook estimated the Department of the Platte's costs at $1,319,720. Sioux War–related costs totalled $2,312,531, of which $1,892,311 represented charges against the Quartermaster Department, $23,798 charges to the Subsistence Department, and $70,466 war-related expenses of the Ordnance Department.[1]

E. D. Townsend, adjutant general of the army, provided a summary of casualties. By his tally, 16 commissioned officers were killed in the Sioux War and 2 wounded, while 267 enlisted men were killed and 123 were wounded. Aggregate casualties among the regular forces totaled 408. Townsend did not provide data on Indian casualties, and even today estimates are woefully lacking.[2] Curiously, none of the casualty figures provided in the official tally included the war-related statistics at Fort Laramie. With one Second Cavalry trooper killed by Indians at Richard Creek on October 1876 and the wounding of three Third Cavalrymen on Elkhorn Creek in January 1877 as specific examples, these casualty totals would surely be increased significantly if detailed studies existed for all the military posts in the northern plains war zone.

The Sioux War of 1876 had a profound impact on the national deployment of the United States Army. Line strength was fixed at five regiments of artillery, ten regiments of cavalry, and twenty-five regiments of infantry, totaling just over 1,500 officers and 24,000 enlisted men in 440 scattered companies. A year before the war General Terry had controlled in his department 63 companies of cavalry and infantry totaling 3,647 officers and men. Crook's Department of the Platte was of comparable size: 60 companies of cavalry and infantry comprising 3,537 officers and men. At the height of the war one year later, deployment of the nation's 440 army companies had shifted dramatically. In 1876 Terry, bolstered by the transfer of all or parts of several infantry regiments, commanded 92 companies totaling 4,686 men. Increases in Crook's department came as a result of the transfer of the entire Fifth Cavalry and parts of the Fourth Cavalry and Fourth Artillery, these movements bringing his authorized totals to 82 companies and 4,391 men.

In effect, two-fifths of the entire United States Army was deployed on the strife-torn northern plains. Troop rotations, particularly evident in the Department of the Platte, brought nearly every one of Crook's companies into the fray. Though not all could campaign with their department chief, to serve at Medicine Bow Station, Wyoming, at Red Canyon, Dakota Territory, or at Camp Sheridan, Nebraska, was every bit as war related as to fight at Powder River or plod through the famous starvation march.[3]

By the final quarter of 1877, statistics for Crook's Department of the Platte clearly reflected a return to normal. In this fiscal year his troops garrisoned one additional military post, Cantonment Reno, soon to be called Fort McKinney, yet he met his obligations with only 54 companies comprising 3,026 officers and men. Terry, meanwhile, reported sizable increases in troop strength—109 companies and 5,100 men—but his figures can easily be misleading. The Department of Dakota boasted two new military posts, known in mid-1877 as Bighorn Barracks and Tongue River Barracks and soon as Forts Custer and Keogh, and it had abandoned one in Minnesota. But Terry's department now bore the brunt of the Nez Perce flight from Oregon and Idaho toward Canada, and dozens of these companies were involved in that emergency.[4]

The establishment of these new military posts in the very midst of the unceded lands was trumpeted by General Sheridan as a leading success of the Sioux War. He had bargained for this action at least since 1874, when he sent Custer and his Seventh Cavalry into the Black Hills to find, among other objectives, a location for a new military post in the heart of Sioux country. In his annual report for 1875 Sheridan begged authority to construct posts at the mouths of the Bighorn and Tongue rivers in Montana as essential to the "settlement of the Sioux Indian question." In recounting the disasters of 1876 Sheridan again raised the issue. "This advice, if adopted," he wrote, "would have given us abundant supplies at convenient points, to operate in the very heart of the country from whence all our troubles came." It took the debacle at the Little Bighorn for Congress to authorize the desired expenditures, but by mid-1877 three permanent posts were under construction, and in the next several years Sheridan was also provided with Fort Meade in the northern Black Hills, Fort Assiniboine on the Milk River in northern Montana, Fort Maginnis in the Judith basin of central Montana, and Fort Niobrara in northern Nebraska. Each watched over various bands of the Sioux or further isolated Sitting Bull's followers in Canada.[5]

Without belaboring the obvious, the war had a profound impact on the Teton Sioux. The rights and privileges guaranteed these people by the Fort Laramie Treaty of 1868 had little or no meaning in the clash of cultures coming, inevitably, on the heels of railroad expansion, gold discoveries in the Black Hills, and the nationalistic impulse to settle the northern plains. The ethnocentricity of these actions revolts Americans a century later, but as they actually occurred they seemed only part of an orderly evolutionary process, carrying the land from Indian to soldier to railroad and pioneer.[6] Leaders like Red Cloud or Spotted Tail, even though their loyalties were questioned early on, ultimately exhibited a wisdom that made the most of this culturally shocking time. Gains were only temporary; the old world could not be restored.[7]

For five more years the residency of Sitting Bull and his followers in Canada remained the final unfinished business of the Great Sioux War. Throughout the winter of 1876–77 small bands of Hunkpapa Sioux, hounded continuously by Miles's dogged infantry, drifted northward across the international border. Sitting Bull arrived in the spring of 1877, and many Oglalas came from the Red Cloud Agency after the killing of Crazy Horse. In the winter of 1877–78 some four thousand Indians in six hundred lodges, representing all the bands of the Teton Sioux and even some Nez Perce, were scattered over the Canadian prairies near Wood Mountain and the Cypress Hills in what is today southwestern Saskatchewan.[8]

While the Canadian and United States governments worked toward a political solution, the red-coated Northwest Mounted Police actually welcomed the Sioux but laid down strict rules that, to their supreme credit, were followed with firmness and consistency. Feeding so large a number of refugees, however, methodically destroyed the Sioux. There were not enough buffalo for even the Canadian natives, and increasingly in the late 1870s bands of Sioux returned to Montana to hunt. In 1879 Colonel Miles, seemingly ever present, clashed with one party of hunters, including Sitting Bull himself, on the Milk River and chased them back to Canada. Broken in spirit and poverty stricken, the Sioux camps dwindled in 1879 and 1880 as chiefs surrendered their hungry people. Sitting Bull resisted to the last. Destitute, he and his followers—forty-five men, sixty-seven women, and seventy-three children—surrendered at Fort Buford, Dakota Territory, on July 19, 1881. The last of the mightly alliance that had shocked Crook and crushed Custer just five years before was no more.[9]

Officers like Edwin Franklin Townsend and Andrew Wallace Evans probably paid little heed to the larger implications of the Great Sioux War. Issuing supplies, guarding the telegraph, and campaigning in the field were all matters of duty for these regular army soldiers. Still, they were probably amazed when equipment lost by Company K, Second Cavalry, in the fight with Cheyennes at the Powder River on March 17 was recovered just north of Fort Laramie on August 3 and when Company K recovered two horses at the Dull Knife battlefield on November 26 that had been lost by a detail of its troopers in the October 16 Richard Creek fight southwest of the Hunton ranch.

Beyond battlefield surprises like these, the Fort Laramie garrison may have equated the war mostly with garrison, regimental, or army casualties. The American army of the 1870s was not so large that the loss of a single soldier went unnoticed. During the various movements of the Sioux War every company in Fort Laramie's garrison took a turn in the field with General Crook. Although casualties in the general's three expeditions were not as numerous as those borne by the Seventh Cavalry at the Little Bighorn, both of Fort Laramie's Second Cavalry companies and their replacements, five companies from the Third Cavalry, experienced combat deaths or multiple woundings at Powder River, Rosebud Creek, or Slim Buttes. These were in addition to the local casualties already noted. Of the various officers killed or wounded in Crook's campaigns, Captain Guy V. Henry and First Lieutenant A. H. Von Luettwitz nominally belonged to the Third Cavalry companies garrisoning the post after the summer operation. Campaign grief was felt at every station. At nearby Camp Robinson, for example, Second Lieutenant Frederic S. Calhoun, Fourteenth Infantry, lost his brother, First Lieutenant James Calhoun, Seventh Cavalry, who died with Custer at the Little Bighorn.[10]

Beyond the recognition all soldiers warranted for actual field and combat service, Fort Laramie's garrison held a number of recognized heroes. Charles A. Bessey, the dashing corporal of Company A, Third Cavalry, who commanded an outnumbered detail at Elkhorn Creek in an aggressive action against Indians in mid-January 1877, was later awarded the Medal of Honor for supreme valor. Two other Third Cavalrymen, Joseph Robinson and Michael A. McGann, first sergeants of Companies D and F, respectively, also received the Medal of Honor for their coolness and gallantry under fire at the Battle of the Rosebud.[11]

For all the attention given the actions in the north, Fort Laramie's most obvious role in the Great Sioux War was not that of a combat post, a status in the whole of the Department of the Platte most nearly accorded only Fort Fetterman. Rather, Fort Laramie emerged with a combination of three roles that was unique to the department and the Sioux War.

Fort Laramie's protectorate duties during the Black Hills gold rush constituted its most obvious success in 1876. With the iron bridge nearby, Fort Laramie lay astride the most popular route to the new El Dorado. Over this Cheyenne to Custer City and Deadwood route traveled the first scheduled stage service to the Hills. Paralleling this same road, the first telegraph connected Cheyenne and Custer City by November and the "magic city" and Deadwood by December 1,

1876. These were significant accomplishments. "The coming of the Cheyenne and Black Hills Telegraph Line was welcomed by everyone and this, with the running of regular coaches, made us feel that we were not altogether out of touch with the outside world," remarked pioneer Richard B. Hughes.[12]

The road and telegraph line north of Fort Laramie were mostly built by others, but Townsend's and Evans's plucky cavalrymen made these efforts as secure as possible through routine patrols, repeated dashes after renegade raiders, and the routine escort of civilian wagon trains. The Fort Laramie subposts at Sage Creek and Red Canyon also offered incalculable protection to travelers. Moreover, these hearty troops investigated their own share of emergencies, participated in several clashes with Indians, and with a good measure of sweat helped construct and maintain the telegraph. The tedium of that chore is evident in bare statistics recorded about the telegraph line: poles averaged eighteen feet long, with four-inch diameter tops; they were planted three and one-half feet deep; placement averaged twenty poles per mile; 50 percent of the poles were cottonwood.[13]

Important too was Fort Laramie's position on the main road to the Red Cloud and Spotted Tail agencies. The powerful Oglala and Brule Sioux lived there, along with Northern Cheyennes and some Arapahoes. Despite the peaceable intent of Chiefs Red Cloud and Spotted Tail, many of their people belonged to the northern camps during the war, and the coming and going of these roamers and others was a constant worry to the army. Legislative action in 1877 safeguarded a western Dakota home for the Oglalas and Brules, despite interest in moving them to the Indian Territory or to the Missouri River. But before the agencies were relocated to the lands we know today as the Pine Ridge and Rosebud reservations, Fort Laramie protected the advance of annuities, beef herds, agency supplies, and Indian commissioners and other emissaries as they came north from the Union Pacific Railroad in Cheyenne.[14]

Interaction at the agencies included direct military intervention as well. Fort Laramie's commanders exercised administrative oversight over the two army camps adjacent to the agencies until Ranald Mackenzie removed headquarters of the District of the Black Hills to Camp Robinson in August 1876. Telegraphic connection to Camp Robinson was not completed until April 1877, and until then the Fort Laramie station remained the end of the line, with official dispatches forwarded by courier. Fort Laramie's soldiers shared with their Robinson counterparts the duty of protecting the Laramie-Robinson road, safeguarding the mails, and escorting notables like Crook and Sheridan to and from the agencies. Before transferring into Fort Laramie, Major Evans and companies of the Third Cavalry participated in the initial disarmings and unhorsings at the Red Cloud Agency in October 1876, and in September 1877 many of these same cavalrymen dashed from Laramie northeastward as the Crazy Horse saga drew to its tragic conclusion.

The tempo of the Great Sioux War was measured at Fort Laramie in various other ways as well. After most of the fort's resident infantry and cavalry had been dispatched to General Crook's Big Horn, Big Horn and Yellowstone, and Powder River expeditions, the remaining small corps of soldiers attended to a sometimes overwhelming range of duties. Crook used Fort Laramie as the initial staging area for his third campaign, but the springboard for each of these movements was Fort Fetterman. Supplies bound for Fetterman during warm months came directly from Cheyenne or Medicine Bow. During cold months these roads were blocked by snow, and nearly all shipments traveled via Fort Laramie. Its soldiers protected these wagon trains, dug them out when they were snowbound, and guided them to their destinations. Often the transshipment of stores required that an official board of survey consisting of three officers inspect and inventory goods. No fewer than forty-nine such boards were assembled in 1876 to attend supply shipments. While some of this material was routine stock intended for internal use, much more went to outfit Crook's soldiers during the formation of his expeditions, to resupply units like the Fifth Cavalry when they paused on the way north after their month of patrolling on the Black Hills road, or to reequip the general's depleted forces after their starvation march.[15]

Although no battles on the scale of the Rosebud were fought in the environs of Fort Laramie, its resident garrison saw ample field service against elusive Indians. Captain James Egan's chance encounter with eight hundred or nine hundred Indians in late May 1876 illustrated the overwhelming odds of the Sioux War. Egan's company did not clash with these agency defectors, but men from Company K did in October 1876 at Richard Creek, and one cavalryman was killed. Corporal Bessey and his small detachment of Third Cavalrymen had their own sharp clash in January 1877. These troopers had already survived unscathed the battles at Rosebud Creek and Slim Buttes, but on the Elkhorn Bessey and two others were seriously wounded. Captain William Collier led his Company K, Fourth Infantry, against marauding Indians south of their Red Canyon camp on August 1. First Lieutenant George Taylor's men of the Twenty-third Infantry had their own combat experience protecting Wesley Merritt's wagon train during the movement and fight at Warbonnet Creek, Nebraska, in mid-July 1876. Between these significant reported incidents were dozens of sorties in the wake of massacred civilians, wrecked stagecoaches, stolen horses, or frightened emigrants. During the war Fort Laramie's extended garrison responded to twenty-one such emergencies. In these cases Indians were rarely seen, but their trails were often obvious, and booty and stolen horses were occasionally recovered.

Stories of Indian harassment were much the same elsewhere in Nebraska and Wyoming. At Fort Fetterman, for instance, Captain Coates's troops often responded to minor emergencies. Some indeed were real, but just as many were Indian "scares" that caused Coates to complain to Omaha that these "extravagant rumors" regarding the Indians only caused him unnecessary work.[16]

Major Townsend met his military obligations in 1876 with a skeleton garrison. At the peak of the summer he had only two companies at his immediate disposal. From mid-June forward a detachment, usually from Company K, Second Cavalry, was posted to the Chugwater valley, other subunits from that company or from Company F, Ninth Infantry, were dispatched as escorts, telegraph repairmen, and messengers, and a small reserve was always maintained for internal security.

Small as this garrison occasionally was, the remaining residents were treated to "America on parade." Thousands of Hillers streamed through on the Cheyenne to Black Hills road. Many were worthy of mention—men and women like Bill Hickok, Calamity Jane, Jack Langrishe, Spotted Tail, Bill Cody, and Jack Crawford, or newsmen and writers like Robert "Alter Ego" Strahorn, Reuben Davenport, Leander Richardson, and John Finerty, and the military chroniclers John Bourke, Charles King, and Anson Mills. George Crook was nearly a permanent resident, and General Sheridan visited Fort Laramie in 1876 more often than any other post in the war zone. Merritt and Mackenzie both passed through repeatedly, and the men in the charge of these senior commanders represented each branch of the United States Army and nine different regiments including the Second, Third, Fourth, and Fifth Cavalry, Fourth, Ninth, Fourteenth, and Twenty-third Infantry, and Fourth Artillery.

If these soldiers fought the Great Sioux War, women like Cynthia Capron, Mary Anna Egan, and Elizabeth Burt also endured it. Remembering Burt's melancholy note about how hard it was "to sit and think and think and imagine all kinds of disasters," one can easily picture the apprehension in a northern plains garrison while troops were on campaign.[17] No Fort Laramie husbands were lost at the hands of the Sioux or Cheyennes, but death was always tragic, and the loss of Cynthia Capron's two-year-old son to disease and the drowning of First Sergeant John McGregor, Company K, Second Cavalry, while chasing deserters were reminders of the fragility of life.

Historians delight in comparative studies. It is often postulated that Fort Laramie, Wyoming, reached its greatest importance during the Sioux War of 1876–77. Fort Laramie, of course, already had a long and illustrious history. It had a central role in the American fur trade, during the great overland migrations to Oregon, Utah, and California, as an Indian treaty ground and annuity distribution point, and as a station for the pony express and the first transcontinental telegraph. Its role as a base for military campaigning following the Grattan debacle of 1854, during the uprisings of the Civil War, and through the terrible Bozeman Trail War also made it nationally significant. But after examining Fort Laramie's role in the events of 1876, we can see that the warmly debated postulate may well be fact. In no earlier period was there such an aggregation of duties as Fort Laramie handled in the centennial year. Serving as the gateway to the Black Hills goldfields was by itself an illustrious accomplishment. Yet Townsend and Evans also advanced communications and transportation. They had direct interactions with two of the most important agencies in the whole of the Great Sioux Reservation. And they shared in every facet of General Crook's varied field operations originating in the Department of the Platte. In this multifaceted story lies the prime significance of the venerable army post nestled in a bend of the Laramie River, on the ragged edge of the American frontier. Indeed, 1876 was a grand year for Fort Laramie, as no other.

Appendix

The Fort Laramie Telegraph:
1861–76

Quartermaster General, U.S. Army. Washington, D.C.

December 5th 6.

Sir:

In accordance with your instructions of October 26, 1876, I have the honor to submit the following report relative to the telegraph line between Cheyenne, and Forts Laramie and Fetterman, Wyoming.

On an examination of information obtained from several sources I learn that under an Act of Congress of 1860–61, chartering the Pacific Telegraph Company, a telegraph line was built from Omaha to San Francisco, which was completed about October 24, 1861, and over which line government messages were transmitted free for ten years, i.e. to July 1, 1871.

This line ran from Omaha through Fort Kearny, Julesburg, Fort Sedgwick, Fort Laramie, Fort Fetterman, Granger, and so on to San Francisco.

In 1860–4–&5, another line was built, under the same management, leaving the old line at Julesburg, running through Denver, and re-uniting with the old line at Granger: this second line became the main-line, and in 1866 all of the first line between Fort Fetterman, and Granger, was abandoned; but that part between Julesburg and Forts Laramie and Fetterman, was maintained.

Some time in 1867—probably September 30th—an agreement was entered into between the General C. C. Augur, Commanding this Department, and W. B. Hibbard, Esqr., Division Superintendent of the Western Union Telegraph Company, under which agreement the Quartermasters Department early in 1868, moved so much of the old line as lay between the Union Pacific Railroad, (at or near Lodge Pole station) and Fort Laramie, over onto the line as it now runs from Cheyenne to Fort Laramie.

Under this agreement the Quartermasters Department has kept the line from Cheyenne to Forts Laramie and Fetterman, in good condition, and has paid the operators at these posts: up to July 1, 1871, government messages went free; since then the Western Union Telegraph Company has been paid the established rates, (those fixed by the Postmaster General) for public messages transmitted, and has collected its tolls on commercial business.

The operators have, for part of the time, also served as clerks in the Quartermasters Department, at the two posts named. On October 21, 1876, however, the Quartermasters Department ceased to pay the operator at Fort Laramie, the business of the Western Union Telegraph Company, at Fort Laramie, having increased to such an extent (in consequence of the establishment of telegraphic communication with Custer City and Deadwood) as to justify them in assuming that expense.

The foregoing shows that the line to Forts Laramie, and Fetterman, was built by what is now known as the Western Union Telegraph Company: was removed to its present location by the Quartermasters Department, has been maintained and kept in working condition by the Quartermasters Department, excepting that the Telegraph Company has supplied the office-instruments: the removal and maintenance being under the direction of the Department Commander.

The Depot Quartermaster, at Cheyenne, has been charged with the repair of the present line from Cheyenne to Chug station; the Commanding Officer at Fort Laramie, keeps the line in order from Chug station to Horse Shoe Creek; and thence to Fort Fetterman is in charge of the Commanding Officer at that post. The cost of these repairs cannot be even approximately ascertained, extending as they do over a period of nine years, and requiring an examination of the papers of at least four officers who have served as Depot Quartermasters at Cheyenne, (one of whom is dead) and of many other officers who have served as Post Quartermasters at Forts Laramie and Fetterman.

There is no such record in this office. It is not believed however that since the removal of the line to its present location that the actual outlay has been much, the repairs having generally been made by enlisted men, or by the civilian employees at Cheyenne Depot. . . .

Very respectfully
your obedient servant,
Major Marshall I. Ludington
Chief Quartermaster.

Notes

Chapter One

1. James C. Olson, *Red Cloud and the Sioux Problem* (Lincoln: University of Nebraska Press, 1965), pp. 59, 74.
2. Ibid., pp. 74–75.
3. Ibid., pp. 75–76; George E. Hyde, *Red Cloud's Folk: A History of the Oglala Sioux Indians* (Norman: University of Oklahoma Press, 1975), pp. 164, 182–83.
4. The entire text of the 1868 treaty appears in Charles J. Kappler, *Indian Treaties, 1778–1883* (New York: Interland, 1972), pp. 998–1007. Unless otherwise noted, this work is cited in the discussion of the treaty.
5. Better described as the Republican River, which flows into the Kansas River, not the Smoky Hill.
6. Robert M. Utley, *Frontier Regulars: The United States Army and the Indian, 1866–1890* (New York: Macmillan, 1973), p. 237.
7. Ibid., p. 239; Remi Nadeau, *Fort Laramie and the Sioux Indians* (Englewood Cliffs, N.J.: Prentice-Hall, 1967), pp. 250–51; *Outline Description of the Posts in the Military Division of the Missouri* (Chicago: Headquarters Military Division of the Missouri, 1876; reprinted Bellevue, Nebr.: Old Army Press, 1969), p. 111.
8. Richard Guentzel, "The Department of the Platte and Western Settlement, 1866–1877," *Nebraska History* 56 (Fall 1975): 401.

9. B. William Henry, Jr., "Record of Skirmishes That Took Place between Soldiers, both Regular Army and State Militia, and Indians within a Seventy Mile Radius of Fort Laramie, June 1849–March 1890," Fort Laramie National Historic Site, Wyoming, May 1970 (typescript).

10. *Chronological List of Actions, etc., with Indians from January 15, 1837 to January, 1891* (Fort Collins, Colo.: Old Army Press, 1979), pp. 38–61; *Record of Engagements with Hostile Indians within the Military Division of the Missouri, from 1868 to 1882* (Washington, D.C.: Government Printing Office, 1882; reprinted Bellevue, Nebr.: Old Army Press, 1969), pp. 19–29.

11. *Record of Engagements*, p. 35; Arnold O. Goplen, *The Historical Significance of Fort Lincoln State Park* (Bismarck: State Historical Society of North Dakota, n.d.), p. 58.

12. Roger T. Grange, Jr., *Fort Robinson: Outpost on the Plains* (Lincoln: Nebraska State Historical Society, 1965), pp. 194–95.

13. Utley, *Frontier Regulars,* p. 240; Grange, *Fort Robinson,* pp. 194–99; Paul A. Hutton, *Phil Sheridan and His Army* (Lincoln: University of Nebraska Press, 1985), pp. 287–88.

14. Robert M. Utley and Francis A. Ketterson, Jr., *Golden Spike* (Washington, D.C.: National Park Service, 1969), is an excellent introduction to this first transcontinental railroad. American military-railroad relations in the West are discussed by Robert G. Athearn, "The Firewagon Road," *Montana: The Magazine of Western History* 20 (April 1970): 2–19.

15. Utley, *Frontier Regulars,* p. 242; Mark H. Brown, "A New Focus on the Sioux War," *Montana: The Magazine of Western History* 11 (October 1961): 76–85.

16. Watson Parker, *Gold in the Black Hills* (Norman: University of Oklahoma Press, 1966), pp. 10–13.

17. Ibid., pp. 16–17, 20.

18. Ibid., p. 23.

19. Donald Jackson, *Custer's Gold: The United States Cavalry Expedition of 1874* (New Haven: Yale University Press, 1966), p. 14.

20. Ibid., pp. 14–15.

21. Ibid., p. 83.

22. John S. Gray, "News from Paradise: Charley Reynolds Rides from

the Black Hills to Fort Laramie," *By Valor and Arms: The Journal of American Military History* 3 (1978): 38–42.

23. Grant K. Anderson, "Samuel D. Hinman and the Opening of the Black Hills," *Nebraska History* 60 (Winter 1979): 524–27. Hinman's report was published in the 1874 *Report of the Commissioner of Indian Affairs*. It is excerpted with an introduction by Watson Parker in "Report of the Reverend Samuel D. Hinman of an Expedition to the Black Hills during August, 1874," *Bits and Pieces* 5 (November 1969): 5–9. Hinman, a reappearing Fort Laramie figure, died in 1890 and is buried at the Bishop Whipple Mission near Morton, Minnesota.

24. Quoted in Utley, *Frontier Regulars*, p. 244.

25. The story of these early attempts to enter the Black Hills and the army's countermeasures is ably told by Watson Parker in *Gold in the Black Hills*, pp. 28–37, and in his "The Majors and the Miners: The Role of the U.S. Army in the Black Hills Gold Rush," *Journal of the West* 11 (January 1972): 104–7. Documentary evidence of Fort Laramie's role in this policing effort, a worthy episode not explored in here, is found in General and Special Orders, Black Hills Expedition, 1875, and General and Special Orders, District of the Black Hills, 1875, both in Record Group 393, National Archives and Records Service, Washington, D.C. See also Jane Conard, "Charles Collins: The Sioux City Promotion of the Black Hills," *South Dakota History* 2 (Spring 1972): 131–46.

26. Conard, "Charles Collins," pp. 146–50; Watson Parker, "The Report of Captain John Mix of a Scout to the Black Hills, March–April 1875," *South Dakota History* 7 (Fall 1977): 385–401.

27. Lesta V. Turchen and James D. McLaird, *The Black Hills Expedition of 1875* (Mitchell, S. Dak.: Dakota Wesleyan University Press, 1975), p. 1.

28. Ibid., pp. 2, 30.

29. Ibid., p. 15.

30. Ibid., p. 45.

31. Richard I. Dodge, *The Black Hills* (Minneapolis: Ross and Haines, 1965), pp. 104–5.

32. Turchen and McLaird, *Black Hills Expedition of 1875*, p. 19.

33. Ibid., p. 47.

34. Ibid., p. 50; Parker, "Majors and Miners," p. 106.

35. Hutton, *Phil Sheridan and His Army,* pp. 297–98; Olson, *Red Cloud and the Sioux Problem,* p. 201; Anderson, "Samuel D. Hinman and the Opening of the Black Hills," pp. 529–35.

36. Olson, *Red Cloud and the Sioux Problem,* p. 207.

37. Ibid., pp. 208–11; Harry H. Anderson, "A Challenge to Brown's Indian Wars Thesis," *Montana: The Magazine of Western History* 12 (January 1962): 46.

38. Olson, *Red Cloud and the Sioux Problem,* p. 212.

39. John G. Bourke to George Crook, June 15, 1875, Philip Sheridan Papers, Library of Congress, cited in Joseph C. Porter, *Paper Medicine Man: John Gregory Bourke and His American West* (Norman: University of Oklahoma Press, 1986), p. 26.

40. John G. Bourke, *On the Border with Crook* (New York: Charles Scribner's Sons, 1902), p. 244.

41. Olson, *Red Cloud and the Sioux Problem,* p. 215.

42. Hutton, *Phil Sheridan and His Army,* pp. 298–99; Philip H. Sheridan to Alfred H. Terry, November 8, 1875. Philip Sheridan Papers, Library of Congress; John S. Gray, *Centennial Campaign: The Sioux War of 1876* (Fort Collins, Colo.: Old Army Press, 1976), pp. 25–57; Utley, *Frontier Regulars,* pp. 246–47.

43. Quoted in Hutton, *Phil Sheridan and His Army,* pp. 299–300.

44. Utley, *Frontier Regulars,* p. 247.

Chapter Two

1. Department of the Platte Telegrams Sent, November 8, 1875, Record Group 393, National Archives and Records Service, Washington, D.C.; Fort Laramie Post Return, November 1875, Record Group 393, National Archives and Records Service, Washington, D.C.

2. Parker, *Gold in the Black Hills,* p. 73; Bradley Diary, Luther P. Bradley Papers, U.S. Army Military History Institute, Carlisle Barracks, Pa.

3. Unless otherwise noted, the discussion of roads to and from Fort Laramie is based upon W. S. Stanton, *Table of Distances and Itineraries of Routes between the Military Posts in, and to Certain Points Contiguous to, the Department of the Platte* (Omaha: Headquarters De-

partment of the Platte, 1877); U.S. Congress, House, *Annual Report of Capt. W. S. Stanton,* Ex. Doc. no. 1, pt. 2, 45th Congress, 3d session, pp. 1704–47; J. H. Triggs, *A Reliable and Correct Guide to the Black Hills, Powder River, and Big Horn Gold Fields!* (Omaha: Herald Steam Book and Job Printing House, 1876), p. 14.

4. E. B. Robertson, "The Ninth Regiment of Infantry," in Theo. F. Rodenbough, ed., *The Army of the United States* (New York: Argonaut Press, 1966), pp. 526–29.

5. Alfred E. Bates and Edward J. McClernand, "The Second Regiment of Cavalry," in Rodenbough, *Army of the United States,* pp. 173–83.

6. Francis B. Heitman, *Historical Register and Dictionary of the United States Army,* 2 vols. (Washington, D.C.: Government Printing Office, 1903; reprinted Urbana: University of Illinois Press, 1965), 1:967; Colonel Thomas M. Anderson, "Fourteenth Regiment of Infantry," in Rodenbough, *Army of the United States,* p. 589. Townsend retired as a colonel in 1895. He died in 1909 and is buried at Arlington National Cemetery, Virginia.

7. Fort Laramie Post Return, January 1876; Thomas Wilhelm, *A Military Dictionary and Gazetteer* (Philadephia: L. R. Hamersly, 1881), pp. 12, 111, 468, 559.

8. J. W. Vaughn, "Captain James Egan," *Westerners (New York Posse) Brand Book* 13 (1966): 1–3, 6–7, 18; Don Rickey, Jr., and James W. Sheire, *The Cavalry Barracks Fort Laramie Furnishing Study* (Washington, D.C.: National Park Service, 1969), pp. 5–7; Fort Laramie Post Return, October 1875. Egan retired in 1879, a worn-out soldier. He died in 1883 and was buried in Arlington National Cemetery.

9. Fort Laramie Post Return, January 1876; Thomas E. White, "Post Surgeons at Fort Laramie, June 16, 1849 to March 19, 1890," Fort Laramie National Historic Site, Wyoming, April 1972 (Typescript); W. Thornton Parker, ed., *Records of the Association of Acting Assistant Surgeons of the United States Army* (Salem, Mass.: Salem Publishing and Printing, 1891), pp. 41–45.

10. John D. McDermott, "Fort Laramie's Silent Soldier, Leodegar Schnyder," *Annals of Wyoming* 36 (April 1964): 4–13; Wilhelm, *Military Dictionary and Gazetteer,* pp. 111, 229, 393.

11. *Cheyenne Daily Leader,* January 12, 1876; "Roster of Troops Serving in the Department of the Platte, May, 1876," filed with Department of the Platte General Orders, 1876, RG 393.

12. Utley, *Frontier Regulars,* p. 239; Harry H. Anderson, "Cheyennes at the Little Big Horn—a Study of Statistics," *North Dakota Historical Society Quarterly* 27 (Spring 1960): 5.

13. Charles King, "Long Distance Riding," *Cosmopolitan,* January 1894, p. 297.

14. *Outline Description of the Posts in the Military Division of the Missouri,* p. 97; "Roster of Troops Serving in the Department of the Platte, May 1876."

15. The description of Fort Laramie here and following is based upon a careful analysis of a base map in *Outline Description of the Posts in the Military Division of the Missouri,* pp. 93, 95–97, which is accurate for 1876, and a fort plat dated 1874 in the Fort Laramie NHS Collections.

16. Capron Journal no. 12, p. 14, Thaddeus Hurlbut Capron Collection, Archives–American Heritage Center, University of Wyoming, Laramie, Wyoming; Fort Laramie Medical History, Supplementary Report dated December 31, 1874, RG 393; John D. McDermott and James Sheire, *1874 Cavalry Barracks Historic Structures Report: Historical Data Section* (Washington, D.C.: National Park Service, 1970), pp. 35, 49.

17. John D. McDermott, "Fort Laramie's Iron Bridge," *Annals of Wyoming* 34 (October 1962): 136–44; Merrill J. Mattes and Thor Borresen, "The Historic Approaches to Fort Laramie," Fort Laramie National Monument, Wyoming, October 1947 (Typescript). For some months in early 1876 tolls were collected from nonmilitary users of the bridge. Rates were $1.50 for teams of six to eight yokes of oxen, $1 for teams of four to six mules, 50¢ for teams of two horses, and 25¢ for single horsemen (*Cheyenne Daily Sun,* April 14, 1876).

18. J. H. Triggs, *History of Cheyenne and Northern Wyoming Embracing the Gold Fields of the Black Hills, Powder River and Big Horn Countries* (Omaha: Herald Steam Book and Job Printing House, 1876), p. 11.

19. Edwin A. Curley, *Curley's Guide to the Black Hills* (Chicago: Author,

1876; reprinted Mitchell, S.Dak: Dakota Wesleyan University Press, 1973), p. 12; Norbert R. Mahnken, "The Sidney–Black Hills Trail," *Nebraska History* 30 (September 1949): 208–11.

20. John S. Collins, *Across the Plains in '64* (Omaha: National Printing, 1904), p. 39.

21. Paul L. Hedren, "Captain [Charles] King's Centennial Year Look at Fort Laramie, Wyoming," *Annals of Wyoming* 48 (Spring 1976): 104, 106.

22. Capron Journal no. 12, p. 5.

23. Ibid., pp. 8–9.

24. Merrill J. Mattes, *Indians, Infants and Infantry: Andrew and Elizabeth Burt on the Frontier* (Denver: Old West, 1960), p. 197.

25. Capron Journal no. 12, p. 14.

26. Fort Laramie General Orders no. 56, October 2, 1872, Record Group 94, National Archives and Records Service, Washington, D.C.

27. Capron Journal no. 12, p. 7; Clyde C. Walton, ed., *An Illinois Gold Hunter in the Black Hills: The Diary of Jerry Bryan, March 13 to August 20, 1876* (Springfield: Illinois State Historical Society, 1960), p. 5.

28. Persons and Articles Hired, Fort Laramie, November 1875, and January 1876, Record Group 92, National Archives and Records Service, Washington, D.C.

29. The dimensions of the reservation and extensions are given in *Outline Description of Posts*, p. 97. The January 30 *Cheyenne Daily Leader*, in a call for the opening of the extended reservation, claimed it embraced over 360 square miles, stretching for three miles on either side of the North Platte east as far as Scott's Bluff, Nebraska.

30. Olson, *Red Cloud and the Sioux Problem*, pp. 97, 150, 158.

31. Triggs, *History of Cheyenne and Northern Wyoming*, pp. 53–54.

32. John G. Bourke Diary, vol. 19, January–April 1877, pp. 1848–49, United States Military Academy, West Point, New York.

33. Agnes Wright Spring, *The Cheyenne and Black Hills Stage and Express Routes* (Lincoln: University of Nebraska Press, 1967), pp. 110–11; Triggs, *History of Cheyenne and Northern Wyoming*, pp. 53–54; L. G. Flannery, ed., *John Hunton's Diary*, vol. 2, 1876–'77 (Lingle, Wyo.: Guide-Review, 1958), p. 291.

Chapter Three

1. Hutton, *Phil Sheridan and His Army*, p. 301; Utley, *Frontier Regulars*, pp. 158, 219–20, 248; *Report of the Secretary of War* (1876), p. 440.
2. *Report of the Secretary of War* (1876), p. 441.
3. Fort Laramie General Orders no. 56, December 1, 1875.
4. Fort Laramie Special Orders no. 8, January 11, and no. 13, January 23, 1876, RG 393; and Fort Laramie Letters Sent, December 4, 1875, RG 393.
5. Triggs, *History of Cheyenne and Northern Wyoming*, pp. 124–25.
6. *Cheyenne Daily Leader*, January 11, 19, and 21, 1876.
7. Ibid., February 3, 1876; Spring, *Cheyenne Stage and Express Routes*, p. 81.
8. *Cheyenne Daily Leader*, February 24, March 8, 9, 1876.
9. Department of the Platte Telegrams Sent, December 29, 1875.
10. Ibid., February 10, 11, 15, 1876; Department of the Platte Chief Quartermaster Letters Sent, January 29, 1876; Bourke, *On the Border with Crook*, pp. 150–51.
11. Department of the Platte Letters Sent, January 21 and February 7, 1876, RG 393.
12. *Report of the Secretary of War* (1876), p. 502.
13. J. W. Vaughn, *The Reynolds Campaign on Powder River* (Norman: University of Oklahoma Press, 1961), p. 26; "Roster of Troops Serving in the Department of the Platte, May 1876," filed with Department of the Platte General Orders, 1876.
14. Mattes, *Indians, Infants and Infantry*, p. 209.
15. Flannery, *John Hunton's Diary*, p. 56; Fort Laramie Post Return, February 1876.
16. Fort Laramie Special Orders no. 35, February 22, 1876.
17. "Roster of Troops Serving in the Department of the Platte, May, 1876"; Camp at Cheyenne Depot Post Returns, January–December 1876, RG 393.
18. "Persons and Articles Hired, Fort Laramie," February 1876; Department of the Platte Telegrams Sent, February 10 and 15, 1876.
19. Department of the Platte Chief Quartermaster Letters Sent, February 18, 1876.
20. Bradley Diary, January 2–February 16, 1876.
21. Fort Laramie Medical History, 1876; Fort Laramie Post Returns,

January–February 1876; Parker, *Records of the Association of Acting Assistant Surgeons of the United States Army*, pp. 25–26.

22. Bourke, *On the Border with Crook*, pp. 247–48.

23. Bourke Diary, vol. 3, February 20, 1876, p. 4.

24. Ibid., February 22, 1876, p. 5; Flannery, *John Hunton's Diary*, pp. 59–60.

25. Bourke Diary, vol. 3, February 23, 1876, p. 6.

26. Vaughn, *Reynolds Campaign*, pp. 40–41; Joe DeBarthe, *The Life and Adventures of Frank Grouard* (Norman: University of Oklahoma Press, 1958), pp. 88–89.

27. Vaughn, *Reynolds Campaign*, p. 25.

28. Mattes, *Indians, Infants and Infantry*, p. 209.

29. Utley, *Frontier Regulars*, pp. 248–49, 252.

30. Department of the Platte Telegrams Sent, February 27, 1876.

31. Department of the Platte General Orders no. 6, February 28, 1876.

32. Mattes, *Indians, Infants and Infantry*, p. 211.

33. These specifics are detailed in Fort Laramie Special Orders.

34. Department of the Platte Telegrams Sent, November 10 and 19, 1875.

35. Fort Laramie Letters Received, March 11, 1876, RG 393; Department of the Platte Letters Sent, March 11, 1876.

36. *Report of the Commissioner of Indian Affairs* (1876), pp. 382–83, with subreport of Agent Hastings, p. 437; U.S. Congress, House, *Supplies for Indians at Red Cloud*, Exec. Doc. no. 103, 44th Congress, lst session, pp. 1–2; U.S. Congress, House, *Sioux Indians*, Exec. Doc. no. 145, 44th Congress, lst session, pp. 1–2.

37. Don E. Alberts, *Brandy Station to Manila Bay: A Biography of General Wesley Merritt* (Austin: Presidial Press, 1981), pp. 222, 224–25; U.S. Congress, House, *Sioux Indians*, pp. 3–6 (this is Merritt's official report).

38. Fort Laramie Medical History, March 1876; National Archives and Record Service, microfilm publication 665, roll 104, Ninth Infantry Regimental Return, March 1876; Department of the Platte Special Orders no. 28, March 6, 1876, RG 393; Bradley Diary, March 17, 1876.

39. Bradley Diary, March 8–9, 1876; Flannery, *John Hunton's Diary*, pp. 59, 66.

40. *Cheyenne Daily Leader*, February 6 and March 5, 1876; Doug En-

gebretson, *Empty Saddles, Forgotten Names: Outlaws of the Black Hills and Wyoming* (Aberdeen, S.Dak.: North Plains Press, 1982), pp. 81–91.

41. Department of the Platte Telegrams Sent, March 18, 1876.
42. See Fort Laramie Special Orders no. 59, March 28, 1876, for a typical Board of Survey order.
43. Bourke Diary, vol. 3, March 17, 1876, p. 112.
44. The quotation is Robert Utley's in *Frontier Regulars,* p. 251. Utley discusses the Big Horn Expedition on pp. 248–51. Vaughn provides comprehensive treatment in *The Reynolds Campaign on Powder River.*
45. Vaughn, *Reynolds Campaign,* pp. 119–20, 143.
46. The dispatch is printed in ibid., p. 156. The failings of the expedition according to Crook are detailed in *Report of the Secretary of War* (1876), pp. 502–3.
47. The court-martial preceedings against Reynolds and Moore are analyzed by Vaughn, *Reynolds Campaign,* chap. 10. Reynolds was found guilty of most of the charges and suspended from rank and pay for one year. Citing a long and distinguished career, President Grant remitted the sentence, but Reynolds, his reputation ruined, retired in June 1877. He died in 1899 and is buried in Arlington National Cemetery. Moore, found guilty of conduct to the prejudice of good order and military discipline in failing to cooperate fully in the attack, was sentenced to be suspended for six months and to be confined to his post for that period. This too was remitted by Grant. See also Utley, *Frontier Regulars,* p. 264, n 36.
48. Vaughn, *Reynolds Campaign,* p. 159.
49. Ibid., pp. 166–67; Bourke Diary, vol. 3, March 17, 1876, p. 121; Bradley Diary, March 30–31, 1876.
50. Bradley Diary, March 31, 1876; Bourke Diary, vol. 3, March 18, 1876, p. 142; Martin F. Schmitt, ed., *George Crook: His Autobiography* (Norman: University of Oklahoma Press, 1960), p. 193.
51. The report of wounded and killed at Powder River is ir Vaughn, *Reynolds Campaign,* pp. 119–20.

Chapter Four

1. These investigations are discussed in Hutton, *Phil Sheridan and His*

Army, pp. 306–10; William S. McFeeley, *Grant: A Biography* (New York: W. W. Norton, 1981), pp. 427–29.

2. Parker, *Gold in the Black Hills*, pp. 75–76, 89–90.

3. Spring, *Cheyenne and Black Hills Stage and Express Routes*, p. 94; *Cheyenne Daily Leader*, April 11, 1876.

4. Spring, *Cheyenne and Black Hills Stage and Express Routes;* Stanton, *Table of Distances*, pp. 28, 30.

5. *Cheyenne Daily Leader*, February 24, 1876; Walton, *Illinois Gold Hunter in the Black Hills*, p. 15.

6. Fort Laramie Post Returns, March 1876; Fort Laramie Medical History, 1876. As for many contract doctors during this period, little biographical data is readily available on Petteys. His death in 1933, however, makes him one of the longest survivors of the Great Sioux War. He is buried at Arlington National Cemetery.

7. Fort Laramie Register of Sick and Wounded, April 1876, RG 393; Fort Laramie Special Orders no. 83, April 24, 1876.

8. Parker, *Gold in the Black Hills*, pp. 135–36; Jesse Brown and A. M. Willard, *The Black Hills Trails* (Rapid City, S.Dak.: Rapid City Journal Company, 1924), p. 75; *Cheyenne Daily Leader*, April 21, 1876.

9. Spring, *Cheyenne and Black Hills Stage and Express Routes*, pp. 83, 138–39; Department of the Platte Telegrams Sent, April 23, 1876; Fort Laramie Medical History, 1876; *Cheyenne Daily Leader*, April 25 and 26, 1876. Traditionally, the station where Brown was taken was known as Hat Creek, a geographical misnomer, since the development properly stood on Sage Creek. To confuse the issue, a Hat (also known as Warbonnet) Creek did flow thirty miles or so east of this location.

10. Spring, *Cheyenne and Black Hills Stage and Express Routes*, pp. 138–39.

11. *Cheyenne Daily Leader*, April 26 and 29, 1876; Department of the Platte Telegrams Sent, April 14 and 28, 1876.

12. Department of the Platte Telegrams Sent, April 27, 28, 29, 1876.

13. Bradley Diary, April 18 and 27, 1876; Fort Laramie General Orders no. 29, April 27, 1876; Dee Brown, *The Year of the Century: 1876* (New York: Charles Scribner's Sons, 1966), pp. 129–33.

14. Vaughn, in *Reynolds Campaign*, p. 167, also includes Luther Brad-

ley as a court member, but this is at variance with the travel itinerary described in his own diary.

15. Department of the Platte General Court Martial Orders no. 29, May 2, 1876, filed with Department of the Platte General Orders, 1876.
16. Vaughn, *Reynolds Campaign*, p. 169.
17. Department of the Platte Telegrams Sent, April 1876, and Fort Laramie Special Orders, April 1876, document this springtime activity.
18. Department of the Platte Chief Quartermaster Letters Sent, April 16, 1876.
19. Fort Laramie Letters Sent, April 23, 1876; Department of the Platte Letters Sent, May 3, 1876.
20. Collins, *Across the Plains in '64,* pp. 36–38.
21. Ibid., p. 39; Fort Laramie Special Orders no. 92, May 5, 1876.
22. Collins, *Across the Plains in '64,* pp. 40–41. There are other accounts of Hunton's death that are at variance with the one cited here. I have followed Collins's version, since he was most nearly there. But see also Flannery, *John Hunton's Diary,* pp. 84–90.
23. Flannery, *John Hunton's Diary,* p. 84.
24. *Cheyenne Daily Leader,* May 7 and 9, 1876; *Record of Engagements with Hostile Indians,* p. 51.
25. Fort Laramie Special Orders no. 94, May 7, 1876; Fort Laramie Medical History, 1876; "Persons and Articles Hired, Fort Laramie," April 1876.
26. Utley, *Frontier Regulars,* p. 252.
27. Department of the Platte Special Orders no. 68, June 2, 1876; "Roster of Troops Serving in the Department of the Platte, May 1876"; J. W. Vaughn, *With Crook at the Rosebud* (Harrisburg, Pa.: Stackpole, 1956), p. 11.
28. Ibid.
29. David R. Robrock, "A History of Fort Fetterman, Wyoming, 1867–1882," *Annals of Wyoming* 48 (Spring 1976): 52.
30. *Rand McNally's Pioneer Atlas of the American West* (Chicago: Rand McNally, 1956), pp. 77–78; *Tables of Distances,* p. 20.
31. Fort Laramie Medical History, 1876; *Cheyenne Daily Leader,* May 9, 1876.

32. *Cheyenne Daily Leader,* May 3, 1876.

33. Department of the Platte Letters Sent, May 5, 1876; Fort Laramie Letters Received, May 6, 1876.

34. Fort Laramie Letters Received, May 10, 1876.

35. Ibid., May 11, 1876.

36. Ibid., May 10, 1876; Department of the Platte Chief Quartermaster Letters Sent, May 11, 1876.

37. Bourke Diary, vol. 3, May 12–[13], 1876, pp. 222–23; George Crook to Philip H. Sheridan, May 1876, Walter S. Schuyler Papers, Huntington Library; Fort Laramie Medical History, 1876; Fort Laramie Special Orders no. 99, May 12, 1876.

38. Thomas W. Dunlay, *Wolves for the Blue Soldiers: Indian Scouts and Auxiliaries with the United States Army, 1860–90* (Lincoln: University of Nebraska Press, 1982), pp. 48, 89. For a more complete view of tribal warfare and its implications for individual warriors, see John C. Ewers, "Intertribal Warfare as the Precursor of Indian-White Warfare on the Northern Great Plains," *Western Historical Quarterly* 6 (October 1975): 397–410; and Richard White, "The Winning of the West: The Expansion of the Western Sioux in the Eighteenth and Nineteenth Centuries," *Journal of American History* 65 (September 1978): 319–43.

39. Crook to Sheridan, May 1876; Bourke, *On the Border with Crook,* pp. 286–87; Hyde, *Red Cloud's Folk,* p. 259; Olson, *Red Cloud and the Sioux Problem,* pp. 217–18.

40. Crook to Sheridan, May 1876; Olson, *Red Cloud and the Sioux Problem,* p. 218.

41. Crook to Sheridan, May 1876; Bourke, *On the Border with Crook,* pp. 288–89; *Cheyenne Daily Leader,* May 18, 1876.

42. Gracc L. Schaedel, "Isaac Bard Stage Station—Little Bear, Wyoming, with Notes from His Diaries 1874–1876," *Annals of Wyoming* 37 (April 1965): 87.

43. Department of the Platte Telegrams Sent, May 16, 1876. The Dakota Column actually left on May 17.

44. *Cheyenne Daily Leader,* May 16, 1876; Fort Laramie Letters Received, May 16, 1876; Department of the Platte General Orders no. 18, May 2, 1876.

45. Fort Laramie Circular, May 18, 1876, RG 393.

46. Cynthia J. Capron, "The Indian Border War of 1876," *Journal of the Illinois State Historical Society* 13 (January 1921): 477; Mattes, *Indians, Infants and Infantry,* pp. 213–14.

47. Fort Laramie Letters Sent, May 19, 1876; Fort Laramie Post Returns, May 1876.

48. Oliver Knight, *Following the Indian Wars: The Story of Newspaper Correspondents among the Indian Campaigners* (Norman: University of Oklahoma Press, 1960), pp. 171–74; John F. Finerty, *War-Path and Bivouac* (Norman: University of Oklahoma Press, 1961), pp. 20–24.

49. *Cheyenne Daily Leader,* May 24, 1876.

50. Ibid., May 23 and 25, 1876.

51. Department of the Platte Telegrams Sent, May 27 and 29, 1876; Crook to Townsend, May 27, 1876, Crook Collection, University of Oregon, Eugene; Military Division of the Missouri Letters Sent, May 29, 1876, RG 393.

52. Fort Laramie Special Orders no. 108, May 25, 1876.

53. Ibid., no. 109, May 26, and no. 110, May 27, 1876; Fort Laramie Letters Sent, May 17, 1876.

54. *Cheyenne Daily Leader,* May 25 and 28, 1876.

55. Division of the Missouri Letters Sent, May 31, 1876; *Cheyenne Daily Leader,* May 30, 1876.

Chapter Five

1. Alberts, *Brandy Station to Manila Bay,* p. 225; Fort Laramie Special Orders no. 117, June 3, 1876.

2. Fort Laramie Post Returns, June 1876.

3. Capron Journal no. 12, pp. 20–21, 23–24.

4. Ibid., p. 33.

5. Ibid., pp. 34, 36–37.

6. Ibid., pp. 35–36, 39.

7. Ibid., pp. 38, 77–77A. Cynthia Capron twice referred to a Chaplain Taylor as conducting the burial service, but in her bereavement she was mistaken. Records clearly identify Jeremiah Porter as having come from Fort D. A. Russell. See Fort Laramie Letters Sent, June 9, 1876; Department of the Platte Special Orders no. 76, June 14, 1876.

8. Department of the Platte Telegrams Sent, June 5, 1876.
9. Fort Laramie Special Orders no. 122 and 123, June 10 and 11, 1876; Fort Laramie Letters Sent, June 10, 1876; Fort Laramie Post Return, June 1876.
10. Fort Laramie Special Orders no. 121 and 122, June 9 and 10, 1876; Fort Laramie Letters Received, June 8, 1876; Fort Laramie Post Return, June 1876.
11. The stories of the army camp on Sage Creek and of Company H, Twenty-third U.S. Infantry, in the Great Sioux War are told by Paul Hedren in "Cp. Hat Creek, Wyo.," *Periodical: Journal of the Council on Abandoned Military Posts* 6 (Winter 1974–75): 29–32, and idem, "An Infantry Company in the Sioux Campaign, 1876," *Montana: The Magazine of Western History* 33 (Winter 1983): 30–39.
12. Robert A. Murray chronicles the story of Collier's station in "The Camp at the Mouth of Red Canyon," *Periodical: Journal of the Council on Abandoned Military Posts* 1 (January 1967): 2–9.
13. Fort Laramie Letters Received, June 8, 1876; and Orders no. 6, August 18, 1876, in Letters Sent, Endorsements, &c., Camp at the Mouth of Red Canyon, Filed with Fort Laramie Records, RG 393.
14. William A. Dobak, "Yellow-Leg Journalists: Enlisted Men as Newspaper Reporters," *Journal of the West* 13 (January 1974): 95; *Cheyenne Daily Leader,* June 10 and 11, 1876.
15. Don Russell, *The Lives and Legends of Buffalo Bill* (Norman: University of Oklahoma Press, 1960), pp. 204, 219–20; Dobak, "Yellow-Leg Journalists," pp. 97–98.
16. *Cheyenne Daily Leader,* June 11, 1876; Dobak, "Yellow-Leg Journalists," p. 96; Alberts, *Brandy Station to Manila Bay,* pp. 225–26; Hutton, *Phil Sheridan and His Army,* p. 314.
17. Dobak, "Yellow-Leg Journalists."
18. Department of the Platte Telegrams Sent, June 12, 1876.
19. Alberts, *Brandy Station to Manila Bay,* p. 225; *Cheyenne Daily Leader,* June 14, 1876.
20. Hutton, *Phil Sheridan and His Army,* pp. 153–54, 312–13; Fort Laramie Special Orders no. 124, June 14, 1876.
21. Fort Laramie Letters Received, June 10 and 12, 1876; Fort Laramie Letters Sent, June 13, 1876.
22. Department of the Platte Chief Quartermaster Letters Sent, June

16, 21, 22, 1876; Department of the Platte Register of Contracts, June 26, 1876, RG 393; *Cheyenne Daily Leader,* June 4, 1876. Other rates included Ferris's transportation contract at $1.20 per 100 pounds, July–October 1876, and May–June 1877; $1.50 per 100 pounds during November–December 1876 and January–February 1877; and $1.75 per 100 pounds during March–April 1877. Murrin's wood contract specified that at least half of the 3,000 cords had to be pine. The prevailing rate was $7.27 per cord. Stacked hay cost variously $17.43 and $17.25 per ton, and baled hay cost $21.50 per ton.

23. "Persons and Articles Hired, Fort Laramie," April and June 1876.

24. Letter dated August 28, 1876, Capron Papers, University of Wyoming, Laramie; *Cheyenne Daily Leader,* June 4, 1876.

25. Flannery, *John Hunton's Diary,* pp. 109–11; *Cheyenne Daily Leader,* June 20, 1876. Cannary's participation in the opening movements of the Big Horn and Yellowstone Expedition is discussed in Vaughn, *With Crook at the Rosebud,* pp. 13, 158.

26. Capron, "Indian Border War of 1876," p. 487; George E. Hyde, *Spotted Tail's Folk* (Norman: University of Oklahoma Press, 1974), p. 223. The story of Mini-Aku, her alleged love for a white man at Fort Laramie, and her death and burial is chronicled by Wilson P. Clough, "Mini-Aku, Daughter of Spotted Tail," *Annals of Wyoming* 39 (October 1967): 187–216; Bourke, *On the Border with Crook,* pp. 399–400.

27. Military Division of the Missouri Letters Sent, June 18, 1876.

28. Ibid., Department of the Platte General Orders no. 18, May 2, 1876, and no. 22, June 19, 1876; Paul L. Hedren, *First Scalp for Custer: The Skirmish at Warbonnet Creek, Nebraska, July 17, 1876* (Glendale, Calif.: Arthur H. Clark, 1980), p. 36.

29. Military Division of the Missouri Letters Sent, June 18, 1876; Mahnken, "Sidney–Black Hills Trail," pp. 210–11.

30. Fort Laramie Letters Received, June 13, 1876; Military Division of the Missouri Letters Sent, June 18 and June (undated, but thought to be 17 or 18), 1876.

31. Fort Laramie Letters Received, June 17, 1876; Capron, "Indian Border War of 1876," p. 486; *Cheyenne Daily Leader,* June 21, 1876.

32. Fort Laramie Letters Sent, June 18, 1876.

33. Department of the Platte Telegrams Sent, June 20, 1876; Fort Laramie Letters Received, June 19, 1876.

34. Dobak, "Yellow-Leg Journalists," p. 98, Capron Journal no. 12, p. 78.

35. Biographies of Fifth Cavalry officers are found in George F. Price, *Across the Continent with the Fifth Cavalry* (New York: Antiquarian Press, 1959). A roster of officers campaigning with the Fifth in June is found in Hedren, *First Scalp for Custer,* appendix, pp. 96–97. The novel referred to here is Captain Charles King's *Laramie; or, The Queen of Bedlam* (Philadelphia: J. B. Lippincott, 1889), reprinted in 1986 by the Fort Laramie Historical Association. Notes on King's writings are found in *First Scalp*; Hedren, "Captain King's Centennial Year Look at Fort Laramie, Wyoming," pp. 102–8; and Paul L. Hedren, *King on Custer: An Annotated Bibliography* (College Station, Tex.: Brazos Corral of the Westerners, 1982).

36. Fort Laramie Medical History, June 1876.

37. Utley, *Frontier Regulars,* p. 256. The principal secondary source on Crook's operations in May and June is Vaughn, *With Crook at the Rosebud.* The bibliographies of these two books identify the important primary sources.

38. Vaughn, *With Crook at the Rosebud,* pp. 152–53.

39. Department of the Platte Telegrams Sent, June 23, 1876; Division of the Missouri Letters Sent, June 23, 1876.

40. Capron Journal no. 12, p. 98; Vaughn, *With Crook at the Rosebud,* pp. 115, 199–200, 212.

41. Hedren, *First Scalp for Custer,* p. 40; James T. King, *War Eagle: A Life of General Eugene A. Carr* (Lincoln: University of Nebraska Press, 1963), pp. 156–57; Fort Laramie Letters Sent, June 26, 1876.

42. *Cheyenne Daily Leader,* June 23, 1876.

43. Ibid., June 22 and 28, 1876; Alice Cochran, "The Gold Dust Trail: Jack Langrishe's Mining Town Theaters," *Montana: The Magazine of Western History* 20 (Spring 1970): 58–69.

44. AGO General Orders no. 51, June 21, and no. 69, July 26, 1876, in *General Orders, Adjutant General's Office, 1876* (Washington, D.C.: Government Printing Office, 1877); Hutton, *Phil Sheridan and His Army,* p. 314; Fort Laramie Special Orders no. 136, June 28, 1876.

45. Bourke, *On the Border with Crook,* p. 319; Ray Meketa, ed., *Marching with General Crook, Being the Diary of Lieutenant Thaddeus Hurlbut Capron Company C, Ninth Infantry* (Douglas, Alaska: Cheechako Press, 1983), p. 23.

46. Meketa, *Marching with General Crook,* pp. 23–25.

47. Fort Laramie Letters Sent, July 3, 1876.

48. Adjutant General's Office General Orders no. 49, June 21, 1876; Fort Laramie General Orders no. 42, July 3, 1876.

49. Capron, "Indian Border War of 1876," p. 490; General Charles King, "Faster Than the Fastest Pony," *Youth's Companion,* February 9, 1911, p. 71.

50. Meketa, *Marching with General Crook,* p. 27.

51. Fort Laramie Letters Sent, July 3, 1876.

52. Fort Laramie Letters Received, July 2, 1876.

53. *Cheyenne Daily Leader,* July 2, 1876; Fort Laramie Letters Sent, July 4, 1876.

54. AGO General Orders no. 49, June 21, 1876; Capron Journal no. 12, p. 105; Fort Laramie General Orders no. 42, July 3, 1876.

55. Capron Journal no. 12, pp. 102–3.

56. Fort Laramie Special Orders no. 140, July 2, no. 142, July 5, and no. 145, July 8, 1876; Fort Laramie Post Return, July 1876.

57. Capron Journal no. 12, p. 197. In Cynthia Capron's 1925 reminiscence "Indian Border War of 1876," she reports the day when only thirteen soldiers came on duty as July 4, but this is contradicted in her journal transcription as well as by official post records. Although the actual day referred to is unclear, it may have been either July 9 or 10, since this coincides with the absence of Company K, Second Cavalry, and most of the infantry, who were off on scouts or details.

58. Thomas R. Buecker, "The Post of North Platte Station, 1867–1878," *Nebraska History* 63 (Fall 1982): 394.

59. In 1950 an old-timer, George O. Reid, reminisced to National Park Service personnel at Fort Laramie National Monument about 1876. As a child he knew Ordnance Sergeant Leodegar Schnyder, and Reid alleged that Schnyder kept loaded cannons about the post at those times when few troops were available. Further, Schnyder was said also to have placed stovepipes around the fort to simulate even more cannons. The story seems fanciful at best.

See George O. Reid Interview, September 23 and 25, 1950, Fort Laramie National Historic Site Research Collections.

60. *Cheyenne Daily Leader*, July 4, 1876; Hedren, *First Scalp for Custer*, pp. 47, 49, 51; Captain Charles King, *Campaigning with Crook and Stories of Army Life* (New York: Harper, 1890), pp. 23–24.

61. James T. King, "General Crook at Camp Cloud Peak: 'I Am at a Loss What to Do.'" *Journal of the West* 11 (January 1972): 121, 123; Big Horn and Yellowstone Expedition Telegrams, July 12, 1876, RG 393.

62. Department of the Platte Telegrams Sent, July 12, 1876; Fort Laramie Letters Received, July 14, 1876.

63. Fort Laramie Special Orders no. 151, July 17, 1876; Department of the Platte Telegrams Sent, July 17, 1876.

64. King, *Campaigning with Crook,* pp. 26–29; Hedren, *First Scalp for Custer,* pp. 59–61; Hedren, "Infantry Company in the Sioux Campaign, 1876," pp. 36–38.

65. Hedren, *First Scalp for Custer,* pp. 63–68; King, *Campaigning with Crook,* pp. 32–39.

66. *Cheyenne Daily Leader*, July 20, 1876; Hedren, *First Scalp for Custer,* pp. 77–80, 83.

67. Fort Laramie Special Orders no. 153, July 19, 1876; *Cheyenne Daily Leader,* July 20, 1876.

68. *Helena Daily Independent*, June 30, 1876; *Cheyenne Daily Leader,* July 20, 1876; *Army and Navy Journal*, August 5, 1876. Townsend incorrectly identified the errant newspaper as the *Helena Herald*.

69. King, *Campaigning with Crook,* p. 43; *New York Herald*, July 23, 1876; Russell, *Lives and Legends of Buffalo Bill,* pp. 229, 237.

70. Price, *Across the Continent with the Fifth Cavalry,* p. 159; *Cheyenne Daily Leader,* July 19, 1876.

71. *Cheyenne Daily Leader,* July 9 and 11, 1876; Military Division of the Missouri Letters Sent, July 20, 1876.

72. King, *Campaigning with Crook,* pp. 43–44.

73. Hedren, "An Infantry Company in the Sioux Campaign, 1876," p. 39; Fort Laramie Medical History, July 1876; Fort Laramie Special Orders no. 155, July 22, 1876.

74. *Tables of Distances*, p. 20; Robrock, "History of Fort Fetterman," p. 57; *Cheyenne Daily Leader*, October 5, 1876.

75. James Willert, ed., *The Cuthbert Mills Letters to New York Times dur-*

ing the Indian War of 1876 (La Mirada, Calif.: James Willert, 1984), p. 10.

76. Leander P. Richardson, "A Trip to the Black Hills," *Scribner's Monthly*, April 1877, pp. 748–56; *Cheyenne Daily Leader*, July 19, 21, 27, 28, 30, August 2, 9, 12, 16, 1876.

77. *Cheyenne Daily Leader*, July 28, 1876; Jack Crawford, *The Poet Scout* (San Francisco: H. Keller, 1879), p. 25.

78. *Black Hills Pioneer*, July 22, 1876.

79. *Cheyenne Daily Leader*, July 27, 1876.

80. Fort Laramie Letters Received, July 15, 1876; Fort Laramie Letters Sent, July 18 and 20, 1876.

81. Capron, "Indian Border War of 1876," p. 494.

82. Camp at the Mouth of Red Canyon Letters Sent, August 2, 1876.

83. Ibid.; Fort Laramie Letters Received, August 4, 1876; Hedren, "Infantry Company in the Sioux Campaign, 1876," p. 39; *Cheyenne Daily Leader*, August 6, 1876.

84. *Cheyenne Daily Leader*, August 5, 1876.

85. J. W. Vaughn, *Indian Fights: New Facts on Seven Encounters* (Norman: University of Oklahoma Press, 1966), chap. 6; Department of the Platte Telegrams Sent, August 3, 1876; Flannery, *John Hunton's Diary*, pp. 132–36.

86. Department of the Platte Telegrams Sent, August 3 and 8, 1876; Fort Laramie Special Orders no. 164, August 3, 1876.

87. *Cheyenne Daily Leader*, August 6, 1876; Department of the Platte Telegrams Sent, August 5, 1876; Capron, "Indian Border War of 1876," p. 494.

88. *Cheyenne Daily Leader*, August 6, 1876; Robrock, "History of Fort Fetterman, Wyoming," pp. 57–58.

89. Hutton, *Phil Sheridan and His Army*, pp. 321–22.

90. Fort Laramie Special Orders no. 152, July 18, and no. 165, August 4, 1876; Fort Laramie Letters Sent, August 2 and 4, 1876; Department of the Platte Telegrams Sent, August 4, 1876.

91. "Persons and Articles Hired, Fort Laramie," April, July, and August 1876; Department of the Platte Chief Quartermaster Letters Sent, August 5, 17, 18, 1876; Fort Laramie Letters Received, August 6, 1876; Department of the Platte Letters Sent, August 7, 1876.

92. *Cheyenne Daily Leader*, July 22, August 2 and 6, 1876; Spring, *Cheyenne and Black Hills Stage and Express Routes*, p. 155.

93. Joseph G. Rosa, *They Called Him Wild Bill: The Life and Adventures of James Butler Hickok* (Norman: University of Oklahoma Press, 1964), chap. 15; *Cheyenne Daily Leader*, August 12, 1876.

94. *Cheyenne Daily Leader*, August 6, 15, and 16, 1876.

95. Ibid., August 5, 7, 15, and 16, 1876.

96. Dale E. Floyd to Mrs. Duane M. Kline, June 11, 1976, Collections, Wyoming State Archives; Christian C. Hewitt Diary, August 7, 9–10, 12, 1876, microfilm copy in Collections, Wyoming State Archives.

97. Fort Laramie Post Return, September 1876; Hewitt Diary, August 13–17, 1876.

98. *Cheyenne Daily Leader*, August 11, 1876. Curiously, Wagner was not officially hired as a Fort Laramie courier until August 22, 1876, yet the paper specifically mentions his name. Perhaps he was on the quartermaster employee rolls at Camp Robinson. See "Persons and Articles Hired, Fort Laramie," August 1876.

99. *Cheyenne Daily Leader*, August 13, 1876; Fort Laramie Special Orders no. 170, August 13, 1876.

100. *Cheyenne Daily Leader*, August 19, 1876. The unnamed correspondent is most assuredly Cynthia Capron.

101. Price, *Across the Continent with the Fifth Cavalry*, p. 159; Department of the Platte Telegrams Sent, July 10 and 26, 1876.

102. *Cheyenne Daily Leader*, August 4, 1876; Fort Laramie Post Return, August 1876; Fourth Cavalry Regimental Returns, August 1876, microfilm publication 744, roll 42, National Archives and Records Service, Washington, D.C.

103. Hutton, *Phil Sheridan and His Army*, pp. 220, 322–23; Fort Laramie Letters Received, August 13, 1876; Department of the Platte Telegrams Sent, August 14, 1876; Department of the Platte Letters Sent, August 15, 1876.

104. Fort Laramie Medical History, August 1876; Fort Laramie Special Orders no. 172, August 15, 1876.

105. Hutton, *Phil Sheridan and His Army*, p. 323; Richard N. Ellis, *General Pope and U.S. Indian Policy* (Albuquerque: University of New Mexico Press, 1970), p. 202; Rodenbough, *Army of the United States,*

p. 326; *Cheyenne Daily Leader,* August 15, 1876; Fourth Artillery Regimental Return, August 1876, microfilm publication 727, roll 30, National Archives and Records Service, Washington, D.C.

106. Fort Laramie Post Return, August 1876; Fourteenth Infantry Regimental Return, August 1876, microfilm publication 665, roll 155, National Archives and Records Service, Washington, D.C.

107. *Cheyenne Daily Leader,* August 22 and 23, 1876.

108. AGO General Orders no. 90, August 22, 1876.

109. Fort Laramie Letters Received, August 23, 1876; Hedren, "Infantry Company in the Sioux Campaign, 1876," p. 34; *Cheyenne Daily Leader,* August 26, 1876.

110. *Cheyenne Daily Leader,* August 4 and 26, 1876.

111. Fort Laramie Letters Received, August 22, 1876.

Chapter Six

1. Olson, *Red Cloud and the Sioux Problem,* pp. 222–23; *Report of the Secretary of War* (1876), p. 445; Department of the Platte Telegrams Sent, July 26, 1876.

2. Olson, *Red Cloud and the Sioux Problem,* pp. 223–34.

3. Hyde, *Spotted Tail's Folk,* p. 251.

4. Olson, *Red Cloud and the Sioux Problem,* pp. 220–21; Hyde, *Red Cloud's Folk,* p. 279; Hyde, *Spotted Tail's Folk,* p. 251; Department of the Platte Telegrams Sent, September 1, 1876; Anderson, "Cheyennes at the Little Big Horn," pp. 11–13.

5. Olson, *Red Cloud and the Sioux Problem,* pp. 224–45. For the text of the Agreement of August 15, 1876, see Jackson, *Custer's Gold,* pp. 137–41. See also Richmond L. Clow, "The Sioux Nation and Indian Territory: The Attempted Removal of 1876," *South Dakota History* 6 (Fall 1976): 456–73.

6. Olson, *Red Cloud and the Sioux Problem,* pp. 224–25; Gray, *Centennial Campaign,* p. 261; Anderson, "Samuel D. Hinman and the Opening of the Black Hills," pp. 535–37.

7. *Cheyenne Daily Leader,* August 26, 1876.

8. Department of the Platte Telegrams Sent, August 25, 1876; Capron Journal no. 13, pp. 47–48; Fort Laramie Special Orders no. 182, September 2, 1876; Department of the Platte Chief Quartermaster Letters Sent, September 5, 1876.

9. *Cheyenne Daily Leader,* September 8, 1876; Olson, *Red Cloud and the Sioux Problem,* p. 225.

10. Olson, *Red Cloud and the Sioux Problem,* pp. 225–26. The articles in question were numbers 3 and 4; see Jackson, *Custer's Gold,* pp. 138–39.

11. For a discussion of Crook's midsummer campaign hiatus, see King, "General Crook at Camp Cloud Peak," pp. 114–27.

12. Utley, *Frontier Regulars,* pp. 269–70.

13. Bourke, *On the Border with Crook,* pp. 365–66; Big Horn and Yellowstone Expedition Telegrams, September 5, 1876.

14. Bourke Diary, vol. 8, September 5, 1876, p. 878.

15. Department of the Platte Telegrams Sent, September 8–9, 1876; Department of the Platte Letters Sent, September 7, 1876. The telegram to Mackenzie is particularly interesting for its description of the variety and measure of rations ordered for General Crook: 50,000# grain, 9,000# bacon, 18,000# flour, 6,000# hard bread, 3,000# beans, 200# rice, 2,200# coffee, one-half chest green tea, 3,300# sugar, 2 barrels vinegar, 2 boxes candles, 480# soap, 4 barrels salt, 60# pepper, 600# tobacco, 100# smoking tobacco, 200# cornmeal, 10# citric acid, 200# dried apples, 200# butter, 50# chocolate, 300# sugar-cured ham, 288 cans milk, 72 cans peaches, 100# dried peaches, 100# dried prunes, 48 cans Damson preserves, 72 cans salmon, 72 cans mock turtle soup, 2 barrels granulated sugar, 432 cans tomatoes, 144 cans yeast powder, and 1 barrel syrup.

16. Department of the Platte Telegrams Sent, September 8, 11, 1876.

17. Capron Journal no. 13, pp. 2, 41–47.

18. Mattes, *Indians, Infants and Infantry,* p. 230.

19. Department of the Platte Telegrams Sent, September 10, 1876; Finerty, *War-Path and Bivouac,* p. 152; Meketa, *Marching with General Crook,* p. 39.

20. Department of the Platte Telegrams Sent, September 10, 1876.

21. Fort Laramie Special Orders no. 191, September 19, 1876.

22. Department of the Platte Telegrams Sent, September 8 and 11, 1876; Fort Laramie Special Orders no. 190, September 9, and no. 192, September 11, 1876; "Persons and Articles Hired, Fort Laramie," September, 1876.

23. Fort Laramie Letters Received, September 10, 1876.

24. Fort Laramie Special Orders no. 192, September 11, 1876; *Cheyenne Daily Leader,* September 20 and 24, 1876; Hutton, *Phil Sheridan and His Army,* p. 323.

25. Fort Laramie Special Orders no. 193, September 12, 1876; Department of the Platte Telegrams Sent, September 11 and 12, 1876; District of the Black Hills Special Orders no. 13, September 13, 1876. Record Group 393, National Archives and Records Service, Washington D.C.; *Cheyenne Daily Leader,* September 12, 1876.

26. Fort Laramie Medical History, September 1876; Paul L. Hedren, ed., "Eben Swift's Army Service on the Plains, 1876–1879," *Annals of Wyoming* 50 (Spring 1978): 143–44.

27. The best telling of the fight at Slim Buttes is Jerome A. Greene's *Slim Buttes, 1876: An Episode of the Great Sioux War* (Norman: University of Oklahoma Press, 1982).

28. Ibid., pp. 127–29.

29. See the books by Charles King, Finerty, and Bourke, cited above, as well as Greene, *Slim Buttes, 1876,* and Paul L. Hedren, *With Crook in the Black Hills: Stanley J. Morrow's 1876 Photographic Legacy* (Boulder, Colo.: Pruett, 1985).

30. Big Horn and Yellowstone Expedition Orders and Telegrams, September 10, 1876; Greene, *Slim Buttes, 1876,* pp. 105–7; Fort Laramie Letters Received, September 15, 1876; Crawford, *Poet Scout,* p. xv; Knight, *Following the Indian Wars,* pp. 276–79; DeBarthe, *Life and Adventures of Frank Grouard,* pp. 159–63.

31. *Cheyenne Daily Leader,* September 16, 1876.

32. Military Division of the Missouri Letters Sent, September 16, 1876; Capron, "Indian Border War of 1876," p. 499.

33. Department of the Platte Chief Quartermaster Letters Sent, September 9 and 15, 1876. A descriptive list of equipment shipped to Fort Laramie is revealing: 2,000 pair woolen stockings, 200 woolen blankets, 25 wall tents, flies, and sets poles, 200 common tents and sets poles, 4,699 assorted tent pins, 700 pairs mounted trousers, 500 pairs foot trousers, 800 lined blouses, 500 pair boots, 200 cavalry jackets, 100 uniform coats, 1,250 pair drawers.

34. Fort Laramie Letters Received, September 5 and 17, 1876.

35. Fort Laramie Letters Sent, September 11 and 17, 1876.

36. Big Horn and Yellowstone Expedition Letters Sent, September 15, 1876; Finerty, *War-Path and Bivouac*, p. 206; Bourke Diary, vol. 9, September 15, 1876, pp. 918, 920–21.

37. Bourke, *On the Border with Crook*, pp. 383–87; Bourke Diary, vol. 9, September 18, 1876, p. 950.

38. Hedren, *With Crook in the Black Hills*, p. 29; Bourke, *On the Border with Crook*, p. 387; Big Horn and Yellowstone Expedition Letters Sent, September 18, 1876.

39. Finerty, *War-Path and Bivouac*, p. 216.

40. Bourke Diary, vol. 9, September 20, 1876, p. 953; Bourke, *On the Border with Crook*, p. 387; Fort Laramie Medical History, September 1876.

41. Hutton, *Phil Sheridan and His Army*, p. 325.

42. Ibid.; *Cheyenne Daily Leader*, September 28, 1876.

43. *Cheyenne Daily Leader*, September 22, 1876; Big Horn and Yellowstone Expedition Letters Sent, September 15, 1876; Department of the Platte Letters Sent, September 23, 1876; Fort Laramie Letters Received, September 22, 1876; Department of the Platte Telegrams Sent, September 18 and 19, 1876.

44. Mattes, *Indians, Infants and Infantry*, p. 233; Capron Journal no. 13, pp. 51, 55.

45. John S. Collins, *My Experiences in the West* (Chicago: Lakeside Press, 1970), pp. 157–59.

46. Mattes, *Indians, Infants and Infantry*, p. 232.

47. Bourke Diary, vol. 9, September 24, 1876, p. 954; Bourke, *On the Border with Crook*, p. 388; Fort Laramie Medical History, September 1876.

48. Knight, *Following the Indian Wars*, pp. 173, 184, 280–81; King, *Campaigning with Crook*, pp. 130, 153.

49. Fort Laramie Special Orders no. 201, September 23, 1876; *Cheyenne Daily Leader*, September 28, 1876; Ninth Infantry Regimental Return, September 1876; Fort Laramie Post Returns, September 1876; Fort Laramie Medical History, September 1876.

50. Fort Laramie Letters Sent, September 25, 1876; Big Horn and Yellowstone Expedition Memorandum, September 25, 1876.

51. Big Horn and Yellowstone Expedition Letters Sent, September

27 and 28, 1876; Bourke Diary, vol. 10, September 28, 1876, p. 980; Department of the Platte Letters Sent, September 28, 1876.

52. Olson, *Red Cloud and the Sioux Problem,* pp. 226–28.

53. Ibid., p. 228; Hyde, *Spotted Tail's Folk,* pp. 254–56.

54. Olson, *Red Cloud and the Sioux Problem,* p. 229.

55. Gray, *Centennial Campaign,* pp. 263–64; Olson, *Red Cloud and the Sioux Problem,* pp. 228–29.

56. Although Department of the Platte Special Order no. 132, September 25, 1876, declared that Major Thaddeus H. Stanton would pay these troops and it was so reported by the *Daily Leader* on September 29, other information suggests that Major Arthur from Omaha made the rounds. See Fort Laramie Letters Received, September 25, 1876, and Fort Laramie Post Return, September 1876.

57. King, *Campaigning with Crook,* p. 147.

58. Ibid., p. 146; Paul L. Hedren, ed., "Campaigning with the Fifth Cavalry: Private James B. Frew's Diary and Letters from the Great Sioux War of 1876," *Nebraska History* 65 (Winter 1984): 456; Willert, *Cuthbert Mills Letters,* p. 56.

59. King, *Campaigning with Crook,* p. 148.

60. Fort Laramie Special Orders no. 210, October 2, 1876; Collins, *Across the Plains in '64,* pp. 69–71 (Collins mistakenly dates this hunt as occurring in the "fall previous to the beginning of the Sioux Indian war of '76" when actually it occurred in the fall during the war); Bourke, *On the Border with Crook,* p. 388.

61. Harry H. Anderson, "Charles King's 'Campaigning with Crook,'" *Chicago Westerners Brand Book* 32 (January 1976): 66; Knight, *Following the Indian Wars,* pp. 282–83; Wesley Merritt to George Crook, October 8, 1876. George Crook Letters, Special Collections, University of Oregon Library, Eugene.

62. Department of the Platte Chief Quartermaster Letters Sent, October 3, 4, and 19, 1876.

63. *Cheyenne Daily Leader,* October 7, 1876. The indexes on the reverse of Mitchell's stereographs describe the many views taken during his travels and serve as our guides to those 1876 scenes awaiting discovery. See also Hedren, *With Crook in the Black Hills,* p. 29.

64. Fort Laramie Letters Sent, October 7, 1876; McDermott, "Fort Laramie's Silent Soldier, Leodegar Schnyder," pp. 16–17. Schnyder was finally transferred in 1886 to the fort at Clark's Point, Massachusetts.

65. Fort Laramie Medical History, October 1876; *Cheyenne Daily Leader,* October 11, 1876.

66. Fort Laramie Medical History, October 1876.

67. Fort Laramie Special Orders no. 209, October 1, 1876; *Cheyenne Daily Leader,* October 15, 17, 18, 19, 1876; Rickey and Sheire, *Cavalry Barracks Fort Laramie Furnishing Study,* pp. 59, 61.

68. *Cheyenne Daily Leader,* October 19, 1876; Fort Laramie Medical History, October 1876; Capron Journal no. 13, p. 78.

69. *Cheyenne Daily Leader,* October 12, 14, 1876; Fort Laramie Special Orders no. 218, October 14, 1876.

70. *Cheyenne Daily Leader,* October 19, 1876.

71. Olson, *Red Cloud and the Sioux Problem,* p. 232.

72. "Roster of Troops Serving in the Department of the Platte, September, 1876," filed with Department of the Platte General Orders, 1876; Bourke Diary, vol. 19, p. 989.

73. Olson, *Red Cloud and the Sioux Problem,* pp. 232–33.

74. Ibid., pp. 233–34.

75. Big Horn and Yellowstone Expedition Telegrams, October 23, 1876.

76. Hutton, *Phil Sheridan and His Army,* pp. 325–26; Richmond L. Clow, "General Philip H. Sheridan's Legacy: The Sioux Pony Campaign of 1876," *Nebraska History* 57 (Winter 1976): 465.

77. Clow, "General Philip H. Sheridan's Legacy," pp. 466–67.

78. Donald F. Danker, ed., *Man of the Plains: Recollections of Luther North, 1856–1882* (Lincoln: University of Nebraska Press, 1961), p. 204; *Cheyenne Daily Leader,* October 1876.

79. King, *Campaigning with Crook,* pp. 166–67.

80. Department of the Platte Special Orders no. 152, November 11, 1876.

81. Fort Laramie Post Returns, October 1876.

82. Ibid.; Fort Laramie Special Orders no. 230, October 27, 1876; Danker, *Man of the Plains,* pp. 205–6.

83. Fort Laramie Letters Received, October 27, 1876.

84. *Cheyenne Daily Leader,* October 22, 27, 28, 31, 1876.
85. Fort Laramie Letters Received, October 27, 1876; Fort Laramie Special Orders no. 230, October 27, 1876.
86. Camp Mouth of Red Canyon Telegrams, October 24, 1876.
87. *Cheyenne Daily Leader,* October 7 and November 4, 1876; Spring, *Cheyenne and Black Hills Stage and Express Routes,* p. 122.
88. Fort Laramie Letters Sent, September 30, 1876; Department of the Platte Telegrams Sent, October 31, 1876; Fort Laramie Letters Received, October 19 and 24, 1876; Camp Mouth of Red Canyon Order no. 16, October 7, 1876.

Chapter Seven
1. Bourke Diary, vol. 14, November 2, 1876, p. 1352.
2. Bourke, *On the Border with Crook,* pp. 389–90; Department of the Platte Telegrams Sent, October 30, 1876; John G. Bourke, *Mackenzie's Last Fight with the Cheyennes* (New York: Military Service Institution, 1890; reprinted Bellevue, Nebr.: Old Army Press, 1970), pp. 4–5.
3. Fort Laramie General Orders no. 53, October 29, no. 55, October 31, and no. 56, November 1, 1876.
4. Fort Laramie Post Return, November 1876.
5. Fort Laramie Special Order no. 236, November 2, 1876; Ninth Infantry Regimental Return, November 1876; Fort Laramie Post Return, November 1876.
6. Danker, *Man of the Plains,* p. 206; Bourke Diary, vol. 14, November 2, 1876, p. 1353; Clow, "General Philip H. Sheridan's Legacy," p. 466.
7. Olson, *Red Cloud and the Sioux Problem,* p. 235.
8. Bourke, *On the Border with Crook,* p. 390; Danker, *Man of the Plains,* p. 206.
9. Bourke, *On the Border with Crook,* p. 390; Bourke Diary, vol. 14, November 5, 1876, p. 1364; Knight, *Following the Indian Wars,* p. 290.
10. *Cheyenne Daily Leader,* August 29, November 2, and 4, 1876; Capron Journal no. 13, p. 43.
11. Department of the Platte Telegrams Sent, November 2, 1876; Fort Laramie Post Return, November 1876.

12. *Cheyenne Daily Leader,* November 5, 1876; *Rand McNally's Pioneer Atlas of the American West,* p. 79.

13. *Cheyenne Daily Leader,* November 10, 1876.

14. Fort Laramie General Order no. 58, November 8, 1876.

15. Fort Laramie Post Return, November 1876.

16. *Cheyenne Daily Leader,* November 8, 1876; Camp Mouth of Red Canyon Telegrams, October 24, November 20, 1876.

17. Fort Laramie Letters Sent, November 20, 1876; Department of the Platte Chief Quartermaster Letters Sent, November 20, 1876.

18. Department of the Platte Chief Quartermaster Letters Sent, November 1 and 20, 1876. A letter from the department's chief quartermaster to the quartermaster general of the army, dated December 5, 1876, has a detailed history of the Fort Laramie telegraph line, 1861–76, and this is reprinted in its entirety in the Appendix.

19. Fort Laramie Medical History, November 1876; Greene, *Slim Buttes, 1876,* pp. 127–29; Fort Laramie Letters Received, October 17, 1876; Fort Laramie Register of Sick and Wounded, November 1876; Fort Laramie Special Orders no. 235, November 1, 1876.

20. Fort Laramie Register of Sick and Wounded, November 1876; Fort Laramie Letters Received, November 22, 1876; Department of the Platte Telegrams Sent, November 23, 1876; Flannery, *John Hunton's Diary,* p. 158. Curiously, Hunton claims that Von Luettwitz stayed overnight at his ranch on November 24, but both the Fort Laramie Medical History and the Post Returns for November 1876, indicate that he left the fort on November 25.

21. Fort Laramie Register of Sick and Wounded, November 1876; Vaughn, *With Crook at the Rosebud,* pp. 95, 201; Third Cavalry Regimental Return, March 1877, microfilm publication 744, roll 31, National Archives and Records Service, Washington, D.C.

22. *Cheyenne Daily Leader,* November 28, 29, December 2, 1876; Olson, *Red Cloud and the Sioux Problem,* pp. 97, 120, 160.

23. Flannery, *John Hunton's Diary,* p. 159; *Cheyenne Daily Leader,* November 29, 1876; Bourke Diary, vol. 14, November 18, 1876, p. 1391; Bourke, *Mackenzie's Last Fight,* p. 9. A structural history of Cantonment Reno is found in Robert A. Murray, *Military Posts*

in the Powder River Country of Wyoming, 1865–1894 (Lincoln: University of Nebraska Press, 1968), pp. 110–14.

24. George B. Grinnell, *The Fighting Cheyennes* (Norman: University of Oklahoma Press, 1955), p. 362; Bourke, *Mackenzie's Last Fight,* pp. 12–13.

25. Bourke, *Mackenzie's Last Fight,* pp. 13, 28–31; Lessing H. Nohl, Jr., "Mackenzie against Dull Knife: Breaking the Northern Cheyennes in 1876," in *Probing the American West,* ed. K. Ross Toole et al. (Santa Fe: Museum of New Mexico Press, 1962), pp. 87–89; *Cheyenne Daily Leader,* December 29, 1876. Bourke, Nohl, and Grinnell, cited above, are the principal sources for this fight, but see also Homer W. Wheeler, *Buffalo Days: Forty Years in the Old West* (New York: A. L. Burt, 1925), chaps. 17–18.

26. Bourke, *Mackenzie's Last Fight,* pp. 27–28; Grinnell, *Fighting Cheyennes,* pp. 264, 382.

27. Bourke, *Mackenzie's Last Fight,* pp. 33–34; Nohl, "Mackenzie against Dull Knife," p. 91.

28. Department of the Platte Chief Quartermaster Letters Sent, October 30, November 28, December 12, 1876; Department of the Platte Telegrams Sent, November 29, 1876; Fort Laramie Letters Sent, December 15, 1876.

29. DeBarthe, *Life and Adventures of Frank Grouard,* p. 172; Agnes W. Spring, "Dr. McGillycuddy's Diary," in *The Denver Westerners 1953 Brand Book,* ed. Maurice Frink (Denver: Westerners, 1954), p. 295; *Cheyenne Daily Leader,* December 2, 1876; Flannery, *John Hunton's Diary,* p. 162.

30. *Cheyenne Daily Leader,* November 25, December 2, 7, 1876.

31. Fort Laramie Letters Received, December 3, 1876; Fort Laramie Special Order no. 268, December 5, 1876; Third Cavalry Regimental Returns, November and December 1876.

32. Department of the Platte Telegrams Sent, December 5, 6, 1876.

33. *Cheyenne Daily Leader,* December 3, 1876.

34. Ibid., December 7, 1876.

35. Department of the Platte Telegrams Sent, December 5, 12, 1876; Fort Laramie Letters Received, December 13, 1876.

36. Fourteenth Infantry Regimental Return, December 1876.

37. Fort Laramie Letters Received, December 6, 13, 16, 1876.

38. Twenty-third Infantry Regimental Return, December 1876, microfilm publication 665, roll 237, National Archives and Records Service, Washington, D.C.; Fort Laramie Letters Sent, December 18, 1876.

39. Courts-martial were convened pursuant to special orders, and the findings were published in general orders. In the McLean case see Fort Laramie Special Order no. 57, March 25, 1876, and Fort Laramie General Order no. 18, March 28, 1876. Wilhelm, *Military Dictionary and Gazetteer*, p. 119.

40. Department of the Platte General Court Martial Order no. 71, December 14, 1876, filed with Department of the Platte General Orders.

41. Fort Laramie Special Order no. 276, December 16, 1876; Third Cavalry Regimental Return, December 1876.

42. *Cheyenne Daily Leader,* December 10, 17, 23, 1876.

43. Fort Laramie Letters Received, December 20, 1876; *Cheyenne Daily Leader,* December 21, 1876.

44. Ibid.; Fort Laramie Letters Received, December 21, 1876; Hyde, *Red Cloud's Folk,* pp. 287–88.

45. *Cheyenne Daily Leader,* December 28, 1876; *Cheyenne Daily Sun,* January 6, 21, 1877.

46. Department of the Platte Telegrams Sent, December 29, 1876; *Cheyenne Daily Leader,* December 31, 1876.

47. Fort Laramie Letters Sent, December 30, 1876.

48. Ibid., January 6, 1877.

49. *Cheyenne Daily Sun,* January 12, 1877; Elizabeth McGinnis Snow Interview, August 1, 1950, Fort Laramie National Historic Site Research Collections.

50. Department of the Platte Special Orders no. 5, January 12, 1877.

51. Bourke Diary, vol. 16, December 31, 1876–January 3, 1877, pp. 1549–51; *Cheyenne Daily Sun,* January 4, 1877.

52. Ibid.; Bourke, *Mackenzie's Last Fight,* p. 43; Vaughn, *Reynolds Campaign on Powder River,* p. 172.

53. *Cheyenne Daily Sun,* January 5, 1877.

54. Vaughn, *Reynolds Campaign on Powder River,* pp. 172–78; *Cheyenne Daily Sun,* January 14, 1877.

55. Vaughn, *Reynolds Campaign on Powder River,* pp. 178, 183–86.

56. Fort Laramie Special Orders no. 4, January 4, 1877; Red Canyon Telegrams Received, January 8, 1877. Recovery of this weaponry is not reported in any subsequent post records.

57. Red Canyon Telegrams Sent, January 11, 1877; Red Canyon Telegrams Received, January 12, 1877; Fort Laramie Letters Sent, January 14, 1877.

58. Fort Laramie Special Orders no. 2, January 2, 1877, no. 8, January 8, and no. 9, January 9, 1877; *Cheyenne Daily Sun,* January 16, 1877; Fort Laramie Post Return, January 1877; Third Cavalry Regimental Return, January 1877.

59. Fort Laramie Special Orders no. 13, January 14, 1877; Fort Laramie Post Return, January 1877; Third Cavalry Regimental Return, January 1877.

60. Department of the Platte General Orders no. 9, March 16, 1877.

61. Flannery, *John Hunton's Diary,* pp. 172–73; *Cheyenne Daily Sun,* January 16, 24, 1877.

62. Fort Laramie Letters Sent, January 18, 1877.

63. Harry H. Anderson, "Indian Peace-Talkers and the Conclusion of the Sioux War of 1876," *Nebraska History* 44 (December 1963): 236.

64. Ibid., pp. 233–35; *Cheyenne Daily Sun,* January 7, 1877; Hyde, *Spotted Tail's Folk,* pp. 264–65.

Chapter Eight

1. Utley, *Frontier Regulars,* pp. 276–79; Olson, *Red Cloud and the Sioux Problem,* pp. 237–38.

2. Anderson, "Indian Peace-Talkers," pp. 239–45; Hyde, *Spotted Tail's Folk,* pp. 266–67; Oliver Knight, "War or Peace: The Anxious Wait for Crazy Horse," *Nebraska History* 54 (Winter 1973): 526. See also Clow, "Sioux Nation and Indian Territory," pp. 456–73.

3. Department of the Platte Letters Sent, March 13, 1877; Anderson, "Indian Peace-Talkers," pp. 245–46.

4. Bourke Diary, vol. 19, pp. 1837–38.

5. Ibid., pp. 1844–49. Bourke mistakenly identified the headquarters stables as the remains of the American Fur Company's Fort John from thirty years earlier. In fact, Fort John was long gone by 1876, and the reference is to the fortified quartermaster corral near the storehouses.

6. Ibid., pp. 1851–52.
7. Ibid., April 4, 1877, p. 1852; Anderson, "Indian Peace-Talkers," pp. 249–51.
8. "Red Cloud's Mission to Crazy Horse, 1877: Source Material," *Museum of the Fur Trade Quarterly* 22 (Spring 1986): 9–13; Olson, *Red Cloud and the Sioux Problem,* p. 238; Bourke Diary, vol. 19, April 10, 1877, p. 1858, and undated, p. 1918; Anderson, "Indian Peace-Talkers," pp. 250–52.
9. *Cheyenne Daily Sun,* May 6, 1877; Bourke Diary, vol. 19, April 28, 1877, p. 1919; Knight, "War or Peace," 538; Olson, *Red Cloud and the Sioux Problem,* p. 239. Olson incorrectly identifies the officer as a Lieutenant Rosecrans.
10. Knight, "War or Peace," pp. 539–41; Olson, *Red Cloud and the Sioux Problem,* p. 239; Bourke Diary, vol. 20, May 6, 1877, pp. 1948–87; Anderson, "Indian Peace Talkers," p. 235; Bourke, *On the Border with Crook,* p. 412.
11. Bourke Diary, vol. 20, p. 1994; Hyde, *Red Cloud's Folk,* p. 292.
12. Department of the Platte Letters Sent, December 9, 1876; Department of the Platte Chief Quartermaster Letters Sent, December 8, 1876.
13. Department of the Platte Telegrams Sent, January 9, 1877; Fort Laramie Post Returns, January–December 1877.
14. Fort Laramie Special Orders no. 31, February 2, 1877; Fort Laramie Letters Sent, February 7, 1877; Department of the Platte General Orders no. 4, February 19, 1877.
15. Fort Laramie Special Orders no. 37, February 19, and no. 50, February 25, 1877.
16. Fort Laramie Special Orders no. 44, February 19, and no. 59, March 10, 1877.
17. Parker, *Gold in the Black Hills,* pp. 184–87.
18. Ibid., p. 119; Spring, *Cheyenne and Black Hills Stage and Express Routes,* pp. 196–97.
19. Spring, *Cheyenne and Black Hills Stage and Express Routes,* pp. 127–28, 164–65, 207.
20. Camp Mouth of Red Canyon Telegrams Received, April 9, 1877, and Telegrams Sent, April 9, 1877.
21. Camp Mouth of Red Canyon Telegrams Received, June 1, 1877, and Telegrams Sent, June 2, 1877; Fort Laramie Special Orders

no. 128, June 1, and no. 129, June 2, 1877; Murray, "Camp at the Mouth of Red Canyon," pp. 8–9.

22. Fort Laramie Post Return, June 1877; Fourth Infantry Regimental Return, June 1877, microfilm publication 665, roll 47, National Archives and Records Service.

23. Spring, *Cheyenne and Black Hills Stage and Express Routes,* pp. 208–18; Fort Laramie Letters Sent, June 30, 1877.

24. Fort Laramie Special Orders no. 149, June 22, and no. 168, July 15, 1877; Fourteenth Infantry Regimental Return, June 1877; Hedren, "Cp. Hat Creek, Wyo.," p. 30; Third Cavalry Regimental Return, July and December 1877.

25. Hyde, *Red Cloud's Folk,* pp. 294–96; Olson, *Red Cloud and the Sioux Problem,* pp. 241–43.

26. Olson, *Red Cloud and the Sioux Problem,* p. 243; Bourke, *On the Border with Crook,* p. 420; Fort Laramie Special Order no. 205, September 1, 1877; Third Cavalry Regimental Return, September 1877.

27. Olson, *Red Cloud and the Sioux Problem,* pp. 243–44; Bourke, *On the Border with Crook,* pp. 420–21.

28. Olson, *Red Cloud and the Sioux Problem,* p. 244; E. A. Brininstool, ed., *Crazy Horse: The Invincible Oglalla Sioux Chief* (Los Angeles: Wetzel, 1949), pp. 30–34, 50; John M. Carroll, Foreword in Richard G. Hardorff, *The Oglala Lakota Crazy Horse: A Preliminary Genealogical Study and an Annotated Listing of Primary Sources* (Mattituck, N.Y.: J. M. Carroll, 1985), pp. 9, 15. See also Robert A. Clark, ed., *The Killing of Chief Crazy Horse* (Glendale, Calif.: Arthur H. Clark, 1976); and Julia B. McGillycuddy, *McGillycuddy Agent* (Stanford, Calif.: Stanford University Press, 1941).

29. Bourke, *On the Border with Crook,* p. 423.

Epilogue

1. U.S. Congress, Senate, *Cost of the Late War with the Sioux Indians,* Exec. Doc. no. 33, 45th Congress, 2d session, pp. 1–4.

2. Ibid., p. 3. See also Don Russell, "How Many Indians Were Killed?" *American West* 10 (July 1973): 42–47, 61–63, for additional insightful analysis.

3. *Report of the Secretary of War* (1875), p. 56; *Report of the Secretary of War* (1876), pp. 42–45, 48–49.

4. *Report of the Secretary of War* (1877), pp. 16–21.

5. *Report of the Secretary of War* (1875), pp. 57–58; *Report of the Secretary of War* (1876), p. 442; Utley, *Frontier Regulars,* pp. 290–91; Robert M. Utley, "War Houses in the Sioux Country," *Montana: The Magazine of Western History* 35 (Autumn 1985): 18–25.

6. Utley, *Frontier Regulars,* p. 291.

7. Olson, *Red Cloud and the Sioux Problem,* p. 246.

8. Utley, *Frontier Regulars,* pp. 284–85.

9. Ibid., pp. 285–88; Christopher C. Joyner, "The Hegira of Sitting Bull to Canada: Diplomatic Realpolitik, 1876–1881," *Journal of the West* 13 (April 1974): 12–16.

10. Fort Laramie Post Return, November 1876; Hardorff, *Oglala Lakota Crazy Horse,* p. 14.

11. *American Decorations: A List of Awards of the Congressional Medal of Honor, the Distinguished-Service Cross and the Distinguished-Service Medal Awarded under the Authority of the Congress of the United States, 1862–1926* (Washington, D.C.: Government Printing Office, 1926), pp. 7, 67, 90; Vaughn, *With Crook at the Rosebud,* pp. 158–59; John M. Carroll, ed., *The Medal of Honor: Its History and Recipients for the Indian Wars* (Bryan, Tex.: Privately published, 1979), pp. 5–6, 59, 75.

12. Richard B. Hughes, *Pioneer Years in the Black Hills* (Glendale, Calif.: Arthur H. Clark, 1957), p. 194.

13. Fort Laramie Letters Received, February 6, 1880.

14. Clow, "Sioux Nation and Indian Territory," 470–72; George E. Hyde, *A Sioux Chronicle* (Norman: University of Oklahoma Press, 1956), chap. 1.

15. Boards of survey were convened by special order. By comparison Fort Laramie special orders for 1871 were scanned, and fewer than twenty supply shipments were received from Cheyenne Depot.

16. Robrock, "History of Fort Fetterman, Wyoming," p. 56.

17. Mattes, *Indians, Infants and Infantry,* p. 230.

Bibliography

Manuscripts

Carlisle Barracks, Pennsylvania. United States Army Military History Institute. Luther P. Bradley Diary.

Cheyenne, Wyoming, Wyoming State Archives. Christian C. Hewett Diary and File.

Eugene, Oregon. University of Oregon. George Crook Papers.

Fort Laramie, Wyoming. Fort Laramie National Historic Site. George O. Reid Interview; Elizabeth McGinnis Snow Interview; Research Collections.

Laramie, Wyoming, University of Wyoming. Archives-American Heritage Center. Thaddeus Hurlbut Capron Collection.

San Marino, California. Henry Huntington Library. Walter S. Schuyler Papers.

Washington, D.C., Library of Congress. Philip H. Sheridan Papers.

Washington, D.C., National Archives and Records Service. Microfilm publication 665, roll 47. Fourth Infantry Regimental Returns, 1876–85.

―――. Microfilm publication 665, roll 104. Ninth Infantry Regimental Returns, 1870–79.

―――. Microfilm publication 665, roll 155. Fourteenth Infantry Regimental Returns, 1873–82.

―――. Microfilm publication 665, roll 237. Twenty-third Infantry

Regimental Returns, 1874–82.

———. Microfilm publication 727, roll 30. Fourth Artillery Regimental Returns, 1871–77.

———. Microfilm publication 744, roll 19. Second Cavalry Regimental Returns, 1872–79.

———. Microfilm publication 744, roll 31. Third Cavalry Regimental Returns, 1876–84.

———. Microfilm publication 744, roll 42. Fourth Cavalry Regimental Returns, 1872–76.

———. Microfilm publication 744, roll 53. Fifth Cavalry Regimental Returns, 1872–76.

———. Record Group 92. Records of the Office of the Quartermaster General. Persons and Articles Hired, Fort Laramie, 1875–76.

———. Record Group 393. Records of United States Army Continental Commands, 1821–1920. Big Horn and Yellowstone Expedition, Letters Sent, Memoranda, Orders, Telegrams, 1876.

———. Record Group 393. Black Hills Expedition, General Orders, Special Orders, 1875.

———. Record Group 393. Camp at Cheyenne Depot, Post Returns, 1876.

———. Record Group 393. Department of the Platte, Chief Quartermaster Letters Sent, 1876; General Court-Martial Orders, 1876; General Orders, 1876–77; Letters Sent, 1876–77; Register of Contracts, 1876; Special Orders, 1876–77; Telegrams Sent, 1875–77.

———. Record Group 393. District of the Black Hills, General Orders, Special Orders, 1875–76.

———. Record Group 393. Fort Laramie, Circulars, 1876; Deaths at Post, 1875–77; General Orders, 1872, 1875–76; Letters Sent, 1875–77; Letters Sent, Endorsements, etc., Camp Mouth of Red Canyon, 1876–77; Letters Received, 1876, 1880; Medical History, 1874–76; Post Returns, 1875–77; Record of Burials, 1875–77; Register of Sick and Wounded, 1876; Special Orders, 1871, 1876–77.

———. Record Group 393. Military Division of the Missouri, Letters Sent, 1876.

West Point, New York. United States Military Academy. John G. Bourke Diaries.

Government Documents

U.S. Congress. House. *Annual Report of Capt. W.S. Stanton, Corps of Engineers, for the Fiscal Year Ending June 30, 1878*. Ex. Doc. no. 1, pt. 2, 45th Congress, 3d session. Serial 1846.

———. House. *Report of the Commissioner of Indian Affairs* (1875). Ex. Doc. no. 1, pt. 5, 44th Congress, 1st session. Serial 1680.

———. House. *Report of the Commissioner of Indian Affairs* (1876). Ex. Doc. no. 1, pt. 5, 44th Congress, 2d session. Serial 1749.

———. House. *Report of the Commissioner of Indian Affairs* (1877). Ex. Doc. no. 1, pt. 5, 45th Congress, 2d session. Serial 1800.

———. House. *Report of the Secretary of War* (1875). Ex. Doc. no. 1, pt. 2, 44th Congress, 1st session. Serial 1674.

———. House. *Report of the Secretary of War* (1876). Ex. Doc. no. 1, pt. 2, 44th Congress, 2d session. Serial 1742.

———. House. *Report of the Secretary of War* (1877). Ex. Doc. no. 1, pt. 2, 45th Congress, 2d session. Serial 1794.

———. House. *Sioux Indians*. Ex. Doc. no. 145, 44th Congress, 1st session. Serial 1689.

———. House. *Supplies for Indians at Red Cloud Agency*. Ex. Doc. no. 103, 44th Congress, 1st session. Serial 1689.

———. Senate. *Costs of the Late War with the Sioux Indians*. Ex. Doc. no. 33, 45th Congress, 2d session. Serial 1780.

Newspapers

Army and Navy Journal, 1876.
Black Hills Pioneer, 1876.
Cheyenne Daily Leader, 1876.
Cheyenne Daily Sun, 1876–77.
Helena Daily Independent, 1876.
New York Herald, 1876.

Periodical Articles

Anderson, Grant K. "Samuel D. Hinman and the Opening of the Black Hills." *Nebraska History* 60 (Winter 1979): 520–42.

Anderson, Harry H. "A Challenge to Brown's Indian Wars Thesis." *Montana: The Magazine of Western History* 12 (January 1962): 40–49.

———. "Charles King's 'Campaigning with Crook.'" *Chicago Westerners Brand Book* 32 (January 1976): 65–67, 70–72.

————. "Cheyennes at the Little Big Horn—a Study of Statistics." *North Dakota Historical Society Quarterly* 27 (Spring 1960): 3–15.

————. "Indian Peace-Talkers and the Conclusion of the Sioux War of 1876." *Nebraska History* 44 (December 1963): 233–55.

Athearn, Robert G. "The Firewagon Road." *Montana: The Magazine of Western History* 20 (April 1970): 2–19.

Brown, Mark. "A New Focus on the Sioux War." *Montana: The Magazine of Western History* 11 (October 1961): 76–85.

Buecker, Thomas R. "The Post of North Platte Station, 1867–1878." *Nebraska History* 63 (Fall 1982): 381–98.

Capron, Cynthia J. "The Indian Border War of 1876." *Journal of the Illinois State Historical Society* 13 (January 1921): 476–503.

Clough, Wilson P. "Mini-Aku, Daughter of Spotted Tail." *Annals of Wyoming* 39 (October 1967): 187–216.

Clow, Richmond L. "General Philip H. Sheridan's Legacy: The Sioux Pony Campaign of 1876." *Nebraska History* 57 (Winter 1976): 461–77.

————. "The Sioux Nation and Indian Territory: The Attempted Removal of 1876." *South Dakota History* 6 (Fall 1976): 456–73.

Cochran, Alice. "The Gold Dust Trail: Jack Langrishe's Mining Town Theaters." *Montana: The Magazine of Western History* 20 (Spring 1970): 58–69.

Conard, Jane. "Charles Collins: The Sioux City Promotion of the Black Hills." *South Dakota History* 2 (Spring 1972): 131–71.

Dobak, William A. " 'Yellow-Leg Journalists': Enlisted Men as Newspaper Reporters." *Journal of the West* 13 (January 1974): 86–112.

Ewers, John C. "Intertribal Warfare as the Precursor of Indian-White Warfare on the Northern Great Plains." *Western Historical Quarterly* 6 (October 1975): 397–410.

Gray, John S. "News from Paradise: Charley Reynolds Rides from the Black Hills to Fort Laramie." *By Valor and Arms: The Journal of American Military History* 3 (1978): 38–42.

Guentzel, Richard. "The Department of the Platte and Western Settlement, 1866–1877." *Nebraska History* 56 (Fall 1975): 388–417.

Hedren, Paul L. "Captain King's Centennial Year Look at Fort Laramie, Wyoming." *Annals of Wyoming* 48 (Spring 1976): 102–8.

————. "Cp. Hat Creek, Wyo." *Periodical: Journal of the Council on Abandoned Military Posts* 6 (Winter 1974–75): 29–32.

————. "An Infantry Company in the Sioux Campaign, 1876." *Montana: The Magazine of Western History* 33 (Winter 1983): 30–39.

————, ed. "Campaigning with the Fifth Cavalry: Private James B. Frew's Diary and Letters from the Great Sioux War of 1876." *Nebraska History* 65 (Winter 1984): 442–66.

————, ed. "Eben Swift's Army Service on the Plains, 1876–1879." *Annals of Wyoming* 50 (Spring 1978): 141–55.

Joyner, Christopher C. "The Hegira of Sitting Bull to Canada: Diplomatic Realpolitic, 1876–1881." *Journal of the West* 13 (April 1974): 6–18.

King, Charles. "Faster Than the Fastest Pony." *Youth's Companion,* February 9, 1911, p. 71.

————. "Long Distance Riding." *Cosmopolitan,* January 1894, pp. 295–302.

King, James T. "General Crook at Camp Cloud Peak: 'I Am at a Loss What to Do.'" *Journal of the West* 11 (January 1972): 114–27.

Knight, Oliver. "War or Peace: The Anxious Wait for Crazy Horse." *Nebraska History* 54 (Winter 1973): 521–44.

Larsen, Arthur J., ed. "The Black Hills Gold Rush: Letters from Men Who Participated." *North Dakota Historical Quarterly* 6 (July 1932): 302–18.

McDermott, John D. "Fort Laramie's Iron Bridge." *Annals of Wyoming* 34 (October 1962): 136–44.

————. "Fort Laramie's Silent Soldier, Leodegar Schnyder." *Annals of Wyoming* 36 (April 1964): 4–18.

Mahnken, Norbert R. "The Sidney–Black Hills Trail." *Nebraska History* 30 (September 1949): 203–25.

Murray, Robert A. "The Camp at the Mouth of Red Canyon." *Periodical: Journal of the Council on Abandoned Military Posts* 1 (January 1967): 2–9.

Parker, Watson. "The Majors and the Miners: The Role of the U.S. Army in the Black Hills Gold Rush." *Journal of the West* 11 (January 1972): 99–113.

————. "The Report of Captain John Mix of a Scout to the Black Hills, March–April 1875." *South Dakota History* 7 (Fall 1977): 385–401.

————. "Report of the Reverend Samuel D. Hinman of an Expedition to the Black Hills during August, 1874." *Bits and Pieces* 5 (November 1969): 5–9.

"Red Cloud's Mission to Crazy Horse, 1877: Source Material." *Museum of the Fur Trade Quarterly* 22 (Spring 1986): 9–13.

Richardson, Leander P. "A Trip to the Black Hills." *Scribner's Monthly,* April 1877, pp. 748–56.

Robrock, David R. "A History of Fort Fetterman, Wyoming, 1867–1882." *Annals of Wyoming* 48 (Spring 1976): 4–76.

Russell, Don. "How Many Indians Were Killed?" *American West* 10 (July 1973): 42–47, 61–63.

Schaedel, Grace L. "Isaac Bard Stage Station—Little Bear, Wyoming, with Notes from His Diaries 1874–1876." *Annals of Wyoming* 37 (April 1965): 84–88.

Utley, Robert M. "War Houses in the Sioux Country." *Montana: The Magazine of Western History* 35 (Autumn 1985): 18–25.

Vaughn, J. W. "Captain James Egan." *Westerners (New York Posse) Brand Book* 13 (1966): 1–3, 6–7, 18.

White, Richard. "The Winning of the West: The Expansion of the Western Sioux in the Eighteenth and Nineteenth Centuries." *Journal of American History* 65 (September 1978): 319–43.

Books and Pamphlets

Alberts, Don E. *Brandy Station to Manila Bay: A Biography of General Wesley Merritt.* Austin: Presidial Press, 1981.

American Decorations: A List of Awards of the Congressional Medal of Honor, the Distinguished-Service Cross and the Distinguished-Service Medal Awarded under the Authority of the Congress of the United States, 1862–1926. Washington, D.C.: Government Printing Office, 1926.

Bourke, John G. *Mackenzie's Last Fight with the Cheyennes.* New York: Military Service Institution, 1890; reprinted Bellevue, Nebr.: Old Army Press, 1970.

———. *On the Border with Crook.* New York: Charles Scribner's Sons, 1902.

Brininstool, E. A. *Crazy Horse: The Invincible Oglalla Sioux Chief.* Los Angeles: Wetzel, 1949.

Brown, Dee. *The Year of the Century: 1876.* New York: Charles Scribner's Sons, 1966.

Brown, Jesse, and A. M. Willard. *The Black Hills Trails.* Rapid City, S.Dak.: Rapid City Journal Company, 1924.

Carroll, John M., ed. *The Medal of Honor: Its History and Recipients for the Indian Wars*. Bryan, Tex.: Privately published, 1979.

Chronological List of Actions, etc., with Indians from January 15, 1837 to January, 1891. Fort Collins, Colo.: Old Army Press, 1979.

Clark, Robert A., ed. *The Killing of Chief Crazy Horse*. Glendale, Calif.: Arthur H. Clark, 1976.

Collins, John S. *Across the Plains in '64*. Omaha: National Printing, 1904.

————. *My Experiences in the West*. Chicago: Lakeside Press, 1970.

Crawford, Jack. *The Poet Scout*. San Francisco: H. Keller, 1879.

Curley, Edwin A. *Curley's Guide to the Black Hills*. Chicago: Author, 1876; reprinted Mitchell, S.Dak.: Dakota Wesleyan University Press, 1973.

Danker, Donald F., ed. *Man of the Plains: Recollections of Luther North, 1856–1882*. Lincoln: University of Nebraska Press, 1961.

DeBarth, Joe. *The Life and Adventures of Frank Grouard*. Norman: University of Oklahoma Press, 1958.

Dodge, Richard I. *The Black Hills*. Minneapolis: Ross and Haines, 1965.

Dunlay, Thomas W. *Wolves for the Blue Soldiers: Indian Scouts and Auxiliaries with the United States Army, 1860–90*. Lincoln: University of Nebraska Press, 1982.

Ellis, Richard N. *General Pope and U.S. Indian Policy*. Albuquerque: University of New Mexico Press, 1970.

Engebretson, Doug. *Empty Saddles, Forgotten Names: Outlaws of the Black Hills and Wyoming*. Aberdeen, S.Dak.: North Plains Press, 1982.

Finerty, John F. *War-Path and Bivouac*. Norman: University of Oklahoma Press, 1961.

Flannery, L. G., ed. *John Hunton's Diary*. Vol. 2. *1876–'77*. Lingle, Wyo.: Guide-Review, 1958.

General Orders, Adjutant General's Office, 1876. Washington, D.C.: Government Printing Office, 1877.

Goplen, Arnold O. *The Historical Significance of Fort Lincoln State Park*. Bismarck: State Historical Society of North Dakota, n.d.; reprinted from *North Dakota History* 13 (October 1956).

Grange, Roger T., Jr. *Fort Robinson: Outpost on the Plains*. Lincoln: Nebraska State Historical Society, 1965.

Gray, John S. *Centennial Campaign: The Sioux War of 1876*. Fort Collins, Colo.: Old Army Press, 1976.

Greene, Jerome A. *Slim Buttes, 1876: An Episode of the Great Sioux War*. Norman: University of Oklahoma Press, 1982.

Grinnell, George B. *The Fighting Cheyennes*. Norman: University of Oklahoma Press, 1955.

Hafen, LeRoy R., and Francis M. Young. *Fort Laramie and the Pageant of the West, 1834–1890*. Glendale, Calif.: Arthur H. Clark, 1938.

Hardorff, Richard G. *The Oglala Lakota Crazy Horse: A Preliminary Genealogical Study and an Annotated Listing of Primary Sources*. Mattituck, N.Y.: J. M. Carroll, 1985.

Hedren, Paul L. *First Scalp for Custer: The Skirmish at Warbonnet Creek, Nebraska, July 17, 1876*. Glendale, Calif.: Arthur H. Clark, 1980.

———. *King on Custer: An Annotated Bibliography*. College Station, Tex.: Brazos Corral of the Westerners, 1982.

———. *With Crook in the Black Hills: Stanley J. Morrow's 1876 Photographic Legacy*. Boulder, Colo.: Pruett, 1985.

Heitman, Francis B. *Historical Register and Dictionary of the United States Army*. 2 vols. Washington, D.C.: Government Printing Office, 1903; reprinted Urbana: University of Illinois Press, 1965.

Henry, B. William, Jr. "Record of Skirmishes That Took Place between Soldiers, both Regular Army and State Militia, and Indians Within a Seventy Mile Radius of Fort Laramie, June 1849–March 1890." Fort Laramie National Historic Site, Wyoming, May 1970. Typescript.

Hieb, David L. *Fort Laramie National Monument*. Washington, D.C.: National Park Service, 1954.

Hughes, Richard B. *Pioneer Years in the Black Hills*. Glendale, Calif.: Arthur H. Clark, 1957.

Hutton, Paul A. *Phil Sheridan and His Army*. Lincoln: University of Nebraska Press, 1985.

Hyde, George E. *Red Cloud's Folk: A History of the Oglala Sioux Indians*. Norman: University of Oklahoma Press, 1975.

———. *A Sioux Chronicle*. Norman: University of Oklahoma Press, 1956.

———. *Spotted Tail's Folk*. Norman: University of Oklahoma Press, 1974.

Jackson, Donald. *Custer's Gold: The United States Cavalry Expedition of 1874*. New Haven: Yale University Press, 1966.

Jones, Brian. "Those Wild Reshaw Boys." In *Sidelights of the Sioux Wars*, ed. Francis B. Taunton, pp. 5–46. London: English Westerners' Society, 1967.

Kappler, Charles J. *Indian Treaties, 1778–1883*. New York: Interland, 1972.

King, Charles. *Campaigning with Crook and Stories of Army Life*. New York: Harper, 1890.

———. *Laramie; or, The Queen of Bedlam*. Philadelphia: J. B. Lippincott, 1889.

King, James T. *War Eagle: A Life of General Eugene A. Carr*. Lincoln: University of Nebraska Press, 1963.

Knight, Oliver. *Following the Indian Wars: The Story of Newspaper Correspondents among the Indian Campaigners*. Norman: University of Oklahoma Press, 1960.

Lavender, David. *Fort Laramie and the Changing Frontier*. Washington, D.C.: National Park Service, 1983.

McDermott, John D., and James Sheire. *1874 Cavalry Barracks Historic Structures Report: Historical Data Section*. Washington, D.C.: National Park Service, 1970.

McFeeley, William S. *Grant: A Biography*. New York: W. W. Norton, 1981.

McGillycuddy, Julia B. *McGillycuddy Agent*. Stanford, Calif.: Stanford University Press, 1941.

Mattes, Merrill J. *Indians, Infants and Infantry: Andrew and Elizabeth Burt on the Frontier*. Denver: Old West, 1960.

Mattes, Merrill J., and Thor Borreson. "The Historic Approaches to Fort Laramie." Fort Laramie National Monument, Wyoming, October 1947. Typescript.

Meketa, Ray, ed. *Marching with General Crook, Being the Diary of Lieutenant Thaddeus Hurlbut Capron Company C, Ninth Infantry*. Douglas, Alaska: Cheechako Press, 1983.

Murray, Robert A. *Military Posts in the Powder River Country of Wyoming, 1865–1894*. Lincoln: University of Nebraska Press, 1968.

Nadeau, Remi. *Fort Laramie and the Sioux Indians*. Englewood Cliffs, N.J.: Prentice-Hall, 1967.

Nohl, Lessing H., Jr. "Mackenzie against Dull Knife: Breaking the Northern Cheyennes in 1876." In *Probing the American West*, ed. K.

Ross Toole et al., pp. 86–92. Santa Fe: Museum of New Mexico Press, 1962.

Olson, James C. *Red Cloud and the Sioux Problem.* Lincoln: University of Nebraska Press, 1965.

Outline Description of the Posts in the Military Division of the Missouri. Chicago: Headquarters Military Division of the Missouri, 1876; reprinted Bellevue, Nebr.: Old Army Press, 1969.

Parker, W. Thornton, ed. *Records of the Association of Acting Assistant Surgeons of the United States Army.* Salem, Mass.: Salem Publishing and Printing, 1891.

Parker, Watson. *Gold in the Black Hills.* Norman: University of Oklahoma Press, 1966.

Porter, Joseph C. *Paper Medicine Man: John Gregory Bourke and His American West.* Norman: University of Oklahoma Press, 1986.

Price, George F. *Across the Continent with the Fifth Cavalry.* New York: Antiquarian Press, 1959.

Rand McNally's Pioneer Atlas of the American West. Chicago: Rand McNally, 1956.

Record of Engagements with Hostile Indians within the Military Division of the Missouri, from 1868 to 1882. Washington, D.C.: Government Printing Office, 1882; reprinted Bellevue, Nebr.: Old Army Press, 1969.

Rickey, Don, Jr., and James W. Sheire. *The Cavalry Barracks Fort Laramie Furnishing Study.* Washington, D.C.: National Park Service, 1969.

Rodenbough, Theo. F., ed. *The Army of the United States.* New York: Argonaut Press, 1966.

Rosa, Joseph G. *They Called Him Wild Bill: The Life and Adventures of James Butler Hickok.* Norman: University of Oklahoma Press, 1964.

Russell, Don. *The Lives and Legends of Buffalo Bill.* Norman: University of Oklahoma Press, 1960.

Schmidt, Martin F., ed. *George Crook: His Autobiography.* Norman: University of Oklahoma Press, 1960.

Spring, Agnes Wright. *The Cheyenne and Black Hills Stage and Express Routes.* Lincoln: University of Nebraska Press, 1967.

———. "Dr. McGillycuddy's Diary." In *The Denver Westerners 1953 Brand Book,* ed. Maurice Frink, pp. 277–307. Denver: Westerners, 1954.

Stanton, W. S. *Table of Distances and Itineraries of Routes between the Military Posts in, and to Certain Points Contiguous to, the Department of the Platte*. Omaha: Headquarters Department of the Platte, 1877.

Thian, Raphael D. *Notes Illustrating the Military Geography of the United States*. Washington, D.C.: Government Printing Office, 1881; reprinted Austin: University of Texas Press, 1979.

Triggs, J. H. *History of Cheyenne and Northern Wyoming Embracing the Gold Fields of the Black Hills, Powder River and Big Horn Countries*. Omaha: Herald Steam Book and Job Printing House, 1876.

————. *A Reliable and Correct Guide to the Black Hills, Powder River, and Big Horn Gold Fields!* Omaha: Herald Steam Book and Job Printing House, 1876.

Turchen, Lesta V., and James D. McLaird. *The Black Hills Expedition of 1875*. Mitchell, S.Dak.: Dakota Wesleyan University Press, 1975.

Utley, Robert M. *Frontier Regulars: The United States Army and the Indian, 1866–1890*. New York: Macmillan, 1973.

————. *The Indian Frontier of the American West, 1846–1890*. Albuquerque: University of New Mexico Press, 1984.

Utley, Robert M., and Francis A. Ketterson, Jr. *Golden Spike*. Washington, D.C.: National Park Service, 1969.

Vaughn, J. W. *Indian Fights: New Facts on Seven Encounters*. Norman: University of Oklahoma Press, 1966.

————. *The Reynolds Campaign on Powder River*. Norman: University of Oklahoma Press, 1961.

————. *With Crook at the Rosebud*. Harrisburg, Pa.: Stackpole, 1956.

Walton, Clyde C., ed. *An Illinois Gold Hunter in the Black Hills: The Diary of Jerry Bryan, March 13 to August 20, 1876*. Springfield: Illinois State Historical Society, 1960.

Wheeler, Homer W. *Buffalo Days: Forty Years in the Old West*. New York: A. L. Burt, 1925.

White, Thomas E. "Post Surgeons at Fort Laramie, June 16, 1849 to March 19, 1890." Fort Laramie National Historic Site, Wyoming. April, 1972. (Typescript.)

Wilhelm, Thomas. *A Military Dictionary and Gazetteer*. Philadelphia: L. R. Hamersly, 1881.

Willert, James, ed. *The Cuthbert Mills Letters to New York Times during the Indian War of 1876*. La Mirada, Calif.: James Willert, 1984.

Index

Big Horn and Yellowstone
Expedition (*cont.*)
described, 190; wounded, 200–
201
Bighorn Barracks, 235
Big Horn Expedition, 60, 68, 71,
87, 187; Noyes court-martial,
82; organized, 53; Reynolds
court-martial, 208, 216–17
Big Horn Mountains, 5, 202; mili-
tary posts near, 142; and treaty
rights, 15
Bighorn River, 171, 236
Big Road, 226
Bishop Whipple Mission, 249n23
Bismarck, 7, 9, 60; and Black Hills
routes, 39
Bitter Cottonwood Creek, 67
Black Hills, 4, 11, 13–14; and
Agreement of August 15, 1876,
156; gold, 10, 13–14, 179–80,
216, 221, 228, 236; miners described, 145; newspaper coverage, 42; routes to, 39; and
Sioux Commission, 179; and
Sioux War, 234; traffic to, 73
Black Hills Expedition of 1874,
10–12
Black Hills Expedition of 1875, 14
Black Hills Pioneer, 207
Black Hills Road, 26, 39, 228; described, 138; and Indians, 51,
138–39, 228; military protection for, 99–100, 103, 119, 135;
and Powder River trail, 35; stations, 51; troops on, 98
Black Hills stage, 51–52, 73, 78,
143; attacked, 140; charges, 67;
to Deadwood, 228–29; Indian
trouble and, 125–26, 130; passengers on, 207–8; and road
agents, 230
Black Hills Telegraph, 42, 89, 191,
207, 238–39

Boone, Albert G., 156
Bordeaux, 66, 85, 201
Bourke, John G., 17, 68, 70, 91–
93, 122, 159, 168–69, 173, 177,
193, 205, 224, 242, 278n5; and
agency surrenders, 225; de-
scribes Cantonment Reno, 202;
describes Cheyenne, 57–58;
and Crazy Horse's surrender,
226; describes Cuny and Ecof-
fey brothel, 45–46; on death of
Crazy Horse, 232; and Dull
Knife battle, 203–4; on Fort
Laramie, 223; and Powder
River Expedition, 196; and
Sioux ponies, 195
Bowman, Jack, 191
Box Elder Creek, 179
Bozeman Trail, 3, 53; and Fort
Fetterman, 24; war, 2
Brackett, Albert G., 29
Bradley, Luther P., 29, 56, 58, 63,
65, 78–79, 195, 208, 217, 232,
257–58n14; and agencies, 79;
and Black Hills, 13; at Camp
Robinson, 231; and weather,
20, 50, 70
Brady, George K., 55, 80
Brandt, William E., 57
Breckenridge, George E., 197
Bridger's Ferry, 53, 141
Bridges. *See* Clarke's bridge; Fort
Laramie: iron bridge
Brown, Charlie, 207
Brown, H. E. ("Stuttering"), 77–78
Brown, Jesse, 77
Brown, Rufus P., 103–4, 218
Brown, Theodore V., 33, 116
Budd, John W., 166
Bullis, Henry C., 156
Bullock, William G., 46
Bull's Bend, 26
Burrowes, Thomas B., 30–31, 79,
84, 97, 175

183, 191, 215, 228, 241; military protection for, 120
Clark, Ben, 59
Clark, Charles, 93
Clark, William P., 168, 225, 232; and Crazy Horse's surrender, 226
Clarke, Henry R., 118
Clarke's Bridge, 39, 118–19
Clements, Bennett A., 179, 201
Clinton, R. V., 75
Clymer, Heister, 72
Coad, John F., 113, 143
Coates, Edwin M., 112, 137, 160, 241
Cody, William F. ("Buffalo Bill"), 291; joins campaign, 109–11; and Gen. Sheridan, 112; at Warbonnet Creek fight, 134; and Yellow Hair trophies, 135
Coffee, Charles F., 84
Cold Springs, 74
Collier, William S., 80, 103, 107–8, 139–40, 191–92, 241; and Crook, 229; and telegraph, 167
Collins, John S., 35, 38, 51, 67, 121, 145, 172–73, 214, 272n60; and army contracting, 113; and Crook, 180–81, 223; on goldfields, 114–15; and Hunton murder, 83–84; develops Rustic House, 52
Collins Cutoff, 58
Columbia School of Mines, 14
Coppinger, John J., 80
Corlett, William W., 198
Cottonwood Creek, 74, 131, 214
Cowen, Benjamin R., 17
Crawford, Emmett, 12
Crawford, Jack, 65–66, 138, 166, 241
Crazy Horse, 16, 48, 59, 68, 202, 213, 220, 222, 225; death of,

232; at Red Cloud Agency, 230–31; surrenders, 225–26
Crazy Woman's Fork of Powder River, 202–3
Crook, George, 19, 25, 55, 57–58, 72, 89, 100, 118, 242, 269n15; and Big Horn and Yellowstone Expedition, 52, 82, 87, 91, 94, 187–89; and Black Hills, 168–69; and Black Hills miners, 15–17; and Black Hills road, 78, 86, 102; campaign strategy, 48–49; and Crazy Horse, 231–32; and District of the Black Hills, 94; and Egan, 169; and Elkhorn Creek fight, 219; and Fifth Cavalry, 109, 132; and Fort Laramie, 99, 170–71, 190, 223, 240; hunting expeditions, 172, 180–81, 223; and Indian scouts, 59–60, 91–92, 195–96; and Japanese officers, 171; and mules, 52; nonconformist style of, 172–73; and Powder River battle, 69; and Powder River country, 160; and Powder River Expedition, 193–94, 202–7, 214–15; and press, 181; and quartermaster support, 56, 102; and Red Cloud, 184–86; and Reynolds, 69–70; and Reynolds-Moore courts-martial, 216; and Rosebud Creek fight, 123–24, 126; and Sheridan, 163, 167, 170–71; and Sioux agencies, 79; and Sioux peace missions, 222–23, 225; and Sioux ponies, 195; and Sioux unhorsings and disarmings, 182; and Sioux War, 215–16, 233–34; and Slim Buttes fight, 165; and Spotted Tail, 186; and starvation march, 159, 165; and

Fort Fetterman (*cont.*)
206, 222, 238, 240; and Big
Horn Expedition, 52–53; and
Big Horn and Yellowstone Expedition, 87, 98; commissary
operations, 54; and Fifth Cavalry, 137; freight operations,
50; and Indians, 140, 241; mail
services, 211; and Powder
River Expedition, 207, 214–15;
and quartermaster operations,
54, 68, 82–83, 88, 102, 142;
roads to, 26; and telegraph,
112, 130, 153, 199–200, 213,
215, 218–19, 244–46; and war
materials, 137
Fort Fred Steele, 87–88, 215
Fort Hartsuff: Sioux raiding, 86–
87, 175
Fort John, 33, 278n5
Fort Keogh, 235
Fort Laramie: administrative operations, 30, 50; and agencies, 8,
106–7, 239; and Allison Commission, 15; "Bedlam," 35, 40–
41, 95; and Big Horn Expedition, 53, 58, 70–71; Big Horn
and Yellowstone Expedition,
87, 94–95, 97; and Black Hills,
10, 13, 19, 238; and Black Hills
Expedition of 1875, 14; and
Black Hills gold, 12, 16; and
Black Hills road, 39, 51, 86;
and Bourke, 223; and Bozeman Trail War, 2–3; and Brown
murder, 78; burials, 94–95,
106; and Calamity Jane, 115;
and Camp Mouth of Red Canyon, 229; and Camp Robinson,
240; as cavalry station, 62, 68;
cemetery, 36; and Centennial,
128, 131; and Cheyenne
ponies, 207; and Christmas,
211–12; and commissary oper-

ations, 30, 33, 54, 83; construction, 36; and courier services,
142–43; and Jack Crawford,
138; and Crazy Horse, 232; and
Crook, 102–3; and Custer battle, 129, 131; daily schedule,
42–43, 198; as depot of supplies, 120; description of, 35–
36; and District of the Black
Hills, 94–95, 120, 239; "Dobie
Row," 36, 39; and Elkhorn
Creek fight, 140, 218–19; en-
tertainments at, 58, 62; and escort services, 82–83; and Fifth
Cavalry, 125, 135; and Fort
John, 278n5; and Fourth Artillery, 149; and Fourth Cavalry,
146, 149; freight operations,
50; garrison courts-martial,
210; garrisons, 28, 35, 88, 131–
32, 188–89, 212–13, 237–38;
and Hunton murder, 84; and
Indian scouts, 59; and Indian
trouble, 128, 139–41, 183–84,
190–91, 241; iron bridge, 27,
37–38, 50, 65, 228, 252n17;
and Japanese visitors, 164; and
Charles King, 121, 123; landscape, 39–40; libraries, 42, 233;
and medical services, 32–33,
83, 123, 138, 201; medical staff,
32–33, 75; and Moore court-
martial, 217; and Ninth Infantry, 190, 195; and ordnance operations, 33, and paymaster,
179; and pony packet line, 73;
and Powder River Expedition,
193–94, 196; and protection
duties, 62; and quartermaster
operations, 44, 52, 54, 56, 62,
82, 107, 120, 142, 167, 175,
199, 207, 214, 227, 245–46,
262n22; recruits for, 164; as refitting station, 107; reservation,

302

44–45, 152, 253n29; and Richard Creek fight, 183; roads, 25,
27, 102, 118; robbery at, 217–
18; and Rosebud Creek fight,
124; Rustic Hotel, 67, 157, 165;
and Second Cavalry, 53, 195;
and Sheridan, 117–18, 166;
and Sioux ponies, 187, 195;
and Sioux surrenders, 226–27;
and Slim Buttes casualties,
165–66; social order, 40; and
Spotted Tail, 115–16; and
Spotted Tail Agency, 6; and
squatters, 213–14; "squaw
camp" at, 161; and stage service, 51–52, 208; and subposts,
191; and summer campaign,
99, 124; and supply operations,
160, 281n15; and telegraph,
42, 44, 62, 89–90, 124, 130,
152–53, 199– 200, 213, 215,
218–19, 238–39, 244–46; and
Third Cavalry, 188–89, 197,
199; trader's store, 38, 121,
135; and transportation, 160,
and treaty violations, 67; and
Twenty-third Infantry, 208;
and Western Union, 200;
Wilson's death, 50; and winter
campaigning, 181

Merritt, Wesley (*cont.*)
and agencies, 63, 79, 103, 106–
7; and Big Horn and Yellow-
stone Expedition, 168–69; and
Crook, 132, 135; disarms
Sioux, 184–85; and Fifth Cav-
alry, 111, 118, 126; and tele-
graph, 130
Metz, Charles, 76–77, 123
Miles, Nelson A., 135, 171, 212,
220, 222, 236–37
Military Division of the Atlantic,
57
Military Division of the Missouri,
24, 49, 63, 149; and Japanese
officers, 164; and summer cam-
paign, 160; staffing, 112
Milk River, 236
Mills, Anson, 97, 242
Mills, Cuthbert, 137
Milner, Moses E., 206
Mini-Aku, 116, 262n26
Missouri River, 13, 21, 228; and
Black Hills routes, 39; and
Sioux agencies, 5–6
Mitchell, D. S., 36, 169–70, 181–
82, 216, 272n63
Mix, John, 13
Monahan, Deane, 194, 218, 231;
and the Elkhorn Creek fight,
218–19; and squatters, 213–14
Monroe, Jack, 184
Montana Column, 87
Montgomery, Robert H., 121
Moore, Alexander, 91, 194, 210,
230; and Powder River fight,
69; court-martial, 208, 216–17
Moore, Thomas, 226
Morrow, Stanley J., 169, 182
Morton, Alfred, 83, 97, 107, 142,
157, 175, 194–95; and Fifth
Cavalry, 125; and quartermas-
ter contracting, 113; and quar-

termaster operations, 30, 44,
55, 163; and telegraph, 113
Morton, Charles, 66, 194, 199
Munn, Curtis E., 58
Munson, Samuel, 30–31, 40, 75–
76, 91, 97, 124, 126, 218
Murrin, Luke, 113, 142

Nash, William H., 54
Nebraska: and the Sioux agencies,
12
Newton, Henry, 14
New York Herald, 16, 97, 174, 181,
196; and Warbonnet fight, 135
New York Times, 137
New York Tribune, 13, 174
Nez Perce Indians, 231, 237
Nickerson, Azor H., 17, 171
Ninth U.S. Infantry, 19, 65, 87,
130, 183, 188, 190, 210; band,
43, 76, 145; and Big Horn and
Yellowstone Expedition, 94–
95; and Black Hills Expedition
of 1875, 14; Company C, 126,
223; Company D, 118, 133;
Company E, 97, 128–29, 131,
148–49, 164, 171, 175; Com-
pany F, 54, 86, 109, 112, 131,
164, 175, 194, 241; Company
H, 139, 165, 189; departs Fort
Laramie, 195; escort duty, 50;
history, 28; recruits for, 75; and
Rosebud Creek fight, 124; at
Slim Buttes fight, 165; transfers, 175–76
Niobrara River, 28, 100, 118–19,
140
Norris, William F., 106, 128–29,
131
North, Frank, 187
North, Luther, 190
Northern Cheyenne Indians, 34,
135, 185, 215, 220, 239; and

agency strife, 103; as army
scouts, 196; census, 155; and
Dull Knife battle, 202–26; and
Indian Creek "butchery," 211–
12; and peace missions, 222;
and Powder River battle, 69;
and surrendered ponies, 207;
surrenders, 212, 223, 225–26;
and Warbonnet fight, 133–34
Northern Pacific Railroad, 9, 28,
60
North Platte, Nebr., 30
North Platte River, 1, 4–7, 26, 34,
39, 53, 63, 98, 119, 128, 137,
141, 227, 232; and Fort
Laramie bridge, 37
North Platte Station, 132
Notu, M., 164
Noyes, Henry E., 30–31, 53, 58,
70, 90, 97, 195; court-martial,
80–82; at Powder River battle,
68–69

Ogden, 24
Old Hawk, 226
Old Man Afraid of His Horses, 7
Old Woman's Fork, 51, 74
Omaha, 19, 24–25
Omaha Barracks, 14, 87, 99, 103,
192, 215
Omaha Bee, 66
Omaha Herald, 114–15
Omaha Republican, 51
Otis, Elwell S., 135
Owen Ranch, 141

Pardee, Julius H., 103, 201, 210
Parker, Joseph, 183
Pawnee Scouts, 185, 191, 203; and
Sioux ponies, 195
"Persimmon Bill." *See* Chambers,
William
Petteys, Charles V., 75, 78, 86, 109,

138, 149, 177, 161, 215, 257;
and Powder River Expedition,
194
Philadelphia Press, 174
Phillips, John, 26, 58
Phillips Ranch, 25, 46, 58, 67, 82,
91, 190–91, 218; troops at, 228
Pine Ridge, 107, 162
Pine Ridge Reservation, 239
Pioneer Pony Express, 143
Pleasant Valley, 74, 229
Plum Creek, 39
Poland, Martin L., 65
Pollock, Edwin, 19, 30–31, 50, 97,
103, 120, 131, 148, 157, 164,
172, 175, 202; on Black Hills,
51; establishes Cantonment
Reno, 171
Pope, John H., 109, 135, 149, 207–
8, 215, 217
Porter, Jeremiah, 106, 260n7
Pourier, Baptiste ("Big Bat"), 59
Powder River, 34, 68, 99–100, 106,
118, 202
Powder River country, 2–3, 15, 18,
24, 52; military occupation,
187–88; and Sioux, 8
Powder River Expedition, 193,
202–6, 212–13; contrasted with
Big Horn Expedition, 196; disbanded, 214–15; organized,
196; supplies from, 207
Powder River fight, 68–70, 83, 98,
233; and Egan's company, 141;
and Reynolds-Moore courts-
martial, 216
Powder River Trail, 34–35, 51,
100, 117–19, 132, 134, 191,
225; military oversight of, 107–
8
Powell, J. L., 123
Pratte and Ferris Ranch, 184
Presidio of San Francisco, 149

Price, Curtis E., 149
Promontory Summit, 8
Pumpkin Buttes, 34

Quartermaster Department, 50; and civilian wages, 44; and contracting, 113; and Medicine Bow, 142; and supply operations, 82–83, 88, 162–63. *See also* Camp Robinson; Cheyenne Depot; Department of the Platte; Fort Fetterman; Fort Laramie

Railroads: and army, 8–9; and military posts, 21; and Sioux, 9. *See also* Kansas Pacific Railroad; Northern Pacific Railroad; Union Pacific Railroad
Randall, George M., 168
Rankin, Joe, 115
Rapid City, 228
Rapid Creek, 14, 179
Rawhide Buttes, 74–75
Rawhide Creek, 28, 125, 184, 189
Rawlins, 88
Raynolds, William F., 10
Red Canyon, 74, 85, 99, 104, 191, 199, 229; Metz "massacre," 76–77, 123. *See also* Camp Mouth of Red Canyon
Red Cloud, 7, 45, 60, 92–93, 184, 187, 196, 202, 215, 222, 236, 239; and Allison Commission, 16; and Bozeman Trail war, 2–3; and Crazy Horse, 232; demands agency, 6; disarmed, 185; and peace mission, 225; and Sioux Commission, 158, 178; and Sioux War, 225; and Spotted Tail, 185–86
Red Cloud Agency, 7–8, 11, 17, 21, 51, 53, 59–60, 62–63, 79, 82,

86, 91–92, 94, 99, 107, 111, 118–19, 124, 152, 154, 156, 163–64, 185–86, 188, 219–20, 230–31, 234, 236, 239; and cattle thievery, 141; and Cheyenne surrenders, 205; and Crazy Horse's surrender, 226; and Fourth Cavalry, 135; and Indian Creek "butchery," 211; and Indian ponies, 227; and Indian rumors, 128–29; population, 34, 155; roads to, 27, 39; and Sioux Commissioners, 178; and Sioux defections, 100, 103; and Sioux surrenders, 223; and stage service, 52; and Warbonnet Creek fight, 133
Red Fork of Powder River, 233. *See also* Dull Knife battle
Red Leaf, 3, 187, 196; disarmed, 185
Redmond, John, 210
Red River War, 233
Reel, A. H. ("Heck"), 140
Regan, James, 83, 97, 175, 194; and commissary contracting, 113; and commissary operations, 30; and Crook, 163
Regan, Jimmie, 161
Republican River, 247n5
Reynolds, Bainbridge, 97, 194, 228
Reynolds, Charles A., 12
Reynolds, Joseph J., 61, 91, 195, 210, 256n47; and Big Horn Expedition, 60; court-martial, 208, 216–17; and Powder River battle, 68–69
Reynolds, R. M., 99, 104, 218
Rhodes (civilian), 182
Richard, Louis, 59
Richard Creek fight, 183, 204, 234, 237, 241

Richardson, Leander P., 137, 242
Robertson, Edgar B., 97, 195
Robinson, Joseph, 238
Robinson, Levi H., 7–8
Roche, Jerry, 196
Rockefeller, Charles M., 175, 194
Rock Island Arsenal, 120
Rocky Mountain News, 95
Rogers, William W., 76, 86, 106,
    131, 175
Rosebud Creek, 106, 159, 202
Rosebud Creek fight, 123, 134,
    204, 233, 238; casualties, 124–
    25, 201; evacuation of
    wounded, 126–28; reports,
    124–25
Rosebud Reservation, 239
Rosenquest, J. Wesley, 226
Ross, Horatio N., 12
Royall, William B., 91, 97–98, 189,
    195
Ruggles, George D., 217
Running Water Creek, 51. *See also*
    Niobrara River
Russell, Gerald, 100, 118–19

Sabille Creek, 141
Sage Creek, 34, 74, 78, 100, 103,
    133, 136, 152, 161, 167, 191,
    199, 210–11, 230, 257n9; and
    Indian problems, 138, 219; mil-
    itary camp on, 107
St. Paul, Minn., 19, 187
Salt Lake City, 89, 130, 149, 211
San Francisco Alta California, 174
Santee Sioux Agency, 15
Saville, J. J., 7–8, 17, 63
Schneider, George, 69
Schnyder, Leodegar, 32–33, 182,
    214, 264n59, 273n64
Schuyler, Walter S., 46, 168, 177,
    223
Schwartz Ranch, 25

Scott's Bluff, 253n29
Second U.S. Cavalry, 19, 32, 52,
    87, 188, 191; and Big Horn Ex-
    pedition, 53, 58; and Black
    Hills Expedition of 1875, 14;
    Company I, 58, 60, 68, 70, 84,
    86–87, 90, 94–95, 97, 165, 189,
    195; Company K, 37, 53, 58,
    60, 68–69, 70, 86, 90, 95, 100,
    107, 119, 120, 126, 130–31,
    134, 140, 141, 145, 146, 157,
    163, 169–70, 175, 183, 189,
    194, 204, 215, 237, 241–42,
    264n57; Company history, 28;
    Montana battalion, 61; and
    Rosebud Creek fight, 124; and
    Richard Creek fight, 183
Seton, Henry, 126
Seventeenth U.S. Infantry, 87
Seventh U.S. Cavalry, 11, 87, 157,
    204, 236
Seventh U.S. Infantry, 87
Seymour, Dick, 143
Sheridan, Michael V., 65, 112
Sheridan, Philip H., 8, 12, 24, 49,
    63, 65, 69, 79, 89, 94, 100, 120,
    227; and Black Hills gold, 11,
    138; and Crazy Horse, 231; and
    Crook, 159, 161, 163, 166–67,
    170–71, 223; and Dull Knife
    battle, 206; and Fifth Cavalry,
    132; and Fort Laramie, 111–12,
    166, 242; and Fourth Cavalry,
    135; and Japanese officers,
    171; and Mackenzie, 146–47;
    and Merritt, 126; and new
    forts, 170–71, 235–36; and
    Powder River country, 160–61;
    and Sioux, 154–55; and Sioux
    agencies, 99, 103, 107, 109,
    116–18; and southeast Wyo-
    ming, 119; and summer opera-
    tions, 124; and Terry, 159; and

Sheridan, Philip (*cont.*)
war strategy, 48, 141–42, 170–71, 233; and White House conference, 17–18; and winter operations, 166–67
Sherman, William T., 2, 79; and Black Hills, 11; and costs of Sioux War, 234
Shoshone Indians, 4
Shoshone Reservation, 21
Sibley, Frederick W., 168
Sidney, Nebr., 144, 148, 208, 210, 228, 231; and Black Hills roads, 39, 51
Sidney Barracks, 21, 62–63, 87–88, 171, 188, 190, 195; and Black Hills traffic, 39
Sidney–Black Hills road, 118–19, 133
Sioux City, 13, 39
Sioux Indians, 94, 171, 215, 236; agencies for, 5–6; agency strife, 103; and Agreement of August 15, 1876, 155–56; and Allison Commission, 16; and army administration, 154; as army scouts, 91–92, 196, 231; attack stage, 140; Blackfoot, 5–6; and Black Hills, 14–15, 155; and Bozeman Trail war, 2–3; Brules, 3, 6, 21, 34, 115–16, 158, 178–79, 185, 220, 222, 225, 239; census, 155; and Crazy Horse, 226, 232; and Elkhorn Creek raid, 219; flee agencies, 100–101, 191; and Fort Laramie Treaty of 1868, 3–11; Hunkpapas, 3, 5, 222, 236; and hunting lands, 155; and Hunton murder, 84–85; Lower Brules, 6; and Metz massacre, 77; Miniconjous, 3, 6–7,

226; and Missouri River agencies, 171, 178, 186–87, 222; moderates among, 220; Northern Sioux defined, 4; Oglalas, 2–3, 6, 21, 34, 45, 69, 158, 178–79, 185–86, 202, 222, 225, 230, 236–37, 239; and pony sales, 195; raiding by, 53, 86, 93–94, 107, 125, 140, 146, 152, 184, 190, 228; and railroads, 9–10; and Red Canyon hostilities, 139; Sans Arcs, 6, 53–54, 226; and Sioux Commission, 178–79; and Slim Buttes fight, 165; and telegraph, 199; Two Kettles band, 6; Yanktonais, 3, 6
Sioux Reservation, 4–5
Sioux War of 1876–77: casualties, 234; causes, 4; close, 215–16; costs, 234; strategies, 233; successes and failures, 233. *See also* Crook; Sheridan; Sherman; White House Conference
Sitting Bull (Hunkpapa), 16, 48, 59, 128, 184, 206, 220, 222, 226, 231, 236; in Canada, 236–37; and Custer fight, 131; surrenders, 237
Sitting Bull (Oglala), 7, 178
Six Mile Ranch, 46, 98, 230
Sixth U.S. Infantry, 87
Slemmer, Adam J., 3
Slim Buttes fight, 165–66, 233; casualties, 200–201
Smead, Alexander D. B., 194, 228, 230
Smith, Edward P., 17–18
Smith, Frank G., 169
Smith, John E., 8, 80, 208, 217
Smoky Hill River, 4, 247n5
South Fork Cheyenne River. *See* Cheyenne River

South Pass, 8
Sparks, John, 84
Spotted Tail, 21, 220, 225, 236, 241; and Allison Commission, 16; and Bozeman Trail War, 3; demands agency, 6; as Oglala chief, 185–86; and peace missions, 222–23, 225; visits Fort Laramie, 115–16
Spotted Tail Agency, 7–8, 12, 15, 21, 28, 62, 79, 82, 92, 99, 111, 130, 149, 154, 176, 178, 188, 223, 232, 234, 239; and Indian ponies, 227; population, 34, 155; and Sioux Commission, 178; and Sioux defections, 100, 103; surrenders at, 226
Spring Creek, 14–15
Springfield Republican, 138
Standing Elk, 178
Standing Rock Agency, 5, 179
Stanton, Thaddeus II., 60, 95, 168, 272n56
Stanton, William S., 140–41; and Fort Laramie bridge, 37, 65
Stebbens, Post and Company, 216
Steele, W. R., 198
Stephens, B. C., 211–12
Stephens, Charles, 201
Stephenson, J. W., 165
Stover, George, 163
Strahorn, Robert E., 95, 98, 242
Sully, Alfred, 208
Sumner, Samuel S., 121
Sutherland, Bill, 143
Sutorious, Alexander, 97
Swain, David G., 217
Swift, Eben, 165
Sykes, George, 208, 217

Taggart, James, 218
Tallent, Annie D., 13

Tashro, S., 164
Tasker, Warren C., 183
Taylor, Frank, 230
Taylor, George McM., 103, 107–8, 132, 136, 164, 182, 191, 210, 241; and Indian raiding, 152; and stage attack, 140; and telegraph, 139, 167
Taylor, Nathaniel G., 2
Telegraph. *See* Black Hills Telegraph; Fort Laramie: and telegraph
Ten Mile Ranch, 214
Terry, Alfred H., 17, 60, 87, 94, 118, 233; and Allison Commission, 15; campaign strategy, 48–49; and costs of Sioux War, 234; and Fort Laramie Treaty of 1868, 2; and Missouri River steamboats, 102; reinforcements for, 135; summer campaign, 158–59; and troop deployments, 235; on Yellowstone River, 159; and Yellowstone River forts, 170–71
Terry, John H., 201
Thayer, John M., 78
Third U.S. Cavalry, 34, 52, 60, 87, 99, 118, 164, 187–89, 200–201, 211, 234, 241; band, 223; and Big Horn Expedition, 53, 91; and Big Horn and Yellowstone Expedition, 97; and Black Hills Expedition of 1875, 14; Company A, 218–19, 238; Company E library, 223; Company F, 230; Company G, 218; and Crazy Horse, 231–32; and Elkhorn Creek fight, 218–19; and Fort Laramie, 194, 199; and Indian raiding, 228; and Powder River fight, 68–69; re-

Third U.S. Cavalry (*cont.*)
cruits for, 197; and Reynolds-
Moore courts-martial, 216
Thompson, I. G., 44
Thompson, John C., 194, 218, 223
Three Mile Ranch, 45–46, 59, 161,
197, 206; and Calamity Jane,
115; and Centennial, 128; and
Ecoffey's death, 201
Throstle, George, 140
Tongue River, 34, 68, 118, 171,
222, 236
Tongue River Barracks, 220, 235
Townsend, E. G., 234
Townsend, Edwin F., 29, 32, 79–
80, 90–91, 95, 97, 100, 120,
135, 192, 215, 237, 241, 251n6,
265n68; and Big Horn and Yellowstone Expedition, 179; and
Black Hills road, 99–100, 103,
118; and Black Hills stage, 130;
and Capron's death, 127–28;
and courier services, 142; and
Crook, 102–3, 160; and Custer
aftermath, 131; and District of
the Black Hills, 94–95, 120;
and Elkhorn Creek fight, 140;
and Fifth Cavalry, 125; and
Hunton murder, 84, and Indian raiding, 191; and Japanese visitors, 164; and
Mackenzie, 146; military record, 30; and Powder River Expedition, 194–95; and
Sheridan, 117, 170; and Sioux
Commission, 156; and Spotted
Tail's visit, 116; and supply operations, 163–64; and telegraph, 89, 112, 139, 153, 167
Townsend, Lucy, 58, 106
Triggs, J. H., 45, 51
Twentieth U.S. Infantry, 87

Twenty-second U.S. Infantry, 135
Twenty-third U.S. Infantry, 34, 55,
86–88, 99, 191–92, 206, 215,
241; Company H, 103, 107,
133, 136, 139, 207–10

Union Pacific Railroad, 8, 24, 54,
57, 88, 97, 103, 136, 156, 208,
230, 239; and Black Hills, 39
Upham, John J., 121
Utter, Charlie, 143

Van Vliet, Frederick, 63
Von Luettwitz, Adolphus H., 200–
201, 238, 275n20
Voorhees, Luke, 125, 130

Wagner, Samuel, 146, 267n98
Walters, Joe, 191, 206
Warbonnet Creek, 133, 210, 257n9
Warbonnet Creek fight, 133–34,
234, 241
Warm Springs, 26
Warren, Gouverneur K., 10
Wasson, Joe, 174
Watkins, Erwin C., 18
Weber, Fred, 211
Western Union Telegraph Com-
pany, 42, 89, 130, 245; and Cus-
ter City, 199; and Fort Laramie,
200; and Indian trouble, 138.
See also Black Hills Telegraph
Whetstone Agency, 6
Whipple, Henry B., 156–57, 178
White House conference, 17–18,
48
White River, 6, 28, 93, 116, 119,
130, 133, 227
Whitewood Creek, 73, 179
Williams, Robert, 111, 124, 227
Wilson, Henry, 50

Wolf Mountain fight, 220
Wood Mountain, 237
Wright's brothel, 46

Yankton, 21, 39, 169
Yellow Hair, 135
Yellow Robe, 106

Yellowstone Expedition of 1873, 28
Yellowstone River, 87, 171, 206, 222; and military posts, 142; and Northern Pacific Railroad, 9
Young Man Afraid of His Horses, 178